M000237753

Bloody Women

Bloody Women

Women Directors of Horror

Edited by
Victoria McCollum
Aislínn Clarke

LEHIGH UNIVERSITY PRESS
Bethlehem

Published by Lehigh University Press
Copublished by The Rowman & Littlefield Publishing Group, Inc.
4501 Forbes Boulevard, Suite 200, Lanham, Maryland 20706
www.rowman.com

86-90 Paul Street, London EC2A 4NE, United Kingdom

Copyright © 2022 by The Rowman & Littlefield Publishing Group, Inc.

All rights reserved. No part of this book may be reproduced in any form or by any electronic or mechanical means, including information storage and retrieval systems, without written permission from the publisher, except by a reviewer who may quote passages in a review.

British Library Cataloguing in Publication Information Available

Library of Congress Cataloging-in-Publication Data

Names: McCollum, Victoria, editor. | Clarke, Aislinn, editor.
Title: Bloody women : women directors of horror / edited by Victoria McCollum, Aislinn Clarke.
Description: Bethlehem : Lehigh University Press ; Lanham, Maryland : The Rowman & Littlefield Publishing Group, Inc., [2022] | Series: Critical conversations in horror studies | Includes bibliographical references and index. | Summary: "Bloody Women: Women Directors of Horror is the first book-length exploration of female creators at the cutting edge of contemporary horror, turning out some of its most inspired and twisted offerings"—Provided by publisher.
Identifiers: LCCN 2021052474 (print) | LCCN 2021052475 (ebook) | ISBN 9781611463071 (cloth) | ISBN 9781611463088 (epub)
Subjects: LCSH: Horror films—History and criticism. | Horror films—Production and direction. | Women motion picture producers and directors. | Women in the motion picture industry.
Classification: LCC PN1995.9.H6 B63 2022 (print) | LCC PN1995.9.H6 (ebook) | DDC 791.4302/3309252—dc23/eng/20220120
LC record available at https://lccn.loc.gov/2021052474
LC ebook record available at https://lccn.loc.gov/2021052475

∞™ The paper used in this publication meets the minimum requirements of American National Standard for Information Sciences—Permanence of Paper for Printed Library Materials, ANSI/NISO Z39.48-1992.

Contents

Acknowledgments   vii

Introduction   1
Victoria McCollum and Aislínn Clarke

1   Horror's Founding Mothers: Women in Proto-cinema,
Visual Avant-Gardes, and the Silent Era   21
Erica Tortolani

2   Women's Filmmaking and the Male-Centered Horror Film   39
Alexandra Heller-Nicholas

3   Angela Bettis: Gender in the Space of Collaborative Horror   53
James Francis Jr.

4   Stitches, Screams, and Female Beauty: Canadian Women
Horror Film   69
Shelby Shukaliak, Eve O'Dea, and Ernest Mathijs

SCREENPLAY: *Trim* by Mayumi Yoshida   89

5   "They've Got Something You Haven't. A Cock": Exploring
the Gendered Experience of Horror Filmmaking in Britain   97
Amy Harris

6   At Our Table: Conceptualizing the Black Woman's Horror
Film Aesthetic   115
Ashlee Blackwell

SCREENPLAY: *Paralysis* by R. Shanea Williams   131

7   Women in Horror Film Festivals: Representation, Dark
    Storytelling, and an International Community of Filmmakers   145
    Kate R. Robertson

8   "But Are You Really into Horror?": The Importance of
    Female-Centric Horror Film Festivals, Horror Curators,
    and Industry Champions   167
    Anna Bogutskaya

9   Short Sharp Shocks: An Interview with Women Who
    Make Horror Shorts   181
    Brian Hauser

SCREENPLAY: *Childer* by Aislínn Clarke   197

10 His Canon, Herself: Teaching Horror as Feminist Cinema   213
    Dan Vena, Iris Robinson, and Patrick Woodstock

Appendix: A Cultural Study of the (Western) Horror Film
(Abridged Viewing List)   229

Index   231

About the Editors and Contributors   241

Acknowledgments

To the contributors—a collection like this results only from the contributions of many talented people. Thank you. Your commitment, enthusiasm, and expertise are what made this book possible. Thanks so very much to my coeditor, Aislínn. Working with you has been an honor every step of the way, and you've taught me so much in the process. I am also deeply grateful to Brian for his unwavering support. Kate, Dawn, and Trish, thank you for your patience and understanding.

Here's offering my sincere, heartfelt thanks to my partner for her strength of character and courage of conviction. I am deeply grateful to my folks for their belief in me. I would like to offer my special thanks to Giuliana for her insightful comments and suggestions. Without Giuliana's tremendous understanding and encouragement in the past few years, it would be impossible for me to complete most of my books.

For Bella, a queen among dogs, my muse, and the best friend I could have ever wished for.

—Victoria

Firstly, to my coeditor, Victoria: thank you for inviting me to collaborate with you and for being such a trusty guide across the bridge from industry to academy. It has been a privilege, an education, and a lot of fun.

To the contributors and the contributors we lost along the way: thank you for your push, resolve, and patience. And to the publishing team at Lehigh, thank you for your patience, resolve, and push.

I would also like to acknowledge the extraordinarily important work of those who set up and championed Women in Horror film festivals—particularly International Women in Horror Film Festival, Final Girls

Berlin, and Axwound Film Festival, who have done so much for me. I have been privileged to meet and work with so many brilliant women through the Women in Horror community, and I will treasure those connections. I hope some of your experience is represented here. With special thanks to Sonia Lupher and Colleen O'Holleran.

And, finally, taking my lead from Victoria once again: my family, particularly my husband, who is always supportive and encouraging and knows his place, just below Moose, my own best girl.

—Aislínn

Introduction

Victoria McCollum and Aislínn Clarke

In a 2020 pitch meeting, a US producer suggested we make the lead of my (Clarke) proposed horror film female instead of male. It is not a proposition made often in Hollywood, where the percentage of top-grossing films that featured female protagonists dropped to 29 percent in 2020 (Lauzen 2021, 1). And still, in 2020, a horror film was the most likely place to see a female protagonist, accounting for 39 percent of all female leads (2). Indeed, horror is the only genre in which female characters receive the majority of screen time, if not speaking time. This would have put my character in an established but select lineage of Scream Queens, Final Girls, imperiled virgins, and all-sacrificing mothers, usually in films directed, written, and produced by men. Women have always held a special focus in horror cinema: most frequently looking terrified on posters and VHS sleeves, routinely misrepresented, monstered, and sexualized. But despite horror's fixation on women (or maybe because of the problematic nature of such depictions), it became news, in 2017, when 49 percent of tickets sold for the adaptation of Stephen King's *IT*—a film with an ensemble cast that included only one female character—were to women (Donaldson 2017). Still, women watch horror films. We knew this ourselves—I (Clarke) am a female director of horror films, which is what I always aspired to be. The film's producer is a female producer of horror films. The conversation we had was not really about the protagonist of the film at all; it was a conversation we doubt a male producer has had with any of our male counterparts. Indeed, when Mary Lambert was to make the sequel to her own hit Stephen King adaptation, *Pet Sematary*, in 1992, the male-headed studio quashed her attempts to write a female lead (Dixon 2018). No, the change of protagonist from male to female here was in the room and about the focus of horror itself: women watch it, women make it, and women take the lead.

Today women represent a key market for horror films (if not the main market), just as they did in the nineteenth century for the Gothic and sensation novel or the supernatural romance; and yet the film industry has not granted women the same leadership that their literary predecessors wielded over their medium. There is no equivalent in horror cinema of famed pioneer authors such as Mary Shelley or Ann Radcliffe; there is no established tradition of great practitioners like Margaret Oliphant, Edith Nesbit, and Vernon Lee. Even into the twentieth and twenty-first centuries, few if any female horror filmmakers have the name recognition of their literary counterparts such as Anne Rice, Shirley Jackson, and Susan Hill, to pick but three. What woman has the equivalent status of any male horror filmmaker—a John Carpenter, George A. Romero, or Wes Craven, the "Masters of Horror"?

Bloody Women addresses this discrepancy between the female consumption and production of horror films by taking a theoretical, historical, and critical approach to horror directed by women. Aimed at both scholarly and general readers, the essays in this collection bring together the expertise of filmmakers, festival programmers, and scholars. Writing from their own unique perspectives, the contributors to this volume are allied in exploring the central presence of women as creators, consumers, and critics of horror cinema. While acknowledging the challenges that women have experienced and continue to face in the industry, this book considers how the gender landscape of horror filmmaking is changing and focuses on the varied contributions of women who have worked to define the evolving genre of horror cinema.

In considering how women have shaped the varied methods and aims of horror films, this book asks, most centrally: what does it mean for women to have control over their own enjoyment of horror? Is a horror film directed by a female filmmaker significantly different from one directed by one of her male counterparts? Does a horror film written by a female screenwriter offer more to the significant portion of its prospective audience that is female? On a grander scale, what is horror cinema when directed by women? How is horror shaped as an institution when women run its festivals and conventions? How is it shaped as a scholarly discipline when women become the focus of study and curricula?

In recent years, both scholars and industry leaders have become increasingly interested in exploring women's place in horror cinema. Anna Bogutskaya, cofounder of The Final Girls collective, suggests in her contribution to this volume that 2014 was a turning point for women in horror cinema (see chapter 8). This year saw huge international success for Australian director Jennifer Kent's *The Babadook* and Iranian American Ana Lily Amirpour's Persian-language *A Girl Walks Home Alone at Night*. After the release of these popular and critically acclaimed films, other horror films directed by women and female-focused horror festivals gained visibility, legitimacy, and cultural cachet. While women have always been crucial to the enterprise of horror cinema, the early twenty-first century finally made it clear that women were everywhere in horror: on the screen, in the audience, and behind the camera. This watershed moment for female filmmakers in horror brings with it varying commercial and critical responses. On one side of this watershed, there is the critical reception to Karyn Kusama's *Jennifer's Body*, and on the other the reception to Kusama's *The Invitation*.

The seismic shift in female horror filmmaking is characterized by multiple developments. Like *The Babadook* and *A Girl Walks Home*, many of the most significant recent horror films have been directed by women living and working outside the dominant Anglo-American cinematic sphere. These include Austrian director Veronika Franz's *Goodnight Mommy*, French director Julia Ducornau's *Raw*, and Mexican director Issa López's *Tigers Are Not Afraid*. Mattie Do's 2016 feature, *Dearest Sister*, became the first Laotian film—let alone horror film—submitted for consideration for the Best Foreign Language Film at the Academy Awards.

As these examples suggest, the success of female horror filmmakers is concurrent with the increased visibility (and increased financial support) of film industries outside the main Anglosphere powerhouses of the US, Canada, and the UK. The increase in women-directed horror films is also related to other contemporary developments including the #MeToo movement and the rise of female-focused horror festivals and conventions. Horror cinema has also seen the rise of so-called elevated horror, which foregrounds social and political themes. This development, with films that consider power, victimhood, and identity, does not seem incidental. While no one element here is causal, these developments all contributed to a new era of prominence for women in horror cinema.

And yet we must acknowledge that in spite of such recent success, the industry still has room for progress when it comes to producing work by female filmmakers. Blumhouse, the figurehead horror studio of the day, has been repeatedly criticized for the scant number of female filmmakers on the wall of directors in their LA office. This was compounded when studio founder Jason Blum commented that "there are not a lot of female directors period, and even less who are inclined to do horror" (quoted in Sims 2018). Blum claimed that the company made several offers to Jennifer Kent but she repeatedly turned them down. Choosing to focus on her artistic practice, Kent did not feel pressured to have her work "authorized" by a major film studio. In contrast, the Canadian Mexican director Gigi Saul Guerrero signed a first-look deal with

Blumhouse. These different situations are representative of the current moment for female horror filmmakers: they are on the cusp of joining the world of mainstream cinema even as they show hesitation about the value of that prospect.

Because *Bloody Women* seeks to explore this complex moment in horror cinema, it is important to trace the historical and theoretical developments leading up to the current era. The dynamic and enduringly popular genre of horror cinema has been dominated by male practitioners, presenting male perceptions of female subjectivity and male fears of female sexuality. For these reasons, women have enjoyed (and endured) a central role in horror filmmaking especially in front of the camera and often as "scream queens," known for their iconic roles in the face of terror. While the horror genre has long served as a powerful avenue for young actresses to cut their teeth, women have traditionally played the roles of silent and sexualized screen "vamps" existing in most classic and much contemporary horror only to be looked at (Mulvey 1975).

MISREPRESENTED IN FRONT OF THE CAMERA AND UNDERREPRESENTED BEHIND THE CAMERA

The principal role for most women in the gothic-style classic horror of the 1920 and 1930s was to stare doe-eyed at leading men—and to shriek convincingly on cue (Clark 2003, 183). As fictional filmmaker Carl Denham says to budding actress Ann Darrow in Cooper and Schoedsack's *King Kong* (1933), while tutoring her in the art of terror, "You're helpless, Ann, helpless." Decades later, the archetypal horror victim had narrowly evolved into "an intelligent, often posh, usually virginal lady who, with a queasy sexual undercurrent, is reduced to animalistic bellowing by something big, hulking and male" (Clarke 2012). Take, for instance, the female protagonists of the Hammer horror films of the late 1950s and early 1970s, who were most recognizable for their heaving breasts and see-through garments and who were often preyed upon by (male) monsters—only to be saved by a strong and heroic male stranger. While heroines were more progressive by the 1970s, evolving from the damsel in distress to a more modern "final girl" capable of going toe-to-toe with her aggressor (Clover 1992), female protagonists predominately remained in their traditional exhibitionist role—on display—with their appearance coded for strong visual and erotic impact. For example, in the opening of Wes Craven's *The Last House on the Left* (1972), seventeen-year-old female protagonist Mari is filmed taking a shower. Mari's body, soon to become the site of a brutal, affecting, and utterly monstrous rape, is captured in long, lingering close-ups—wet skin, moistened breasts, and dripping hair. This scene emblematizes Laura Mulvey's theory of the male gaze—that cinematic representations accentuate and duplicate the gaze of the heterosexual man whose sight lingers upon the features of a woman's body. It also speaks to the harsh reality that a "scream queen" often functions as an erotic object to be looked at, not only by the external audience but also by the characters within the film's narrative (Metz 1975). Due to the voyeuristic pleasure of the cinematic apparatus itself, then, and the duplication of this gaze in the horror film, women watching horror often find themselves bearing witness to their own frailty and inadequacy in the face of sexual assault, suffering, and murder (Williams 1984). Thus, the female audience for horror is often framed as "reluctant girlfriends being dragged to the cinema and hiding their face in their hands at every scene" (Donaldson 2017).

In a world ordered by sexual imbalance, the pleasure in looking is split between active men and passive women. As highly recognized and widely renowned horror director Dario Argento horribly puts it, "I like women, especially beautiful ones. If they have a good face and figure, I would much prefer to watch them being murdered than an ugly girl or a man" (cited in Clover 1987, 205). On the face of it, the relation between the sexes could hardly be clearer—women serve as erotic spectacle, thus ensuring a masculinization of the spectatorial position (Doane 1982). When a female protagonist dares to return the gaze of the man who desires her within the horror film (thus expressing desires of her own), she is usually punished for looking. It is interesting to note that monsters too often share a similar status within the patriarchal structures of seeing—they typically exist to be looked at, othered, punished, and victimized. Accordingly then, women traditionally serve not only in the role of victim but also in the role of synergistic double for the monster, sharing a surprising (and at times subversive) affinity with the "freak" (Williams 1984, 62). After all, patriarchal ideologies and structures construct women not only as victims in the horror film but also as abject beings who often horrify their audience through their sexuality, sexual difference, and threat to male power (Kristeva 1982). Thus the most prominent roles historically offered to women—thanks in part to our seemingly "monstrous" bodies, which position us in closer proximity to the abject than our male counterparts (especially through menstruation, pregnancy, and birth)—include archaic mothers, mythical creatures, possessed monsters, witches, and vampires (Creed 1993).

Indeed, it is highly unsurprising that psychoanalytic film criticism of the late 1960s and early 1970s focused on a formal critique of cinema's dissemination of ideology and especially on the role of the cinematic apparatus in this process. Great waves of feminist film criticism would emerge by the mid-1980s to accuse the genre of misogyny, and under-standably so, considering horror's new depiction of women (as bleeders, birthers, gestators, ovulators, among many other demeaning and dehu-manizing things). Yet with monstrosity comes agency. It goes without saying that narratives about the difference of female sexuality, as a dis-tinction that is grounded in monstrousness and which invokes anxious masculinity in the male spectator, may end up being, in fact, quite the opposite of misogynistic. For example, the unforgettable toothed vagina in Mitchell Lichtenstein's *Teeth* (2007) might spring from a primitive masculine dread of the mysteries of women and sexual union, but it is also an incisor-sharp commentary on the cost of male entitlement, enthu-siastic consent, and sexual violence. In other words, horror films driven by men's fear of women's power, troubling as they may be, also repeat-edly and explicitly articulate feminist politics. For example, we might read Brian De Palma's *Carrie* (1976) as a metaphor for anxious masculin-ity shriveling up in the face of female equality. Second-wave feminism is, indeed, the figurative backdrop to *Carrie*, in which a withdrawn and sensitive teenager discovers that her telekinetic powers can be used to wreak revenge on her abusers.

Key watershed moments, such as the upsurge of feminist activity in the early 1970s, enabled a new breed of horror film to emerge, one in which women finally figured as three-dimensional characters, with backstories, wants, needs, and desires—as conceptualizations of archetype as opposed to stereotype. With the cementing of the Final Girl by the 1990s (Clover 1992), women now figured as the relatable sole survivors of contempo-rary horror, who (while eye-rollingly virginal) were now empowered and capable of confronting the killer. Women of contemporary horror were no longer required to gaze into the eyes of leading men, such as Bela Lugosi, Vincent Price, and Peter Cushing. These women, epitomized by Carrie White (*Carrie* [1976]), Laurie Strode (*Halloween* [1978]), Clarice Starling (*Silence of the Lambs* [1991]), and others, were looking outward together in the same direction.

WOMEN PRACTITIONERS AND THE
CONTEMPORARY POLITICAL CLIMATE

Evolving in tandem with women in front of the camera, who were be-coming strong characters able to survive any bloody scenario, women working in artistic and technical roles behind the camera also began to emerge from the rhetorical fog. Take, for example, the timely emergence of Debra Hill, an American film producer and screenwriter, known for cowriting *Halloween* (1978) with John Carpenter and for producing *The*

Fog (1980); or Marianne Maddalena, whose creative production relation-ship with Wes Craven at Craven/Maddalena films started on the set of *The Serpent and the Rainbow* (1988) and resulted in ten films, including the Oscar-nominated non-horror *Music of the Heart* (1999). Then came the groundbreaking women directors of horror: Mary Lambert, an American director best known for her 1989 adaptation of Stephen King's novel *Pet Sematary* and its sequel, and Mary Harron, a Canadian filmmaker and screenwriter renowned for her 2000 adaptation of Bret Easton El-lis's novel *American Psycho*. Of course, this significant breakthrough bled beyond the North American context, as women began to emerge at the forefront of horror filmmaking globally. See the recent visibility of New French Extremity director and writer Claire Denis, known for her bold, sensual, and frequently controversial work, such as *Trouble Every Day* (2001); Japanese filmmaker Kei Fujiwara, who became notable for her sur-real and violent avant-garde films, such as *Organ* (1996); or Italian actress and screenwriter Daria Nicolodi, who cowrote *Suspiria* (1977) with Dario Argento (Paszkiewicz 2017, 61).

Only very recently, however, have women working behind the camera gained discursive visibility and critical and industrial recognition. As we've seen, Anna Bogutskaya, cofounder of The Final Girls collective, marks 2014 as a turning point for women in horror cinema. Despite the increasing visibility of women practitioners working in genre filmmak-ing, however, there remains a significant dearth of academic writing about women working in artistic and technical roles in the horror genre (Paszkiewicz 2017, 61).

Given that the critical landscape tends to replicate the sexual politics invoked by the male gaze, it is highly unsurprising that horror films made by women have received such little scholarly attention. As Paszkiewicz notes, there is a long-standing misconception that horror films are made by men and for men (Hutchings 1993, 84), to indulge their sadistic, ag-gressive, and voyeuristic fantasies against women (Paszkiewicz 2017, 66). While this assumption has been thoroughly interrogated by scholars in-cluding Clover (1992) and Creed (1993), such long-standing notions about supposedly "macho" genres, as Paszkiewicz (2017) rightly contends, are likely the main reason why women at the forefront of horror filmmaking are often the subject of harsh criticism, condemnation, and a severe lack of critical attention (Clover 1992). It is fortunate, however, that scholarship is finally beginning to highlight the significant contributions of women practitioners to the horror genre, both inside and beyond the academy.

In her groundbreaking study *Genre, Authorship and Contemporary Women Filmmakers* (2017), Katarzyna Paszkiewicz outlines the consider-able impact that women filmmakers have had on popular genre cinema, from the war film to the western, offering fresh perspectives on cinema's fraught relationship with women directors. Paszkiewicz deftly grapples with a smorgasbord of debates and controversies that have long circulated around women's participation in popular genres, such as the hotbed of criticism that ensued after Kathryn Bigelow became the first woman to win an Academy Award for Best Achievement in Directing with *The Hurt Locker* (2008). Bigelow was heavily criticized for embracing a hyper-masculine genre (the war film), one which typically includes few female characters, and for her purported "tough-guy" stance (seemingly exemplified during her acceptance speech in which she made no reference to the significance of her accomplishment for feminism [read: she declined to label her film in terms of gender politics]). For Paszkiewicz, however, the contentious and varied responses that Bigelow faced for winning the Oscar exemplified the tension that exists at the conjunction of women's filmmaking, gender, genre, and feminism. This in turn would cause a renewed scholarly and critical interest in women's filmmaking and the role and status of women directors within a predominantly male industry (Paszkiewicz 2015).

Today, women are mobilizing ostensibly masculine genres more than ever before, while at the same time challenging audience expectations and telling stories that transcend gender, despite the discomfort of their detractors. Take, for example, Karyn Kusama's taut and expertly plotted crime drama *Destroyer* (2018). This sun-lit noir dexterously crafted by cinematographer Julie Kirkwood features a career-defining performance from Nicole Kidman who plays a hard-boiled detective, a role that reverses the standard gender polarity. While many critics celebrated *Destroyer* as "an exceptional genre film" (Martín 2019), interestingly said to feature "shades of Kathryn Bigelow" (Friar 2019), others were highly critical of the supposed "grunge feminism laid on with a shovel" (Andrews 2019) not helped by Kidman's "cadaverous countenance" (Paatsch 2019) and "procedural motions in a bad wig" (Ignacio Castillo 2018). As Deborah Ross (2019) of *The Spectator* horribly put it, "I don't know what absorbed more of my attention, the story, her [Kidman's] character, or just how bad she looks. Actually, I can answer that. How bad she looks."

Of course, this was not the first time that Kusama had received a torrent of abuse from critics due to the appearance of a female protagonist coded for strong visual impact. Paszkiewicz's book includes a standout chapter on feminist horror film *Jennifer's Body* (2009), directed by Karyn Kusama and written by Diablo Cody. *Jennifer's Body* remains a highly contentious film among critics, fans, and scholars alike, mostly due to Megan Fox's "to-be-looked-at" celebrity image (the reverse of Kidman in *Destroyer*) and partly due to the film's seeming lack of interest in gender politics (Paszkiewicz 2017, 70–73). As Paszkiewicz suggests, if we follow the assumption that horror is a male-dominated genre and that the cinematic apparatus honors a way of looking that empowers men and objectifies women, then this complicates female spectatorial pleasure in relation to horror films. This dilemma can be observed in Michelle Orange's (2009) article on *Jennifer's Body* for *The New York Times* (emphasis our own):

> And yet recent box office receipts show that women have an even bigger appetite for these films than men. Theories straining to address this particular *head scratcher* have their work cut out for them: Are female fans of "Saw" ironists? Masochists? Or just *dying to get closer to their dates*?

In her latest book, *Women Do Genre in Film and Television* (2020), Paszkiewicz (and Harrod) examines what women engaged in the creative industries do with genre and, in turn, what genre does with them. In another rare chapter centered on women directors of horror, "When the Woman Directs (A Horror Film)," Paszkiewicz tackles the pervasive assumption that women do not derive pleasure from horror films by asking who orchestrates these gaze(s) and for whom, questioning what is at stake when women directors engage with a disreputable genre traditionally seen as masculine. This time, through an analysis of Kimberly Peirce's remake of *Carrie* (2013), Paszkiewicz argues that rather than "undoing" genre, in a way that, say, *Jennifer's Body* does, by "inscribing itself in wider trends of its time and offering—and inflating to the fullest—certain clichés and representations" (2017, 96), *Carrie*'s generative force is activated in the service of women's stories, providing female protagonists access to the violence unleashed by a genre traditionally codified as masculine (Paszkiewicz 2020, 41–56).

The idea that horror cinema and female spectators make uncomfortable bedfellows has at least enjoyed some theoretical attention and intervention (Mulvey 1975, Williams 1984, Clover 1992, Creed 1993, Halberstam 1995, Berenstein 1996, Cherry 2002, Fradley 2013, among others). There remains a dearth of scholarship, however, on women who work in creative and technical roles within horror filmmaking, despite, for instance, *Rolling Stone* heralding "the rise of the modern female horror filmmaker" (Reilly 2016) half a decade ago. Responding to this lack in 2020, Paszkiewicz (2020, 43) advocates, "We need to ask what happens not only when the woman looks, but also *when the woman directs*." In a similar manner, Peirse (2020) also claims that "no scholar has yet asked what happens in horror when sense-making is *done by* women, rather than *done to* women" (emphasis our own).

The recent volume *Women Make Horror: Filmmaking, Feminism, Genre* (2020), edited by Alison Peirse, is the first book-length study to examine women working in horror filmmaking. It is also the first book to call out the male bias in written histories of horror, while illuminating precisely how, and where, these histories are lacking. Peirse's cutting-edge volume is set to reevaluate existing academic literature on the history of horror and on women practitioners working in the film industry. Additionally, it establishes new approaches for studying the work of women creatively and technically engaged in horror filmmaking, while illuminating their hitherto-unexamined contribution to the formation and evolution of the horror genre. *Women Make Horror* focuses on women directors and screenwriters, while acknowledging the importance of women producers, cinematographers, editors, production designers, and so on. The volume came to the fore hot on the heels of a significant global breakthrough of women directors, screenwriters, and producers working in the horror genre and was designed to inspire dialogue among the academy, film-makers, industry gatekeepers, festival programmers, and horror film fans alike. Peirse's volume is underpinned by a trio of interlocking lenses that brilliantly investigate: (1) the cultural perception of horror (and the women who make it), (2) the politics of storytelling, and (3) the politics of authorship. Much like *Women Make Horror*, *Bloody Women* also focuses on women involved in the horror filmmaking process, in various roles. Like-wise, this collection also seeks to inspire dialogue between related parties and to build upon the analysis undertaken by Peirse. *Bloody Women* explores narrative and experimental cinema and short, anthology, and feature filmmaking and offers a dynamic range of case studies on women working in horror filmmaking globally, filmmakers, films, and festivals. It is clear that women directors of horror are becoming increasingly more visible and more difficult to ignore. As Canadian horror filmmaker Jen Soska (cited in Wang 2017) cautions, "A revolution has started."

In *Bloody Women*, we explore the historical and contemporary, the po-litical and aesthetic, the familiar and the underrepresented. Those inter-sections are numerous and complex, and while the book traces the female horror filmmaker from the earliest days of French and German cinema, through American studio and indie output, via a host of international artists—from Kei Fujiwara in Japan, to Svetlana Baskova in Russia, and the Soska Sisters in Canada—to contemporaries vocalizing traditionally marginalized voices (we include three screenplays from a diverse group of screenwriters), it is not possible to cover everything. Sadly, chapters looking more closely at Central American horror were lost along the way. In the end, there is not enough space to capture this moment in only one collection. There is work by many historical directors, emerging national film industries, non-English-language filmmakers, and coalescing schools of cinema, such as the New French Extremity, that we couldn't cover. However, this book does not seek to be comprehensive; it is only a small part of the work that now needs to be done and the critical conversations that need to be enjoined.

Further, as the female horror filmmaker moves from invisibility into visibility, it is worth considering what that visibility means. For the moment, certainly, it is impossible to be a woman who makes horror films without being a "female horror filmmaker"—the current of industry, academic, and consumer conversation brings it up again and again; that is the process of becoming visible. The female filmmaker is identified as such, whether or not the filmmaker wishes to be so identified or whether they consider such a label a useful signpost to understanding their work or useful to them in how they navigate creating work in the industry. This book accepts that the term is, for now, meaningful in a way that has never been required of the term "male horror filmmaker." Despite its limitations, the term has multiple connotations and suggests several different lenses through which to understand female filmmakers who have made or are making horror films.

The female horror filmmaker may primarily be considered as a working individual, but they identify or are identified as female and, thus, their work is examined for female experiences or perspectives and read in the light of a worldview informed by these experiences. Their career is equally understood in this context, contributing to and explaining successes and failures; their being female becomes an explicit element of their industry experience, while the maleness of their counterparts is implicit.

As a result, the label "female filmmaker" places the filmmaker in the middle of a political discourse about representation, about industry practice, or as part of a wider critical debate. This can be intentional on the part of filmmakers, as evidenced by Women in Horror festivals and collectives where a political identity is created to agitate for representation and visibility or to create new spaces of their own. Equally, a female filmmaker may find themselves politicized when a production company hires them, a festival admits them, or a distributor picks them up for the purposes of representation and visibility. That process allows the "female" to be abstracted from the filmmaker in question; it is no longer a quality material to them but to the film or to cinema. Women in Horror Month (WiHM) is an international, grassroots initiative, which showcases the underrepresented work of women in the horror industries during the month of February. WiHM officially retired on March 1, 2021 (its twelfth consecutive year), in the interest of *increasing* engagement, exposure, and opportunities for crossover content "that brings even more attention from communities who haven't previously participated" (WiHM 2021). One might see that a film is marketed on the back of being directed by *a* woman more so than directed by *this* woman. On the other side, a film may be marketed to women on the basis of perceived female themes, characters, experiences, or aspirations. This allows for the abstract notion of female cinema that makes no reference to any individual female filmmaker.

The possibility of female cinema exceptionalizes it to an extent. The female filmmaker may be understood only in opposition to the default male filmmaker, offering a redress or a counterpoint: what they do is different or is made different by the matter of their femaleness; their existence illuminates male filmmaking by exposing it as male filmmaking. However, this lens only allows the female filmmaker to subvert the male gaze and male conventions. Subversion limits efforts to pioneer. What capacity is there to understand female filmmaking without reference to male peers? Can the female filmmaker be a singularity? It is hoped that, through this volume, we might find a clear sense of how the idea of the female filmmaker, especially in horror, works to the advantage and disadvantage of filmmakers themselves and how this may change in the future.

ROADMAP TO THE CHAPTERS

This volume is organized around a quartet of central themes: the female filmmaker as individual, the female filmmaker as group identity, the female filmmaker as oppositional force, and the female filmmaker as an abstract idea. *Bloody Women* kicks off with the founding mothers of horror cinema—those integral to the construction and formation of the genre from its earliest days. In chapter 1, Erica Tortolani provides an intricate historical overview of the female filmmakers working at the dawn of cinema, despite their being regularly misrepresented as rarities in leading accounts of film history. For Tortolani, women directors, such as Alice Guy Blaché, who shot hundreds of films between 1896 and 1920, including several horror films, and Lotte Reiniger, foremost pioneer of the silhouette animation (which was used, for instance, to epitomize the unimaginable horrors of war in the early 1900s), played a key role in the evolution of the genre.

Conventional wisdom tells us that through their lived experience alone, women filmmakers are best equipped to tell women's stories. But what about women filmmakers who choose to tell stories about men? Recent films like Athina Rachel Tsangari's *Chevalier* (2016), which centers on a fishing trip that turns into a struggle for supremacy among six male friends, and Lynne Ramsay's *You Were Never Really Here* (2017), about a traumatized veteran and contract killer's quest for redemption, provide us with an insight equally as valuable and equally as important as the stories women choose to tell about other women. In chapter 2, Alexandra Heller-Nicholas explores what women directors of horror have told us about men and masculinity over a long and rich history, in which horror films by women, about men, have been consistently overlooked in favor of films that focus on the experiences of women.

American filmmaker Lucky McKee is a male director, writer, and actor renowned for telling (horror) stories about women from the perspective of women, often exploring themes of power inequality and gender struggle. McKee is equally renowned for his mutually supportive working relationship with actress and filmmaker Angela Bettis. Bettis starred in McKee's *Masters of Horror* episode "Sick Girl" (2006), *The Woods* (2006), and in his adaptation of Jack Ketchum's *The Woman* (2011). It was Bettis's title role in McKee's *May* (2002), however, that would win her a cult following. In the film, a socially awkward veterinary assistant with a lazy eye and obsession with perfection descends into depravity after developing a crush on a man with perfect hands. Four years later, McKee and Bettis reversed roles, when *he* played a starring role in *her* directorial debut, *Roman* (2006), about a man's dark obsession with the idea of a relationship with his neighbor. In chapter 3, James Francis Jr. conducts a close textual analysis of *Roman*, exploring how Bettis treats the theme of obsession when compared with McKee's exploration and depiction of the same theme in *May*. Through his insightful analysis, Francis demonstrates that Bettis is just as extraordinarily well-equipped to dissect the often-complex world of men and masculinity as McKee is to dissect the experience of women.

In chapter 4, Shelby Shukaliak, Eve O'Dea, and Ernest Mathijs affirm the permanence of female horror filmmaking's place by analyzing the conditions of that place. As the authors rightly assert, horror film scholarship so often journeys down the burrow of sexual politics—grappling with tensions around gender, leaving little room for analysis of cultural context and heritage, regional differences, policy-specific circumstances, and so on, especially as they relate to women horror filmmakers. The analysis in chapter 4 is centered on an important body of women-led Canadian horror, the Soska Sisters' *Rabid* (2019) and *American Mary* (2012) and the *Ginger Snaps* film series (2000–), which, together, the authors suggest, offer a solid understanding of context-specific horror filmmaking by women. Taking an innovative methodological approach, Shukaliak, O'Dea, and Mathijs examine a range of diverse materials, from direct sources, aesthetic analysis, and some reception analysis, demonstrating that Canada remains at the forefront of innovations in mixing political activism, feminism, and the horror film. This chapter is followed by a short screenplay by Mayumi Yoshida entitled *Trim* (2019), a unique and decidedly felt international women-led horror short from Vancouver.

Bloody Women turns its attention to the presumed masculine landscape of specifically British horror in chapter 5, unearthing the unique and undervalued contributions of women to the genre over its long and diverse history. In this chapter, Amy Harris takes an industrial and critical approach to British horror led by women, revealing a unique body of work that responds directly to the UK film industry's stark diversity problem. Unsurprisingly, in Britain, while a hair better than in Hollywood, women remain historically underrepresented as directors and cinematographers. Harris, armed with this data and through the lens of the broader industrial context of the British film industry since the fall of Hammer horror, examines how gendered experiences of horror filmmaking can offer a valuable commentary on the misogyny of the industry. Kate Shenton's *Egomaniac* (2016), a semiautobiographical satire following a women director of horror as she navigates the absurdity of the industry, is one such film that the author incisively reads as a direct response to an industry that privileges, and is dominated by, men.

In chapter 6, pioneering writer and filmmaker Ashlee Blackwell, founder of *Graveyard Shift Sisters*, a site devoted to reviews, interviews, and academic syllabi that aims to educate visitors on the Black experience in horror, journeys deep into the renaissance of Black women's filmmaking. As Blackwell demonstrates, Black women filmmakers whose work could be considered horror are at the forefront of a resurgence of original stories that explore the fears and anxieties unique to Black women through the lens of Black women protagonists. In the chapter, Blackwell calls our attention to several leading Black women filmmakers working in the United States and offers a blueprint for conceptualizing and defining a Black woman's horror film. As the author shrewdly observes, this emerging subgenre finds its roots in previous depictions of Black women on screen, as well as the personal experiential and historical experiences of the Black women filmmakers. Blackwell's findings reveal how these filmmakers are utilizing the genre to give voice to their own distinct stories, in nuanced and complex ways, while showcasing the unique horrors of the Black experience in ways which speak directly to audiences. This chapter is followed by a short horror screenplay by R. Shanea Williams entitled *Paralysis* (2015), which powerfully challenges mental health stigma in the Black community through the supernatural nightmares of a fully developed, central Black woman character.

The growth of film festivals dedicated to women practitioners working in the horror genre is indicative of the recent drive for increased visibility. As Kate Robertson shrewdly observes in chapter 7, women have been at the helm of horror filmmaking throughout cinema history, yet the cultural gatekeepers have had trouble finding (and funding) them. Through a perceptive series of exclusive interviews, this time with festival founders and organizers, Robertson offers insights into the growing global trend for women-led festivals. Highlighting the practical opportunities offered through these initiatives, such as networking, collaboration, and community, the author reveals the history, purpose, goals, and successes of horror film festivals devoted to women.

Where Robertson describes an overview of sympathetic interests and experiences, chapter 8 burrows deep into specifics with Anna Boguts-kaya, cofounder of horror film collective The Final Girls, tracing the timeline of that group from inception to present and, in the process, cap-turing the current climate for the female horror filmmaker and fan. The chapter documents the motivations, challenges, and successes that go into and come out of working outside of conventions of mainstream horror fandom. It presents a rare auto-ethnographical look at the DIY methodol-ogy that informs much of the work around female horror filmmaking, hinting at universal obstacles and regional differences in grassroots film-programming. The careers of many women directors of horror begin—and end—with the making of short and indie films due to institutional bias and a criminal lack of funding opportunities. Women-centric horror events, curatorships, and festivals are springing up across the globe to spotlight new female horror talent, and Bogutskaya brilliantly demon-strates how such events and efforts play a key role in calling attention to women directors of horror through funds, prizes, publicity, and distribu-tion projects, while serving as a quality filter for the horror film industry.

In chapter 9, through a series of exclusive interviews with women directors shaping short-form horror filmmaking—Jennifer Trudrung, Izzy Lee, Aislínn Clarke, and Vanessa Ionta Wright—Brian Hauser dem-onstrates that, due to the relatively low cost and efficiency of the short horror film, it offers one of the most accessible opportunities for diverse voices finding their way into commercial filmmaking. As verified in the insightful interviews, women directors of horror possess a broad range of opinions and perspectives regarding the extent to which they choose to situate their work along the lines of gender identity. Some practitioners would rather be received as a horror filmmaker, as opposed to say, a diverse voice or *woman* director of horror, while others embrace being variously gendered in the discussion and curation of their work. When identity labels are used meaningfully, they can stir a powerful sense of understanding about the world in which certain directors of horror oper-ate and about how their identity exists within various patriarchal struc-tures, not to mention the integral role that this identity can play in the way that filmmakers see and produce their work. Furthermore, Hauser's fascinating findings suggest an explanation for the now-apparent affinity many women have with horror: women horror filmmakers, due to their position within patriarchal societies and systems, which is in itself to partake of horror, recognize an intimate understanding of the emotional content and aesthetic experience of the genre. This chapter is followed by a short screenplay by Aislínn Clarke entitled *Childer* (2016), an inventive and uncanny folk horror film that explores an introverted mother's abject reaction to being haunted by feral children.

Women's participation in horror is so often storied as a subversion of genre rather than an innate part of its offerings. In chapter 10, Dan Vena, Iris Robinson, and Patrick Woodstock reflect on the pedagogical outcomes of teaching horror as feminist cinema from the outset, as opposed to, say, maintaining the illusion that women artists and audiences have been absent in the genre's development. Written collaboratively by a professor and two former students, the authors offer the blueprint for fresh horror syllabi that relies less on recycling canonical male auteurs to students and framing horror as being "undone" by women filmmakers and more on narrating women's contributions to horror as essential to the genre's growth. Vena, Robinson, and Woodstock thus demonstrate how a repatriation of female filmmakers to course syllabi refocuses students' attention to the subversive potential of horror's gendered representations, ultimately fostering a more accurate understanding of the genre's horizons. This chapter is followed by Vena's own syllabus (an abridged viewing list), which demonstrates the importance of treating "women in horror" as a category that includes scholars, filmmakers, and audiences. A feminist horror classroom, as Vena's syllabus implies, is one that profiles all types of women contributors to the genre and one that champions an intersectional approach to both topic and text.

Bloody Women captures that sense of changing perspective: academically, cinematically, professionally, and personally. This is a particular cultural moment in which the label of female filmmaker means many things. It affects how films are made, funded, and marketed. It affects how filmmakers are discussed and who discusses them. It affects the festivals that screen the films and the fans who support them. In horror, especially, these factors are having a profound effect. Where once a female filmmaker was considered an anomaly, they are now a commodity, a totem, an agent, an activist, and an abstraction. Somewhere in that conversation, they are also artists in their own right. This book is not a complete document of that conversation, but it offers many ways into it and points toward the change to come.

In addition to our collection's multifaceted examination of the term "female horror filmmaker," we invited three female horror filmmakers to represent themselves with the inclusion of three short screenplays: *Trim* by Mayumi Yoshida, *Paralysis* by R. Shanea Williams, and *Childer* by Aislínn Clarke. This unique inclusion is in recognition of several things: even at this juncture, the work of many female horror filmmakers—work that is still predominantly short (rather than feature) length—remains less well-known and not easily accessible. Our inclusion of these screenplays allows them to be read alongside criticism that engages with them: Yoshida's screenplay is suggested as a prime example of "felt internationalism" in chapter 4's exploration of Canadian cinema; Williams's screenplay is considered at length in chapter 6's conceptualization of "the Black Woman's Horror Film Aesthetic"; and Clarke's screenplay illustrates the different artistic possibilities available in Europe, as distinct from her American experience, as explored in her chapter 9 interview answers.

In many instances, the female horror director is also the writer—and, in the realm of the short, often the producer—of their work, so study of the screenplay as an artifact offers a rare glimpse into the entire process and vision of the filmmaker. These screenplays also offer an insight into the diverse range of voices among female horror filmmakers, voices that are rarely subject to critical consideration: Mayumi Yoshida is a Japanese-born filmmaker with an international upbringing; R. Shanea Williams explores unique challenges of African American life through horror; and Aislínn Clarke, coming from Northern Ireland's disadvantaged and rural border area, was the first Northern Irish woman to write and direct a horror feature, 2018's *The Devil's Doorway*, a critique of the Magdalene Laundries, Ireland's church-run homes for "wayward" women. Each writer here uses the short format to explore culturally specific issues that lack the universal appeal for feature funding: in *Trim*, it is the Asian Canadian family dynamic; in *Paralysis*, it is the gateway to medical treatment in African American communities; and in *Childer*, it is the ostracization of unwed mothers in rural Ireland. It is hoped that these screenplays will act as objects not just of analysis but of education also.

Notably, *Bloody Women* was written and edited during 2020, a period devastated by the COVID-19 pandemic and global civil unrest—the impacts of which have been disproportionately felt by women and people from marginalized communities. In addition to the personal and political effects of these historic moments on individuals, the film industry and academia have both found themselves radically changed by events, with university campuses thrown into turmoil and film production cancelled. It is too early to tell how the long-term changes may manifest, but the future of film envisaged when we started this book could turn out to be very different.

It is a testament to the dedication and passion of our contributors and the importance of the subject matter that this book comes to you when it does. We were sorry to lose contributors through the tumultuous year: Heidi Honeycutt on Gigi Saul Guerrero, Robin Hershkowitz on Sarah Adina Smith, April Millar on Commodity Feminism in *The Slumber Party Massacre* and *Jennifer's Body*, and Shellie McMurdo on Mary Lambert—although McMurdo's monograph on *Pet Sematary* is strongly anticipated by us all. This only goes to show how vital, diverse, and multilayered the conversation is; there is much to be discussed and much left to do. The horror films and the scholarly works to come will have women visible in the taglines and the bylines, in the director's chair and behind the writer's desk. There is no avoiding it.

Women have always told horror stories, but when it comes to cinema, they have been too often left out of the story of horror itself. This book is about women directing horror in every sense of the word. This collection documents this increased visibility at the same time that it shows how women filmmakers are not to be contained within any label that imposes limits on what they can do and be. While Hollywood still struggles to find its way with "strong female leads" and strong female leaders—many of whom have horror stories of their own in the industry—we are invested in bringing the *Bloody Women* out of the shadows and making them the protagonists of the story of horror films.

BIBLIOGRAPHY

Andrews, Nigel. "Destroyer—Nicole Kidman is a Traumatised Detective in Karyn Kusama's Movie." *The Financial Times*, 2019. https://www.ft.com/con tent/8e10f7c8-1f1e-11e9-b126-46fc3ad87c65.

Berenstein, Rhonda J. *Attack of the Leading Ladies: Gender, Sexuality, and Spectatorship in Classic Horror Cinema*. New York: Columbia University Press, 1996.

Cherry, Brigid. "Refusing to Look: Female Viewers of the Horror Film." In *Horror, the Film Reader*, ed. M. Jancovich. Routledge: London, 2002.

Clark, Mark. *Smirk, Sneer and Scream: Great Acting in Horror Cinema*. Jefferson, NC: McFarland, 2003.

Clarke, Donald. *Queens of the Big Scream*. *The Irish Times*, 2012. https://www.irish times.com/culture/film/queens-of-the-big-scream-1.555436.

Clover, Carol. "Her Body, Himself: Gender in the Slasher Film." *Representations* 20 (1987):187–228.

———. *Men, Women, and Chain Saws: Gender in the Modern Horror Film*. Princeton, NJ: Princeton University Press, 1992.

Creed, Barbara. *The Monstrous-Feminine: Film, Feminism, Psychoanalysis*. London: Routledge, 1993.

Dixon, Zena. "What's Buried in Pet Sematary 2?" *Dread Central*, 2018. https://www.dreadcentral.com/editorials/284397/zenas-period-blood-whats-buried -in-pet-sematary-2/.

Doane, Mary Ann. "Film and the Masquerade: Theorizing the Female Spectator." *Screen* 23, nos. 3–4 (1982):78–87.

Donaldson, Kayleigh. "Women Love Horror: Why Does This Still Surprise So Many Dudes?" *Syfy Wired*, 2017. Available at: https://www.syfy.com/syfy wire/women-love-horror-why-does-this-still-surprise-so-many-dudes.

Fradley Martin. "'Hell Is a Teenage Girl'?: Postfeminism and Contemporary Teen Horror." In *Postfeminism and Contemporary Hollywood Cinema*, ed. Gwynne J. Muller and N. Muller. London: Palgrave Macmillan, 2013.

Friar, Joe. "Destroyer Review." *The Victoria Advocate*, January 19, 2019. https://www.victoriaadvocate.com/blogs/staff/flix/destroyer-review-nicole-kidman-is-riveting-in-karyn-kusama-s/article_e3e8ae22-1bf7-11e9-a39a-fbf7ea8433fe.html.

Halberstam, Judith. *Skin Shows: Gothic Horror and the Technology of Monsters*. Durham, NC: Duke University Press, 1995.

Harrod, M., and Katarzyna Paszkiewicz. *Women Do Genre in Film and Television* (Routledge Research in Cultural and Media Studies). London: Routledge, 2020.

Hutchings, Peter. "Masculinity and the Horror Film." In *You Tarzan: Masculinity, Movies and Men*, ed. Pat Kirkham and Janet Thumim. London: Palgrave Macmillan, 1993.

Ignacio Castillo, Jorge. "Toronto International Film Festival 2018—Day 4: The Lightning Round." *Planet S Magazine*, 2018. https://planetsmag.com/tiff-2018-day-5-the-lightning-round/.

Kristeva, Julia. *Powers of Horror: An Essay on Abjection*. New York: Columbia University Press, 1982.

Lauzen, Martha M. "It's a Man's (Celluloid) World: Portrayals of Female Characters in the Top Grossing U.S. Films of 2020." *Center for the Study of Women in Television & Film*, April 13, 2021. https://womenintvfilm.sdsu.edu/its-a-mans-celluloid-world-portrayals-of-female-characters-in-the-top-grossing-films-of-2020/.

Martín, José. "La Venganza Como Puerta a La Redención." *El Antepenúltimo Mohicano Cinema*, March 2019. https://www.elantepenultimomohicano.com/2019/03/critica-destroyer-una-mujer-herida.html.

Metz, Christian. "The Imaginary Signifier." *Screen* 16, no. 2 (1975): 14–76.

Mulvey, Laura. "Visual Pleasure and Narrative Cinema." *Screen* 16, no. 3 (1975): 6–18.

Orange, Michelle. "Taking Back the Knife: Girls Gone Gory." *The New York Times*, September 6, 2009. https://www.nytimes.com/2009/09/06/movies/06oran.html.

Paatsch, Leigh. "Nicole Kidman Unrecognisable in Grim Slap to the Face." *Herald Sun*, 2019. https://www.heraldsun.com.au/entertainment/movies/destroyer-a-crime-drama-so-grim-and-grotty-it-should-come-with-a-hazmat-rating/news-story/6834070b839b2489a9157c64173bcc7d.

Paszkiewicz, Katarzyna "Hollywood Transgressor or Hollywood Transvestite? The Reception of Kathryn Bigelow's The Hurt Locker." In *Doing Women's Film History: Reframing Cinemas, Past and Future*, ed. Julia Knight and Christine Gledhi. Urbana: University of Illinois Press, 2015.

———. *Genre, Authorship and Contemporary Women Filmmakers*. Edinburgh: Edinburgh University Press, 2017.

———. "When the Women Directs (A Horror Film)." In *Women Do Genre in Film and Television* (Routledge Research in Cultural and Media Studies), ed. M. Harrod and Katarzyna Paszkiewicz, 41–56. London: Routledge, 2020.

Peirse, Alison. "Exciting New Call for Papers: Women Make Horror." *Gothic Feminism*, October 11, 2017. https://gothicfeminism.com/2017/10/11/exciting-new-cfp-women-make-horror/.

————.*Women Make Horror: Filmmaking, Feminism, Genre*. London: Palgrave Macmillan, 2020.

Reilly, Phoebe. "From 'Babadook' to 'Raw': The Rise of the Modern Female Horror Filmmaker." *Rolling Stone*, October 26, 2016. https://www.rollingstone.com/movies/movie-features/from-babadook-to-raw-the-rise-of-the-modern-female-horror-filmmaker-120169/.

Ross, Deborah. "You Don't See the Character, Only a Deglamorised Kidman and That's What the Film Becomes About." *The Spectator*, January 24, 2019. https://www.spectator.co.uk/article/face-time-24-january-2019.

Sims, David. "Horror Cinema Has a Gatekeeping Problem." *The Atlantic*, October 22, 2018. https://www.theatlantic.com/entertainment/archive/2018/10/jason-blum-female-directors-horror-blumhouse/573571/.

Wang, Evelyn. "Welcome to the Golden Age of Women-Directed Horror." *Vice Magazine*, April 14, 2017. https://www.vice.com/en_us/article/zmbnd5/welcome-to-the-golden-age-of-women-directed-horror.

Williams, Linda. "When the Woman Looks." 1984. Reprinted in *The Dread of Difference: Gender and the Horror Film*, ed. Barry Keith Grant. Austin: University of Texas Press, 1996.

Women in Horror Month. "Special Announcement." 2021. https://www.wominhorrormonth.com/special-announcement/.

ONE

Horror's Founding Mothers

Women in Proto-cinema, Visual Avant-Gardes, and the Silent Era

Erica Tortolani

Scholar K. Charlie Oughton (2016, 241) begins their discussion of women in silent filmmaking with the following prompt to the reader[1]:

> [Imagine] you are the director of over 400 of the first films ever made and have work ranging from comedy to horror, yet your name is all but lost in time. The achievements are there, all the more impressive for having been completed in an era without the ease of production enjoyed today, and some have survived a century because people recognised their value. You, however, are ignored because of what amounts to little more than fashion. What's more, your successes are 'given,' by popular assent, to someone else.

While a tad histrionic in style, Oughton does offer a valid point about the status of these pioneering women—that, when compared to their male counterparts, little to no credit is given, their artistic contributions slowly fading into oblivion while more prominent filmmakers take their place. Contributions from women in early horror media—ranging from the amateur to the professional, the well-known to the anonymous—have indeed had a lasting impact on the various forms, styles, and themes present in the broader trajectory of the genre. Most importantly, these foundational figures broke new ground in their experimentation and overall subversion of horror tropes, giving women the opportunity to actually incorporate horror into their cinematic experiments. Yet what is most perplexing about the status of women-made horror, as alluded to by Oughton, is the fact that earlier works made by female creators have been virtually wiped from the horror canon. Women certainly had a complex position in the burgeoning film industry, as described below, but that doesn't necessarily mean that *all* women were absent from horror film production. Where, then, are these early women of women-made horror?

This chapter provides a historical overview of the place of women in the construction of the horror genre—namely, what I term the "founding mothers" of the genre, during its literary, artistic, proto-, pre-, and early-cinematic iterations.[2] Covering horrific imagery and themes at the cross-sections of a wide range of media, this essay accounts for women not only as creators, molding the more recognizable components of the genre as we see it today, but also as communicators, who had an indelible role in the ways in which horror was discussed, understood, and therefore normalized in society at large. Importantly, the works created by these foundational figures—across temporal, geographic, and media lines—all have in common the unique ability to take otherwise commonplace images and subject matter (both within and outside of the cinematic horror genre proper) and give them new meaning. In other words, horror's founding mothers, as I will argue, were transformative and radical figures, in that they had a hand in not only creating horror tropes but subverting them, challenging the very notion of what horror could be in the genre. This transformative role extends into the modern day, where contemporary women-made horror has in common the same types of (re-)creation and subversion.

Beginning with a more general overview of the role of women in horror media, this chapter will then discuss two founding mothers in early cinema, namely film pioneers Alice Guy-Blaché and Lotte Reiniger. While both worked separately, approaching the cinematic medium in varying ways, they were nevertheless crucial in the formation of the horror genre, even before "horror" was understood as a unified genre by audiences and critics alike.

EMERGING HORRORS, EMERGING MEDIA

According to scholar Karen Ward Mahar, the landscape of the earliest days of cinema—namely, the decade leading up to the turn of the twentieth century—is one that was characteristically masculine, that is, marked by "doubly enhanced masculine associations, for not only was the equipment the focus of attention, but so, too, was the knowledgeable male narrator who explained and demonstrated it" (2008, 10). The burgeoning film industry, with its alignment with the "masculinized arena of applied science joined with the masculinized ethos of the marketplace" (11), set a precedent for marginalizing female voices, both behind and especially in front of the camera. To be sure, women did have a limited, and later growing, role in many aspects of the early film industry, notably in those positions like in film processing, editing, and printing (24). Furthermore, the commercialization of the photographic medium amassed a substantial female following, with women making popular the art of amateur photography by the turn of the century (16).[3] Yet, for all of the technological and aesthetic development witnessed during this era, women creators are, by and large, uncredited. Developing a thorough chronicle of women in pre- and proto-horror, due to the shortcomings in this historical record, can therefore seem like an impossible task. However, it is important here to broaden the boundaries of what *exactly* can be defined as pre- and proto-cinema, moving beyond mere visual, photographic apparatuses and instead looking at a variety of media where women actively interrogated (narratively, thematically, and even visually) horror tropes. This practice both casts a wider net, so to speak, when considering the myriad ways that women have approached horror and also takes into consideration the many possible influences of the earliest horror directors, namely Blaché and Reiniger. These pre- and proto-cinematic areas fall into three categories: literature, performance entertainment, and visual modernisms.

Firstly, the body of Gothic literature is an important precinematic influence on horror filmmaking in general, given the genre's narrative and thematic tendencies toward inviting the "readers' fears and anxieties in highly stylized mystery-tales" (Killeen 2009, 2). The so-called Female Gothic,[4] consisting of a collective of works from a range of authors like Ann Radcliffe, Edith Wharton, and others, has an even broader influence on cinematic horror. While not particularly unique in the attention that it pays toward topics like sensationalism, the body, and bodily performance (Shapira 2006, 454–455), the Female Gothic is innovative instead for its ability to transform and subvert such topics. Ann Radcliffe, as the "great inaugurator of the genre" (Fitzgerald 2004, 12), for example, is novel in a variety of ways: through her experimentation with female agency and the "concept of 'delicacy' as a code that seeks to regulate female interaction with the body's verbal representations" (Shapira 2006, 454); with her articulation of "explained supernatural," which not only rationalized the existence of ghosts, but also diverted it, "rerouted, so to speak, into the realm of the everyday" (Castle 1995, 124); and through her subsequent creation of the uncanny, which adds a deeper level of horror by destroying the "distinctions between fantasy and reality, mind and matter, subject and object" (127). Furthermore, Female Gothic authors like Radcliffe are important for their experimental alternatives to linear narratives, a strategy that places "individuals in the no-man's land of an indefinitely extended threshold, a phantom territory which intrudes between action and result, between cause and effect, thus keeping the fugitives in a permanent betwixt-and-between condition" (Aguirre 2008, 10). Beyond mere narrative innovation, the nonlinear textual strategies honed by Radcliffe and others in their Gothic fictions also set a broader precedent for the ways in which horror was realized in fictional media (and, by extension, precinematic media). Ghosts and the supernatural indeed incite fear and fascination in the audience; however, the unease and uncanny brought about by the instability of linear, cohesive time incite horror on an entirely different level, creating new dimensions of horror.

Secondly, theatrical entertainments are another precinematic area that lends itself to the formation of the early horror genre. Because of woman's inscribed place inside the home, and the overall barring of women from cultural and intellectual institutions, women were also limited in their "access to cultural production"; those in wealthy circles could still be seen as patrons at a distance, donating funds to help sustain these institutions, but the arts (and art education) were certainly a means to an end, so to speak, only existing so women could acquire "an honorable education" (Wolff 1990, 24). Despite such denial of female agency outside of the home, it was granted in new capacities by a host of other media, such as home entertainments and parlor games, where women could participate in media that both offered a "specialized and fulfilling type of work that was once congruent with the social life of a class" (Dawson 2008, 101) and, significantly, enabled women to, literally and figuratively, act out of their prescribed societal roles, all within the comfort of their own parlors. Popular in these performances were "isolated, shocking displays" (78); such proto-horror performances involved the active use of the body to cross boundaries between normal and abnormal and to explore the abstract spaces in-between. Examples of these home entertainments range from more improvisational games, where players were freely encouraged to "become giants, 'midnight screechers,' and 'nondescripts,' displacing carpets, furniture, and even the family Bible for a carnivalesque evening of elaboratively prepared revelry" (72), to more scripted performances, in which elaborate adaptations of classic literature were staged in the home. For example, in games like "The Blue Beard Tableau,"

> [The] purpose of the grotesque display was to create the effect of actual decapitation, with participants projecting their heads through holes in a sheet, meanwhile adopting alarmingly slack-jawed, transfixed, and disheveled poses. . . . Bluebeard's wives boast tussled coiffures, unadorned heads, and downcast attitudes vastly different from those of *Harper's* [*Harper's Bazaar* magazine's] complacently fashionable models. (81–82)

Much like Female Gothic authors, female home performers in these instances were given the agency to "deliberately, playfully [work] against normative poses, transforming themselves into bizarre and unsocial spectacles" (74). These women were not the sole creators of grotesque home entertainments, but suffice it to say, they had enough agency in the ways in which these open narratives were presented and most importantly used the female body as an instrument for creating horrific spectacles.[5]

Lastly, visual modernisms developing prior to and at the turn of the twentieth century, in my opinion, play a unique role in the formation of early silent horror. After World War I, movements like dada and, in particular, surrealism heightened their political commentaries by taking dream-like, spectacular imagery at its core and transforming it into images of horror. Referencing Walter Benjamin, Adam Lowenstein offers that modernisms like surrealism experimented with horrific imagery, used the "very real ruptured bodies" (Lowenstein 2005, 18–19) of soldiers, and translated them into the bodily deformities at the center of their pieces. Modernisms like surrealism and dada, as responses to the rapidly modernizing world around them, can therefore be understood as a "violent, embodied assault on the social structures propping up modernity, rather than a romantic retreat within the self" (19). Visual artists outside of film, in this context at least, therefore have a special relationship to the horror genre. German performer, poet, and member of Zurich dada Emmy Hennings, for example, couples the plastic arts with performance in order to represent ideas like the "loneliness, sadness, and oblivion" (Rugh 1981, 3) of postwar society, in pieces like *Puppen* (ca. 1916),[6] and to extend the "shock techniques and disturbing tactics that Dada would develop" to offer an alternative to the superficiality of the modern world (Hemus 2006, 42) in her performances as Arachne, the "truth-speaking spider."[7] In a similar way, Swiss contemporaneous artist and performer Sophie Taeuber combined bodily performance with other plastic media—such as paper masks with elongated and distorted features—to produce "a hybrid of visceral abstraction" that "gives Dada's static art its most physical presence and realness, while also performing its drive toward disintegration and death" (Andrew 2014, 29). These visual artists used horror-adjacent techniques as a response to modernity and all of its political and technological implications. For women artists working within and concurrent to the advent of silent cinema, such a response extended to the shifting role of women in modernity—her place in society, as well as her status as artist within these movements themselves (notably, in movements like surrealism; see Chadwick 1991, 43). Most notably, many female avant-garde artists interrogated "a whole chain of signifiers" dominant in visual iconography, like "the infantile, primitive, unconscious, erotic, monstrous, excessive, abject, and insane" (Latimer 2016, 444). Artists like Frida Kahlo, Leonora Carrington, and others often took on representational strategies like the self-portrait in order to turn "to their own reality" and reveal "their rejection of the idea of woman as an abstract principle, and a substitution of the image in the mirror as a focal point in their quest for greater self-awareness and knowledge" (Chadwick 1991, 74). Placing images of the self into heightened, distorted environments and contrasting them with icons of death, decay, the bestial, and the visceral, these artists communicated personal, internalized states while at the same time critiquing the very visual language used by their male counterparts. While such implicit yet pointed statements about gender relations certainly weren't the collective project of these female artists, horrific images and themes exploited in such artwork helped subvert the very conventions present in the broader movements. These types of representational strategies would later materialize both in concurrent avant-garde cinemas, as well as the broader, future landscape of women-directed horror.

"BITTEN BY THE DEMON OF THE CINEMA"

While many of the pre- and proto-cinematic experiments discussed above carried many of the hallmarks of what we now consider to be the horror genre, upon their creation they were not considered as such.[8] In other words, *horror* as a unified system of conventions was relatively absent from discussions of any and all media, in large part due to the fact that horror itself wasn't as fully formed or coherent as a stand-alone genre category. Instead, the films that were made during the silent era, which, as noted above, are indebted to experiments housed in visual, literary, and performance traditions, have in common what Kendall R. Phillips terms "horrific elements." Phillips argues in part that horrific elements, syntactically, help to describe "the core relationship between [film] elements—in this case, a relationship marked by fear and revulsion" (2018, 4). By this logic, films whose core elements strike negative or repellant feelings can therefore be considered films containing horrific elements. Importantly, horrific elements include discursive frames for film interpretation; that is, they hinge on the ways in which critics and, for Phillips, audiences have linguistically categorized the films that they consume. Moving beyond the mere generic genre classifications that film studios have used to define their films for distribution and exhibition purposes, horrific elements instead consider the narrative and aesthetic expectations that an audience holds while watching a film, how they rationalize what they are seeing, and ultimately how they describe this film to others. Horror in the earliest film-adjacent experiments exhibits the same types of "fluid and corrigible set of historically situated meanings" (19), and in the case of women-made horror, these meanings are unique *because* of their fluidity, of their capacity to transform the very tropes and norms that existed within the mainstream. Horrific elements in pre- and proto-cinemas were not only utilized in early silent cinema but were eventually heightened, taken to creative extremes through their technological innovation, thematic experimentation, and, above all, willingness to exhibit the grotesque, both on the physical and psychological level.

Take, for example, the films of Alice Guy-Blaché, a pioneer of filmmaking well beyond the horror genre. Considered to be one of the first woman filmmakers, Blaché took on many roles in the emerging film industry, first working as secretary for Léon Gaumont's *Comptoir général de Photographie* (Slide 1986, 15) and later establishing firm relationships among film engineers, camera operators, and marketing firms. Her keen interest in the mechanics and industry of film would later lead to her desire to experiment with the art of filmmaking, asking permission from Gaumont himself to "write one or two little scenes and have a few friends in them" (27)—in other words, to create one of the first (if not the first) narrative films.[9] The result, *La Fée aux choux*,[10] not only revolutionized the ways in which films were structured, in part transitioning from actualities to fully formed, linear storylines, but also—important for a study on the genesis of horror—was one of the first experiments with material otherwise recognizable as fantasy. Fantasy, myth, and fairy tale, according to scholars like Carroll, are all valid descriptors that, in a similar way to the more standard fare of the horror genre, entertain the same types of "naturalistic explanations of abnormal incidents" (Carroll 1990, 16). Horrific elements, present in early filmmaking, are cut from the same cloth, so to speak, as the category of fantasy; fantasy can be understood as prefiguring horror, and while the former is not structured in the same way or embedded with the same types of audience response as the latter, both overlap with one another and can describe broader creative tendencies toward representing and sometimes normalizing "unexplainable phenomenon" and the human imagination (Prohászková 2012, 132).

La Fée aux choux is by no means a horror film, nor can it be considered among the larger body of films, both preceding and following it, that have been described as using horrific elements. Nevertheless, *La Fée*—being Blaché's first (surviving) film—is important to consider when outlining the director's larger tendency toward experimenting with fantasy and the marvelous, something that she would approach throughout her career with editing techniques[11] and subject matter. A number of films in Blaché's trajectory as director and producer, while marketed as dramas or thrillers, would stake a much larger claim in the fantastic, the marvelous, and, later, the horrific. These films include 1912's *The Wise Witch of Fairyland*, whose so-called "strong mystic atmosphere" (*Moving Picture World* 1912, 544) is an extension of *La Fée*, and *The Woman of Mystery* in 1914, a film praised (again, as a drama-thriller) for its "unusual air of mystery and adventure" (*Motion Picture News* 1914, 54).[12]

These and other films in Blaché's venture into fantasy-horror are significant for their visual innovation, marked by their radically different
aesthetic and thematic approaches that were dictated, in part, by the
type of tone and the type of subject matter that the director was trying
to achieve. No two films looked alike, and the diversity within Blaché's
fantasy-horror oeuvre run the gamut from the melodramatic, the realistic,
and the lighthearted and childlike to the psychologically and physically
disturbing. The most explicit of these films—and the film that single-
handedly cements Blaché's status as early horror filmmaker—is 1913's
The Pit and the Pendulum, adapted from the Edgar Allan Poe short of
the same name.[13] Following the tradition of such Poe adaptations made
popular during the silent era, Blaché's interpretation of *Pit* would utilize
the same types of "gruesome" and "blood-curdling" (in Rhodes 2018,
350) techniques as both Poe and his cinematic successors and was characterized in reviews, promotions, and even Blaché's personal accounts
on the production of the film as a truly terrifying cinematic experience.
Popularly quoted as having "great pleasures in observing the shivers and
anguished sighs of the public" (Slide 1986, 73), Blaché herself used language connoting fear, terror, and danger during the making of the film,
which no doubt could have extended to the interpretation of the film by
the trade press. "Contrary to general opinion," Blaché described, "filming often offers real dangers. Mortal accidents are not rare. Fortunately
we never had anything of the sort to deplore, as we judged that the best
of films was not worth a man's life" (73). While assuring audiences that
there were no real risks in creating her film, Blaché then changed her tune,
somewhat contradicting herself by detailing ways in which, for instance,
food was smeared on props and the bodies of actors in order to get live
rats to crawl on their bodies (who would later try to escape, infesting the
studio and quashing the attempts of Blaché's bulldog in eradicating them
from the building [72]). The relative abjection taken into consideration
when producing *The Pit and the Pendulum*—handling food waste and raw
meat, employing copious amounts of live vermin—certainly constructs a
mythos around the film that squarely situates it within the realm of horror. Reviews of the film broaden this alignment with the earliest forms of
the horror genre, providing the discursive scaffolding for how these films
were understood, talked about, and indirectly influenced audiences to
react in the same way.

"The literary keynote of this work is suspense," writes a reviewer
from *Exhibitor's Times*, "It is gruesome. It is harrowing. . . . The director
even intensified the suspense by flashing every now and then the rescue
party making its way through the subterranean passageways, so that
the spectators could not help oscillating between fear and hope. It had
the genuine fascination of terror" (1913, 7). Such word choice employed

throughout the review— "suspense," "fear," "terror," "gruesome," "ab-horrent"—communicates not only the tonal quality of the film (that the reviewer feels, and that the audience subsequently *should* feel, upon view-ing the film) but also the visual qualities of its alignment with the gro-tesque and the altogether chilling or horrific. *Pit'*s horrors are discussed at an even greater length toward the end of the article, where the reviewer, despite lauding the film's intricate re-creations of medieval Europe, had an almost visceral reaction to its scenes depicting torture:

> The one great drawback of this film portrayal was the entirely unnecessary torture scene. There was positively no legitimate reason for showing us the agony of a woman on the rack, to say nothing of a man, to all outward intent, being actually racked. After the first shock is over, the spectator reminds himself that it is all pretense anyway, and that the incident consequently loses its real value for him.

Underscoring the extreme brutality of the scene—which, to be fair, was relatively graphic for the time—this review clearly isolates the physical gruesomeness of the film's climactic torture sequence. It also pays consid-erable attention to the psychological thrills and chills woven throughout the overall narrative of the film. Despite critiquing the heavy-handedness that Blaché took in her adaptation of the source text, the advantages of this extreme dramatization result in a final product in which the "cumu-lative intensity . . . is overwhelming. It sweeps the spectator off his feet and deluges him, as it were, in a veritable maelstrom of horror. It does Poe justice, indeed."

It is clear that Blaché was lauded by a variety of critics for her blending of impressive (albeit over-the-top) visuals with renderings of complex psychological states. Certainly, the value of *The Pit and the Pendulum* comes from its "unabashed presentation of dramatic horror" (Rhodes 2018, 350), one of the first of its ilk, at least in the context of early silent film. However, the value of Blaché's contribution to the horror canon—something that I find makes it all the more powerful as an entry into horror—is its experimentations with spectatorial alignment, its blatant efforts to place the viewer in the perspective of the horrors of the fiction-alized torture sequence. According to David Annwn Jones, lobby cards distributed during screenings of the film not only depicted key stills of the protagonist Alonzo's (Darwin Karr) torture but framed these images in a way so as to "allow an intimate audience reaction to the prisoner's growing distress" (Jones 2018, 51). Rather than maintaining a safe inter-personal distance between the camera and the subject, Blaché positions Alonzo in intimately invasive ways—head tilted back toward the camera, limbs outstretched toward the dark abyss of the pit (51–52)—providing the illusion that the audience, too, is trapped alongside the victim. Even before the audience begins watching the film, their perspective is aligned with the victim of torture, and with a few clever cinematic techniques (involving lighting, depth of field, and focal lengths), they are placed squarely into the realm of horror, or rather, the realm of psychological horror. In-theater supplementary materials, alongside these reviews, help set up expectations for the audience on what they will see and how they should react to this cinematic content. Blaché clearly works with horrific elements in *The Pit and the Pendulum*, but it is through these ancillary devices that such horrific elements are heightened to an extreme, pointing to the overall novelty of Blaché's early horror work.

Another innovation present in Blaché's adaptation of *The Pit and the Pendulum* comes from the creative liberties that she takes with how Poe's narrative is structured, as well as how characters are situated within this narrative. In the original source text, the storyline is more free-flowing and dream-like, having very little semblance to a traditional, linear narrative. Blaché, on the other hand, directly sets "the action during the time of the Spanish Inquisition and [adds] a narrative framework to establish reasons why the protagonist would be unjustly subjected to such cruel torture" (Hayes 2001, 37).[14] For sure, Blaché maintains a sort of dream-like (or nightmare-like) structure in the torture sequences, for those provide an eerie break from reality that place the audience in the mindset of Alonzo. However, what is truly impressive about Blaché's interpretation

Figure 1.1.   Screenshot from *The Pit and the Pendulum*.

of *Pit* is her ability to house this more abstract sequence within a larger, more realistic plot structure. This realism, rather than lessening its impact as a horror film, heightens it instead, displaying the horrors of the everyday. In turn, Blaché broadens the definition of horrific elements, expanding the boundaries of cinematic horror that would have reverberations in future subgenres like psychological horror, psycho-thrillers, and even body-related genres like splatter and torture porn.

The German animator Lotte Reiniger is another prominent figure in the landscape of silent cinema, and while many of her works feature lighthearted, childlike images and narratives, they have important implications on the overall development of horrific images in film. Reiniger and Blaché, on the surface, are radically different filmmakers: they worked with different media; they rose to success in different countries and in different time periods;[15] and, above all, whereas Reiniger as a filmmaker adapts "a Victorian pastime, the toy theatre, with its long and deep connection to flights of the imagination" (Warner 2011, 391), Blaché took on a wide range of genres, and approaches to these genres, with a relatively firm stance in realism (or, at the very least, magical realism, as is the case with *La Fée*). Reiniger's work, therefore, is largely valued for its appeal to children in addition to adult audiences, while Blaché stakes no such claims.

Nevertheless, there are some important commonalities between the German animation pioneer Reiniger and the innovative French/American filmmaker Blaché. To start, both Reiniger and Blaché began their careers in cinema by collaborating with other prominent male directors. Reiniger, for instance, frequented Berlin arts circles in the early 1920s, entering personal and professional relationships with the likes of Walter Ruttmann and Paul Wegener; for the latter, she created some of her first animated silhouettes for title sequences in a number of films.[16] Reiniger would later have lasting, professional relationships with the likes of Julius Pinschewer, with whom she would make a number of advertising films; Fritz Lang, who would commission (but would eventually scrap) animated sequences for *Die Nibelungen* in 1923; and, notably, Carl Koch, her future husband (filmportal.de, n.d.). Unlike Blaché, Reiniger would work steadily in the film and television industries well into her old age. Like Blaché, however, Reiniger's talent in silhouette animation led to her success as a filmmaker, where she would gain respect from her peers and eventually gain enough creative agency to make films on her own.

This leads to the second, and perhaps most blatant, connection between Reiniger and Blaché—their experimentation with fantasy, fairy tales, and the marvelous in their debut films. Much like Blaché's fantastical *La Fée aux choux*, Reiniger's first feature film, *Die Abenteuer des Prinzen Achmed* in 1926, portrays a world that follows "a familiar fairy-tale trajectory"

(Ratner 2006, 46) that features magic and the supernatural. Operating in "an *other* world, one that operates according to self-contained but different laws" (author's emphasis; Cleghorn 2019, 43), *Achmed* also contains a thrilling story line, in which the titular character must escape from the clutches of an evil magician and eventually free a benevolent fairy from a tribe of demonic beings.

What's unique about *Die Abenteuer des Prinzen Achmed*—aside from the artistry with which Reiniger crafts her paper silhouettes—is the way that she incorporates horrific elements into an otherwise tame, family-friendly fairy tale. As critics and scholars have pointed out, Reiniger's animations could in fact be read as being "more suited to adult than to child audiences," with their source material implicitly "filled with contradictions, satirical commentary, and often, strong erotic undertones" (Guerin and Mebold, n.d.). And, as mentioned previously, fantasy and the supernatural, for scholars like Carroll, have important connective threads to the horror genre, exploiting the same aesthetic and thematic content as one another. Many sequences in *Achmed* toe the line separating fantasy and horror and, while not wholly entering the realm of horror proper, still contain horrific elements (those elements that are supernatural, grotesque, and abject and that can elicit fear), making it an important precursor to early horror cinema. As Marina Warner offers, Reiniger with *Die Abenteuer des Prinzen Achmed* enters "a universe of different kinds of

Figure 1.2.   Screenshot from *Die Abenteuer des Prinzen Achmed*.

dark" (2011, 402), playing with a number of different fears—both real and fictional, natural and supernatural—which cause it to enter the realm of horror in diverse, and equally interesting, ways.

Critics picked up on similar traits upon viewing *Achmed*, largely using language that emphasized the fantastical, unreal world woven by Reiniger in her silhouettes. Hans Wollenberg (1926, 104) in *Lichtbild-Bühne*,[17] for instance, remarks that the story line itself is "very bizarre," featuring figures like ghosts and monsters that, while frightening, are "particularly beautiful." Described as "one of the most interesting things of the kind ever produced," the English-language *The Educational Screen* (1926, 180) also pays attention to the strangely beautiful way that otherwise monstrous content—"the ugly but good-hearted witch," "hobgoblins," and the like—are portrayed in the film, how "they vie in naturalness of movement, in grace and agility with those of the ordinary film." A reviewer from the Viennese *Der Filmbote* (1926, 27) further praises the "romantic winding path" that Reiniger weaves in her film, equipped with an "exciting, baroque-decorated love story of princes and princesses, battles and adventures, [ghosts] and magic." Such horrific, supernatural elements are further emphasized in other publications, like in reviewer Willy Haas's discussion of the film, noting the film's contrast between "wit and grace" and a more grotesque portrayal of "strictly stylized" atmospheric details like churning winds, fog, and water (1926, 15).

Reiniger's use of horrific elements extend well beyond the fairy-tale dreamscapes found in *Die Abenteuer des Prinzen Achmed*. Critic Rudolph Arnheim, for instance, goes as far as to say that the director's cut-paper techniques in films like *Doktor Dolittle und seine Tiere* (1928) are ideal, in that the "imagination of a child can make a monster more frightening, an exploit more daring and extravagant . . . than the literal representations in puppet or cartoon, which automatically limit and impoverish the visionary, fantastic mental imagery of the viewer" (quoted in Moritz 1996, 15). While children are the focus of Arnheim's review, this notion—that animation heightens horrors in the mind of the spectator—can certainly be grafted onto audiences of all ages. In using animated silhouettes, Reiniger exaggerates the physical features of her fictional monsters, beasts, and other horrific creatures, thereby, to quote Rachel Palfreyman, reveling "in stretching and transforming skins, bizarre births and the unleashing of unknown and powerful beings dwelling deep within" (2011, 15). These techniques not only add a level of grotesquerie to seemingly real, natural objects but lend a sense of hyperreality to those entities that live in the depths of the imagination. As a result, Reiniger's films almost become realer than the real, using exaggerated animations to bring to life those beings that, literally and figuratively, live in the shadows.

Both Blaché and Reiniger are valuable for their contributions to the visual look and feel of early silent horror. Additionally, their engagement with the avant-garde amplifies the horrific content in each of their films. For Reiniger, the avant-garde is realized through the medium of animation and the ways that she incorporated color, rhythm, and movement within films like *Achmed*. As many accounts have offered, Reiniger was heavily involved with Berlin experimental animation circles, becoming acquainted with artist Hans Curlis, among others, in the late 1900s (Cleghorn 2019, 46), and later participated in a German independent film association with the likes of Ruttmann, Hans Richter, and Asta Nielsen in 1930 (Hagener 2007, 101). Reiniger was therefore familiar with film art's capacity to "transpose material forms into moving images . . . and institute the dynamism of graphic forms as the ' . . . basis for a new visual language'" (Cleghorn 2019, 47), which were the common goals of the avant-garde absolute film movement. Importantly, the overly exaggerated silhouettes, with their fluid but nonfigurative gestures, operate within "an *other* world . . . according to self-contained but different laws" (author's emphasis, 43); the manipulation of form, movement, and time lends a sense of unease and uncanniness to the world of the film, therefore entering the territory of the horrific.

CONCLUSION—THE (CONTINUING) LEGACY OF WOMEN IN HORROR

"At first it looked as though the genre would dissipate in the flood of lackluster imitations," scholar Noël Carroll observes of the state of horror in film and literature in his seminal 1990 study, *The Philosophy of Horror or, Paradoxes of the Heart*; "[each] time the health of the genre seemed threatened, suddenly it would revive. The genre seems immensely resilient" (Carroll 1990, 3). Certainly, across the span of some hundred or so years, the horror genre in American filmmaking and beyond has witnessed interesting ebbs and flows that have solidified its place in the popular and critical consciousness. As I have laid out in this chapter, women, and their status within the horror genre, have remained equally resilient, shaping the genre as we have come to know it today. Without the work of early modern artists in dada and surrealism, we would not have such films as Germaine Dulac's *La Coquille et le clergyman* (1928), where disjointed surrealistic narratives are matched by the horrific, sexualized nightmare-scapes of the main characters. Without those experimentations with proto-cinematic visual media—and, later, advancing animation techniques—perhaps we wouldn't have the technologically and thematically groundbreaking *Night on Bald Mountain* (1933), a short by Claire Parker and Alexandre Alexeiff, or *Spook Sport* (1939), by Mary Ellen Bute. Without such theatrical media from women at home and in public, revolutionizing the way that bodily autonomy and gendered performance were understood in daily life, we wouldn't have the contributions of a wide range of avant-garde multimedia, like Maya Deren's incomplete work, *Witch's Cradle* (1944). And, without all of these twentieth century developments, we wouldn't have the radical work from women across all horror media, in all geographic areas, in the context of the present day.

As of the writing of this chapter, the works of foundational figures like Blaché and Reiniger have entered the popular consciousness, with Blaché's work compiled by Kino Lorber in their Blu-Ray series *Alice Guy-Blaché Volume 1: The Gaumont Years* (Smith 2020) and Reiniger receiving attention from *The New York Times* (Lockwood 2019).[18] This uptick in popularity likely points to the ever-changing landscape of horror filmmaking: as more women lend their voices and share their stories in the present day, so too are those voices from the past discovered and welcomed by scholars and audiences alike. And yet there's still much more work that needs to be done, with so many of these creators still marginalized. This chapter catalyzes such discussions of lesser-known, or lesser-discussed, female horror filmmakers, helping to paint a more vivid portrait of horror's founding mothers all-around.

NOTES

1. A more in-depth version of this chapter can be found in my forthcoming dissertation on women-directed horror films.

2. "Precinema" in this case will refer to all media that came before the development of the cinematic medium. "Proto-cinema" instead will refer to the earliest forms of multimedia that incorporate cinematic techniques like projection, movement, special effects, and synchronized sound. The two terms are not mutually exclusive; rather, pre- and proto-cinemas often ran concurrently with one another at various points in time.

3. One could make the argument that there is a correlation between the growth of amateur photography and other visual media and the rise of popular proto-horror entertainments, like spirit photography, trick photography, and other visual illusions.

4. The term "Female Gothic" proves to be a widely contentious one. As Ellen Ledoux offers, the Female Gothic was termed in second-wave feminist circles in order to develop a solid, female canon of literature stemming from the Victorian period. However, as Ledoux and others have attested, this body of female authorship is often devoid of the actual "ideological diversity of women writers" (2017, 2), instead lumping all authors into one overly generalizable category of authorship. Discussions of the Female Gothic in this essay will take these critiques into consideration. For more information, see Ledoux 2017 and Fitzgerald 2004.

5. Outside of home entertainments, several other pre- and proto-cinematic performances paved the way for the early horror genre, like spiritualist media

(seances, hypnotism, mesmerism, other life spectacles, and optical illusions; see Rhodes 2018) and, to a certain extent, public magic shows (see Dawes 2007). Significantly, common to these performances were proto-cinematic innovations, like projected images, electrical effects, and other moving image techniques.

6. According to Thomas F. Rugh, Hennings's puppet work can be described as the following: "The three dolls . . . slump and hang like marionettes. The doll in the center looms above the other two, its arms outstretched in cruciform shape; the one on the right kneels and gestures toward the central figure, shunning it as if it represented an evil power. The doll slumped in the lower left corner is lifeless and oppressed by the doll above. The faces are gaunt and frowning, their bodies angular" (1981, 3).

7. In such performances with the Cabaret Voltaire, Hennings props her head in the middle of large, outstretched arachnid legs, becoming the thorax of a nightmarish human-beast hybrid. For more information, see Hemus 2006, 42.

8. Quoted in Anthony Slide, ed., *The Memoirs of Alice Guy-Blaché* (1986, 27).

9. To be sure, Blaché assisted production on, and was responsible for the prints of, dozens of different films during her time at Gaumont but never received full credit for them.

10. The year of the film's release is up for debate. In some instances, Blaché herself lists the release year as 1896 (hinted at by the remark, "In 1896 unions did not exist"; Slide 1986, 28). According to Slide, film historians like Francis Lacassin date the film at 1900s, due to its placement in the Gaumont film catalog (28n1).

11. Blaché describes the process of filming *La Fée* as one filled with experimentation, noting that she discovered "many little tricks" such as fast-forwarding, reversing, superimposition, fades, and double exposures (Slide 1986, 29). These techniques would prove valuable during her career, as she would employ such techniques in numerous films, like *Chez le Magnetiseur* (1898), *Le Statue* (1905), and *La Vie du Christ* (1906).

12. According to Gary D. Rhodes (2018, 113–114), Blaché's other films within the spectrum of horror-fantasy include *A Message From Beyond* (1912), *The Eyes of Satan* (1913), *The Case of the Missing Girl* (1913), *A Drop of Blood* (1913), *Shadows of the Moulin Rouge* (1914), and *The Dream Woman* 1914).

13. Only the first of three reels exists of *The Pit and the Pendulum*. It can be found at the Library of Congress in Washington, D.C., and (in varying qualities) on online platforms like YouTube.

14. Blaché also adds another dimension of interpersonal conflict to the plot, chronicling a love triangle between Alonzo, his lover Isabelle (Blanche Cornwall), and the rejected Pedro (Fraunie Fraunholz). In the midst of this narrative, Isabelle is falsely accused of being a witch by Inquisitors, who blame her in part for the disappearance of religious jewels and vow to torture her accordingly. Not only does the inclusion of witchcraft further align it with the horror genre, but this plotline also mirrors the general tendency in American filmmaking to bring justice to those accused of witchcraft; that is, to prove that these women have been wrongfully accused. On the Isabelle plotline, see Jones 2018, 50; on the inversion of the witch trope in early horror filmmaking, see Rhodes 2018, 155–156.

15. There is, however, a bit of overlap in terms of when the two women worked: Blaché's career tapered off around the same time as Reiniger's gained momentum, in the early to mid-1920s.

16. For a complete listing of Reiniger's early silhouette contributions, see "Lotte Reiniger," *filmportal.de*, https://www.filmportal.de/person/lotte-reini ger_c94c9327f5cc4ce8ac33debaf05e27e0.

17. All German translations are my own, unless otherwise noted in text.

18. Reiniger was also featured as a "Google Doodle" on June 2, 2016.

BIBLIOGRAPHY

Aguirre, Manuel. "Geometries of Terror: Numinous Spaces in Gothic, Horror, and Science Fiction." *Gothic Studies* 10, no. 2 (2008): 1–17.

Andrew, Nell. "Dada Dance: Sophie Taeuber's Visceral Abstraction." *Art Journal* 73, no. 1 (2014): 12–29.

Carroll, Noël. *The Philosophy of Horror: Or, Paradoxes of the Heart*. London: Routledge, 1990.

Castle, Terry. *The Female Thermometer: 18th Century Culture and the Invention of the Uncanny*. Oxford: Oxford University Press, 1995.

Chadwick, Whitney. *Women Artists and the Surrealist Movement*. London: Thames and Hudson, 1991.

Cleghorn, Elinor. "*In a Tiny Realm of Her Own*: Lotte Reiniger's Light Work." In *Women Artists, Feminism, and the Moving Image: Contexts and Practices*, ed. Lucy Reynolds, 39–55. London: Bloomsbury Academic, 2019.

Dawes, Amy. "The Female of the Species: Magiciennes of the Victorian and Edwardian Eras." *Early Popular Visual Culture* 5, no. 2 (2007): 127–150.

Dawson, Melanie. *Laboring to Play: Home Entertainment and the Spectacle of Middle-Class Cultural Life, 1850–1920*. Tuscaloosa: University of Alabama Press, 2008.

"Die Geschichte des Prinzen Achmed." *Der Filmbote*, October 2, 1926, 27.

Fitzgerald, Lauren. "Female Gothic and the Institutionalization of Gothic Studies." *Gothic Studies* 6, no. 1 (2004): 8–18.

Guerin, Frances, and Anke Mebold. "Lotte Reiniger." *Women Film Pioneers Project*, n.d. https://wfpp.columbia.edu/pioneer/lotte-reiniger/.

Haas, Willy. "Lotte Reinigers Silhouettenfilm." *Lotte Reinigers Silhouettenfilm: Die Geschichte des Prinzen Achmed*. Comenius Film, 1926.

Hagener, Malte. *Moving Forward, Looking Back: The European Avant-Garde and The Invention of Film Culture, 1919–1939*. Amsterdam: Amsterdam University Press, 2007.

Hayes, Kevin. "Alice Guy's 'The Pit and the Pendulum' (1913)." *The Edgar Allan Poe Review* 2, no. 1 (2001): 37–42.

Hemus, Ruth. *The Interventions of Five Women Artists, Writers and Performers in the European Dada Movement*. Edinburgh: Edinburgh University Press, 2006.

"In Berlin." January *The Educational Screen*, January 1926, 180.

Jones, David Annwn. *Re-envisaging the First Age of Cinematic Horror, 1896-1934: Quanta of Fear*. Cardiff: University of Wales Press, 2018.

Killeen, Jarlath. *History of the Gothic: Gothic Literature 1825–1914*. Cardiff: University of Wales Press, 2009.

Latimer, Tirza True. 2016. "Equivocal Gender: Dada/Surrealism and Sexual Politics Between the Wars." In *A Companion to Dada and Surrealism*, ed. David Hopkins and Dana Arnold, 442–459. New York: John Wiley and Sons, 442–459.

Ledoux, Ellen. "Was There Ever a 'Female Gothic'?" *Palgrave Communications* 3, no. 17042 (2017): 1–7.

Lockwood, Devi. "Overlooked No More: Lotte Reiniger, Animator Who Created Magic With Scissors and Paper." *The New York Times*, October 18, 2019. https://www.nytimes.com/2019/10/16/obituaries/lotte-reiniger-overlooked.html.

"Lotte Reiniger." *Filmportal.de*, n.d. https://www.filmportal.de/person/lotte -reiniger_c94c9327f5cc4ce8ac33debaf05e27e0.

Lowenstein, Adam. *Shocking Representation: Historical Trauma, National Cinema, and the Modern Horror Film*. New York: Columbia University Press, 2005.

Mahar, Karen Ward. *Women Filmmakers in Early Hollywood*. Baltimore: Johns Hopkins University Press, 2008.

Moritz, William. "Some Critical Perspectives on Lotte Reiniger." In *Animation: Art and History*, ed. Maureen Furniss, 13–19. Bloomington: Indiana University Press, 1996.

Oughton, K. Charlie. "When the Woman Shoots: Ladies Behind the Silent Horror Film Camera." In *Silent Women: Pioneers of Cinema*. ed. Melody Bridges and Cheryl Robson, 241–254. Twickenham, UK: Supernova Books, 2016.

Palfreyman, Rachel. "Life and Death in the Shadows: Lotte Reiniger's *Die Abenteur des Prinzen Achmed*." *German Life and Letters* 64, no. 1 (2011): 6–18.

Phillips, Kendall R. *A Place of Darkness: The Rhetoric of Horror in Early American Cinema*. Austin: University of Texas Press, 2018.

Prohászková, Viktória. "The Genre of Horror." *American International Journal of Contemporary Research* 2, no. 4 (2012): 132–142.

R.R. "'The Pit and the Pendulum,' A Study in Suspense." *Exhibitor's Times*, 1913, 6–7.

Ratner, Megan. "In the Shadows." *Art on Paper* 10, no. 3 (2006): 44–49.

Rhodes, Gary D. *The Birth of the American Horror Film*. Edinburgh: Edinburgh University Press, 2018.

Rugh, Thomas F. "Emmy Hennings and the Emergence of Zurich Dada." *Woman's Art Journal* 2, no. 1 (1981): 1–6.

Shapira, Yael. "Where the Bodies Are Hidden: Ann Radcliffe's 'Delicate' Gothic." *Eighteenth Century Fiction* 18, no. 4 (2006): 453–476.

Slide, Anthony, ed. *The Memoirs of Alice Guy-Blaché*. Trans. Roberta Blaché and Simone Blaché. Metuchen, NJ: Scarecrow Press.

Smith, Derek. "Alice Guy-Blaché and Julia Crawford Ivers's Films on Kino Lorber Blu-ray." *Slant*, April 6, 2020. https://www.slantmagazine.com/dvd/alice -guy-blache-and-julia-crawford-iverss-films-on-kino-lorber-blu-ray/.

Warner, Marina. *Stranger Magic: Charmed States and the Arabian Nights*. Cambridge, MA: Harvard University Press, 2011.

"The Wise Witch of Fairyland." *The Moving Picture World*, 1912, 544.

Wolff, Janet. *Feminine Sentences: Essays on Women and Culture*. Berkeley: University of California Press, 1990.

Wollenberg, Hans. "Die Geschichte Des Prinzen Achmed." *Lichtbild-Bühne*, May 3, 1926.

"The Woman of Mystery." *The Motion Picture News*, 1914, 54.

TWO

Women's Filmmaking and the Male-Centered Horror Film

Alexandra Heller-Nicholas

Conventional wisdom tells us surely that women filmmakers are best equipped to tell women's stories by virtue of their lived experience alone. But what about women filmmakers who tell stories about men? Celebrated recent films like Athina Rachel Tsangari's *Chevalier* (2016) and Lynne Ramsay's *You Were Never Really Here* (2017) have revealed that some women filmmakers are extraordinarily well-equipped to dissect the complex world of men and masculinity. Although not focusing on women characters, these films reveal a great deal about the broader gender political landscape: when women tell stories about men—particularly violent or aggressive men—we surely gain insight as valuable and as important as the stories they tell about women characters.

In horror, there is a long history of precisely this tradition, which is often overlooked in favor of women-directed features that focus on women characters. Yet as early as Germaine Dulac's *The Seashell and the Clergyman* (1928), women filmmakers have been fascinated with the intersection of horror and masculinity. From Wendy Toye's segment "The Painting" in the British anthology *Three Cases of Murder* (1955) to Greek filmmaker Tonia Marketaki's serial killer film *John the Violent* (1973), women filmmakers looking toward male-centered narratives in horror or horror-aligned cinema are neither new nor culturally specific. It is in this spirit that I turn here to briefly consider six films that illustrate precisely this diversity: Ida Lupino's *The Hitch-Hiker* (1953), Kei Fujiwara's *Organ* (1996), Svetlana Baskova's *The Green Elephant* (1999), Angela Bettis's *Roman* (2006), Karyn Kusama's *The Invitation* (2015), as well as *The Seashell and the Clergyman*.

Clearly, to cover *every* woman-directed horror film that centers on male characters is far too broad in scope to reasonably achieve in one book chapter. Rather, what I am scouting for in this tentative historical sweep are not just trends but also—just as importantly—notable distinctions, identifying them in the spirit of prompting further exploration of this often-overlooked area. While this chapter is historical, as the dates of the films of my six case studies above indicate, this is hardly a balanced decade-by-decade examination: notable omissions here include films made by women horror directors from the 1970s and 1980s in particular. Concrete examples here include perhaps most obviously Brianne Murphy's *Blood Sabbath* (1972) in the case of the former and Fhiona-Louise's *Cold Light of Day* (1989) in that of the latter. While both fascinating (and very different) films in their own right—films that any deeper, lengthier excavation into this subject would be recommended to include—despite centering around a male protagonist, *Blood Sabbath* does seem more interested *thematically* on women and witchcraft, while *Cold Light of Day*'s true crime approach to the story of a real-world serial killer (here Dennis Nilsen) extends the legacy of Lupino's *The Hitch-Hiker* in terms of its factual inspiration and the act of bringing that to life on screen. These are both important films in the history of women's filmmaking, and their omission is not a dismissal but rather a necessary pruning down of case studies in pursuit of making a broader point I hope future researchers and critics will expand further upon.

This is therefore, admittedly, a consciously ambitious chapter in its scope that can in practical terms only skim the surface, but in many ways that is *precisely* the point. While I acknowledge the limitations of the case studies selected here in terms of chronology simply due to lack of space, I have chosen these films precisely *because* they most strongly underscore what I passionately argue should be a much more emphatic focus on male characters in women-directed horror. This is, then, a call to arms of sorts to encourage further exploration of the intersection of gender-and-genre studies regarding exactly *what* women-directed horror and horror-adjacent films have told us about men and masculinity, arguing less for a reductive catch-all that diminishes the uniqueness of the specific films themselves but rather suggesting that the gender of the director influences critical reception itself. When we know a film has been directed by a woman, this often piques interest in its gender politics because we know we are getting that rarest of things: a take on gender politics from outside the dominant male directorial perspective. This surely speaks less to reductively essentializing the content of the film as particularly "feminine" but seeks greater critical value in examining how this awareness draws the critical eye more keenly toward a film's treatment of both masculinity and femininity and the tensions that exist between them.

Women are not divinely compelled to tell the same kinds of stories by virtue of their gender alone. As Jacqueline Levitin, Judith Plessis, and

Valerie Raoul note, "Whether a feminist message, or even a 'woman's point of view,' can still be conveyed without falling into stereotypes is debatable" (2003, 10). Such debates have long been of interest for feminist film critics; in 1975, Molly Haskell argued in her consideration of Liliana Cavani, Lina Wertmüller, and Elaine May that "although distinctly 'feminine' qualities can be discovered in each of these directors, we cannot generalize from these to a 'feminine sensibility'" (1977, 430). She too sees stereotypes as a potential obscuration as an issue, stating "expectations are at the root of the problem, prescriptive definitions of masculine and feminine that have become self-fulfilling prophecies" (435). Offering an alternate critical pathway, she suggested it is "better not to expect or ask for, only observe and describe" (435). She continued, "Polarities do exist, but they don't necessarily correspond to gender. All we can do is hope that women filmmakers become, like their counterparts in the other arts, merely filmmakers" (435).

Responding to Haskell, Teresa de Lauretis further elaborated that "whatever the feminine sensibility may be, it does not appear to be a viable or useful critical category per se" (1976–1977, 37). But at the same time, de Lauretis suggested that "if the criteria have nothing to do with style, subject matter, or technique, might they not consist of (1) ideological awareness (the film as a political act addresses a class rather than an audience), and (2) personal, though not necessarily autobiographical, honesty on the part of the artist who, I'd say, has to be a woman?" (37–38). For de Lauretis, rejecting the notion of an assumed universal feminine sensibility does not necessarily reject the elements that unite women filmmakers as Others to the dominant norm: male filmmakers. There *is* some degree of common ground by virtue of this Othering (i.e., exclusion and oppression in a heavily patriarchal industry), but this does not *necessarily* result in a blanket, unified kind of film that women make.

Regardless of the content of the film or the rejection of a unified "feminine sensibility," this way of thinking allows for the status of women horror filmmakers (by virtue of their being not-men) to be on some level a political or subversive act due to the fact that horror itself is so broadly assumed to be male terrain or a "boys' club." This "act" in practice results in a scenario where women filmmakers have a creative space to express political ideas if they are inclined to do so but *also* has the significant ability to grant critics an insight into the work of women filmmakers through a political lens, regardless of whether the work was intentionally political. Levitin, Plessis, and Raoul's observation that women filmmakers in France in particular have often utilized traditionally "masculine" generic frameworks such as the road movie and thriller underscores precisely this ideological significance, suggesting the use of these genres "may be transgressive in relation to the male models, and they challenge masculine hegemony in the film industry by achieving box office success" (2003, 117). In the case of horror, one need only look at the international success of Jennifer Kent's *The Babadook* (2014) to find a textbook example of this on a global scale. An audience used to mainstream Hollywood fare could perceive *The Babadook*, both an Australian film and a horror film directed by a woman, as doubly transgressive (or at least something far from the assumed norm).

While this gendering of genre is undeniably an important point, my focus on male-centered, woman-directed horror hopes to emphasize how it is perhaps most usefully conceived as a lens to frame critical approaches to these films, rather than casting any reductive, universalizing verdict about their content and themes. The significance of horror films being directed by a woman, for myself at least, functions most successfully as a kind of "reading protocol"[1]; it is less about ghettoizing all women-directed horror films into a crudely simplistic subgenre, but rather it places the emphasis on *reception*. Knowing a horror film—or any film—is directed by a woman makes me think differently about that material, particularly in regard to gender politics. And I am not alone. Writing about Susanne Bier, Belinda Smaill employs gender as a way to frame her approach to the director's work, leading her to "question what her status as a female director might add to a reading of her work's circulation in the contemporary global terrain of film festivals and criticism" (2014, 5–6). In the case of horror specifically, for Katarzyna Paszkiewicz, "addressing women's filmmaking in conjunction with the role of repetition and ongoing cultural recombination already present in the genre can redirect demands for a specifically 'female/feminist sensibility' to an examination of the multiple cultural factors that come into play in the struggle over making sense of particular examples of women's work" (2018, 54).

The "particular examples of women's work" I turn to in this chapter are those within the horror genre that center on male central characters. What fascinates me about these films is how they reveal—from a perspective the film industry has broadly denied a voice—different views of the broader gender political landscape. The construction of masculinity itself is thus presented through these alternate perspectives, which themselves are also multiple. My awareness of the gender of the filmmaker is arguably key here, as it renders *me* more acutely aware or sensitive to the often critical or subversive representations of masculinity within these films. As such, I have deliberately selected a range of films produced across historical, cultural, and industrial contexts to highlight the diversity of these films and filmmakers, seeking to open them up for further critical exploration that celebrates their nuances, their originality, and the voices of their respective creators, and how each in their own way has configured masculinity in a horror context from their own individual perspectives.

MALE MONSTROSITY IN *THE SEASHELL AND THE CLERGYMAN* (GERMAINE DULAC, 1928)

Broadly considered the first surrealist film ever made, Germaine Dulac's *The Seashell and the Clergyman* (*La Coquille et le clergyman*, 1928) contains all the ingredients that permit us to retrospectively consider it as an early precursor to the horror film.[2] While the film's darkly vivid, abstracted imagery is its signature (and far from an orthodox narrative), Dulac is clearly interested in structuring these images around the subjective experience of her eponymous Clergyman, its story documenting his downward spiral. As his psychosexual collapse unfolds—one that we are shown predominantly through the disjointed visions active within his own mind—his repressed desires come to life through the vibrant imagery of surrealism as he succumbs to violence and insanity. The legacy of the film can be felt in the work of filmmakers including David Lynch,[3] but even despite its undeniably enduring impact and quality, Dulac's gender and the role it played on the reception to her film at the time of its original release contain curious parallels with the work of women horror filmmakers today. Based on a screenplay by Antonin Artaud, the film was controversial from its very first screening, where Dulac was called a "cow" (Mounsef 2003, 44). Referred to in shorthand as the *bagarre*[4] ("seashell battle"), the controversy surrounding the film is the stuff of legend, boiling down to a struggle for authorship over the film. Artaud and a number of high-profile male critics were horrified that Dulac in their view so grossly misinterpreted Artaud's screenplay (Mounsef 2003, 44). Instead, Dulac showed much more interest in bringing to life her own vision, an abstract exploration of male violence.

Focusing on the film's final moments, William Van Wert claims that in *The Seashell and the Clergyman*, Dulac demonstrates a clear feminist subversion of the predominantly masculine terrain of surrealism during this period: "She exploits the Freudian symbolism of her male colleagues. She makes film in their style in order, at the end, to expose male fantasies" (1977, 219). The power of Dulac's film, he argues, is how she blurs surrealist fantasy with social critique, as she "chillingly breaks away from Surrealism towards realism, in order to expose the priest's fantasies for what they pathetically are" (221). Focusing on the moments where Dulac's camera jolts between the Clergyman's subjective perspective, where he sees himself strangling a woman, and an external perspective of what he looks like objectively from the outside—"holding, hugging, squeezing, fondling—empty air" (221)—Van Wert concludes that "we are left wondering whether this final shot is Surrealism or realism, a twist of the unreal (or the more than real), or whether it is rather a turn of the everyday world, women as sex objects trapped inside the crystal-ball prisons that are the minds of such men" (222).

Framed by my interest in women-directed horror films about male characters, what rises most emphatically to the surface watching *The Seashell and the Clergyman* today is, as Van Wert observes, the manner with which Dulac flips between the masculine/subjective perspective of the Clergyman and a position Van Wert implies by default is fundamentally *something else*. For Van Wert, this secondary perspective suggested not just a simplistic configuration of "reality" but one very specifically where gendered violence and the objectification of women as an assumed norm have been shockingly defamiliarized. Dulac's film is almost determined in its mission to visually objectify the woman character that the Clergyman is so obsessed with, not to *maintain* these cultural norms but rather to expose them. Dulac's film is in no way about this woman character—she is not telling a "woman's story"—but it does something just as important, if not more so; she seeks to reveal the internal psychological mechanics that lead to precisely this kind of inherently deranged and violent *perception* of women as objects. That Artaud and others in the surrealist scene at the time Dulac's film was first screened were so outraged is perhaps better understood in relation to Van Wert's identification of a dominant tendency in male surrealist art to "portray women as statues, as machines, as half-animals . . . as sexual objects to be fragmented and possessed" (1977, 219). To opt for the contemporary vernacular, Dulac is calling them out: her film was a direct critique of the toxic politics of surrealism itself, leading Van Wert quite rightly perhaps to christen Dulac as the "first feminist filmmaker" (214), or at least one of them.

FEMINIZING FEAR: MALE BODIES AS "ABJECT TERROR PERSONIFIED" IN *THE HITCH-HIKER* (IDA LUPINO, 1953)

While Van Wert celebrated Dulac in the 1970s as a historically significant feminist filmmaker, classical Hollywood film star-turned-director Ida Lupino was not so positively received by feminist film critics more broadly. Wrote Haskell (1974, 201):

> Lupino was tougher as an actress than as a director: the movies she made (*Hard, Fast, and Beautiful, The Bigamist, The Hitchhiker*) are conventional, even sexist; and in her interviews, like so many women who have nothing to complain about, she purrs like a contented kitten, arches her back at the mention of women's lib, and quotes Noël Coward to the effect that woman should be struck regularly like gongs.

While today rightly considered a pioneer in women's filmmaking, Lupino is a curious figure because she refuses to neatly fit into contemporary visions of what that position should entail. Christina Newland (2018) identified a transformation that saw Lupino as a director shift "from relative invisibility to posthumous recognition," but "because she has gone from an oddity in her era to a 'proto-feminist pioneer' in ours, little consideration has been given to how her work and her personality might not fit into neat ahistorical categorization."

Lupino's favorite of all the films she directed was her 1953 film, *The Hitch-Hiker*. Falling broadly under the film noir umbrella (the only one of this period to be directed by a woman), *The Hitch-Hiker* in retrospect can also be clearly recognized in terms of its influence on horror cinema; hitchhiker horror is surely its own identifiable subgenre today, and while Lupino did not invent it, it is difficult to deny its influence on everything from Robert Harmon's cult classic *The Hitcher* (1986) to non-American examples of the trope such as Greg McLean's *Wolf Creek* (2004). Based on real-life serial killer William Cook (a figure Lupino researched in-depth), the film follows two men, Roy (Edmond O'Brien) and Gilbert (Frank Lovejoy), on a fishing trip who pick up the hitchhiker of the title, a traveling serial killer called Emmett Myers (William Talman), who is on the run from police for previous killings and forces the two men to help him escape to Mexico. The opening scene shows an early killing and is drenched in foreboding shadow and an ominous soundtrack, surely foreshadowing precisely the kind of stand-alone horror-vignette-as-hook that would later become typical of slasher films especially. While not referring to horror as such, Wheeler Winston Dixon's description of *The Hitch-Hiker*'s style allows further parallels with horror to be drawn: "There is an atmosphere of real violence in the film—not only in the subject matter but also in Lupino's relentless pacing, hyperkinetic camera setups, and intense use of oppressive close-ups to heighten the film's suspense" (2005, 144).

While Lupino was often linked to the "women's picture" with previous films such as *Never Fear* (1949), *Not Wanted* (1949), and *Outrage* (1950), she notably offered *The Hitch-Hiker* as evidence to the contrary (Weiner 1977, 174, 177). And while the film almost aggressively lacks a central woman character or women characters, in the context of the traditional film noir in particular, it is arguably the very *absence* of women in terms of how they were traditionally cast in these movies that is of interest. If not as straightforwardly "feminist," then certainly Lupino's erasure of the femme fatale figure has at least the potential to be read as leaning toward the progressive; says Mary G. Hurd of the film, "Lupino includes no femme fatale, usually included in more traditional noir films, whose job it is to provide fateful encounters with male characters" (2007, 12).

In *The Hitch-Hiker*, unlike so many other film noirs of its time, men don't need women to get them into trouble—there is, to paraphrase Rita Hayward from *Gilda*, no "mame" to put the blame on. This is important because it allows the focus to be put more explicitly onto what Dixon

noted lies at the heart of the film: Lupino's almost clinical interest in unpacking "the mechanics of male violence" (2005, 134). For myself at least,
it is *precisely* this fascination on Lupino's part that makes *The Hitch-Hiker*
such an important film to consider in the history of women filmmakers
and the representations of toxic masculinity and violence in the generic
context of horror and horror-adjacent film history. In her 1950 rape survivor melodrama, *Outrage*,[5] Lupino looked with profound sensitivity at the
impact of male violence on a woman character, and in many ways *The
Hitch-Hiker* can be understood as a continuation of this interest. What fascinates Lupino in *The Hitch-Hiker* is not merely how male violence manifests in the figure of Emmett Myers, but how his dominance of Roy and
Gilbert in many ways *feminizes* them. These two men adopt characteristics
more typically ascribed to women characters in cinema, and watching
the film today, Roy and Gilbert carry echoes of Carol J. Clover's famous
description of the Final Girl. Swapping the gender in Clover's description,
they are on key points close to a perfect fit: "She is the one who encounters the mutilated bodies of her friends and perceives the full extent of the
preceding horror and her own peril; who is chased, cornered, wounded;
whom we see scream, stagger, fall, rise, and scream again. She is abject
terror personified" (2015, 35). In *The Hitch-Hiker*, Gilbert and Roy may be
male characters, but I would suggest that because Emmett feminizes them
through dominant alpha male violence, they too are ultimately rendered
"abject terror personified."

(MALE) BODY HORROR AND WOMEN DIRECTORS:
ORGAN (KEI FUJIWARA, 1996) AND
THE GREEN ELEPHANT (SVETLANA BASKOVA, 1999)

While very different films, Japanese filmmaker Kei Fujiwara's *Organ*
(1996) and Russian director Svetlana Baskova's *The Green Elephant* (1999)
encourage us to continue thinking about their respective creator's status
as women and the political dimension of gendered bodies within the
films themselves. A long-term collaborator of cult filmmaker Shinya
Tsukamoto, Fujiwara would both star in his splatterpunk classic *Tetsuo:
The Iron Man* (1989) as the title character's unnamed girlfriend, while
also acting as cinematographer alongside Tsukamoto himself. Working
almost solely in theater today, Fujiwara would make two films after *Iron
Man* as director, writer, actor, and cinematographer: *Organ* (1996) and *Id*
(2005). These films in many ways are united by what can be traced back
to her earlier work as such a key collaborator on *Tetsuo: The Iron Man*, as
Fujiwara's work both in front of and behind the camera is marked by an
interest with the visceral meat—the ephemeral, volatile nature of human

fleshiness—that transcends gender and other socio-cultural categories to enter the carnivalesque terrain of her own specific brand of body horror.

Organ follows two male police detectives who are investigating a group of black-market organ dealers, a male schoolteacher and his one-eyed sister (played by Fujiwara herself). Delighting in graphic scenes of live bodies having their organs removed to fuel their illicit trade, the film is a complex web of yakuza, castrating mothers, and sibling bonds that is constructed in a world where human bodies and their component parts have a clear economic value. While Fujiwara has built a complex narrative, however, this is not where the film's primary impact stems—that lies solely in the terrain of its unrestrained levels of gore, guaranteed to delight or disgust (or both), depending on your particular taste. Writes Jim Harper, "*Organ* is not an easy film to watch and it's almost impossible to enjoy"; however, "it's not a bland attempt to shock or gross out, but a complex portrait of moral, physical and psychological decay." He continues, "Everything in the film—from the locations up to the protagonists' morality and even their own bodies—is in a state of decay" (2008, 38). This notion of rot is intrinsic to the film both in terms of its visceral punch and its core thematic drive. Bodies are absolutely gendered in the film, there is no denying that—there are characters that are clearly designated as men's bodies, and those which are clearly that of women. What is so fascinating, however, is how Fujiwara seems driven to literally annihilate these gendered bodies as they melt into puddles of goo and gore and blood and pus and muck. In this sense, if not transcending gender as such, they certainly attain a state of being where the entire notion of gender seems thoroughly beside the point.

Svetlana Baskova's notorious *The Green Elephant* approaches body horror and gender in an altogether different way from Fujiwara, which is equally as shocking, if not more so. Consisting only of male characters, in a manner reminiscent of Lupino's *The Hitch-Hiker*, the absence of women in the film does not mean there are not feminized bodies active within it; in fact, the power struggles between its male characters are explicitly (and graphically) defined by the execution of male violence over other male bodies to render the latter subservient and, by virtue of this, simultaneously feminized by their status as "less masculine." Undeniably a grueling viewing experience, the film follows two men in the Soviet Army during the mid-1980s who are being held in a military prison. Shot in suffocating close-up, they find themselves in uncomfortably intimate proximity, which rapidly leads to rising tensions between not just the two men themselves but the officers guarding them. It's hard to describe the horrors that unfold, suffice to say rape and coprophagia rate highly on the film's most distressing sequences. To give a further sense of the intensity of the film's violence, the "green elephant" of the title refers to one character using the trachea he has just pulled out of his unfortunate victim as a pretend elephant trunk.

As shocking as the violence in *The Green Elephant* is, it has been clearly identified as a significant entry in the Russian *chernukha* subgenre. Alongside films such as Aleksei Baskova's *Cargo 200* (2007) and *The Stoker* (2010), for Greg Dolgopolov, *The Green Elephant* joins films in this category in how it seeks to "mix crime with physical and psychological degradation in fatalistic social denunciations that offer no glimmers of hope" (2015, 157). Described as "one of the most cultish Russian films made after the collapse of the Soviet Union,"[6] for its 2005 screening at the International Film Festival Rotterdam, the program blurb identified the film's specific location in a military prison and depiction of male violence as a direct commentary on then-contemporary issues regarding "the escalation of the war in Chechnya and growing criminality in the Russian army."[7] *The Green Elephant* is useful to consider when approaching the question of women-directed horror films about male characters because despite the centrality of overwhelmingly male violence to the film, in a significant way it demands we ask further questions about how we might assume the gender of a director to influence our reading of a given text. Put simply, I would challenge anyone to watch *The Green Elephant*—or *Organ* for that matter—without prior knowledge and pick them as woman-directed films.

BLURRING THE LINES: *ROMAN* (ANGELA BETTIS, 2006) AND *THE INVITATION* (KARYN KUSAMA, 2015)

I conclude by looking briefly at two films that further challenge and expand the parameters of how the "reading protocol" often subtly dictated by our identification and acknowledgment of a director's gender influences our sensitivity to a given text's gender politics. Both Angela Bettis's *Roman* (2006) and Karyn Kusama's *The Invitation* (2015) pivot around male characters, but in terms of the diegetic world of the films themselves and approached in terms of their broader production contexts, both are in different ways very much able to be conceived as discursive spaces where men and women are in active dialogue. In the case of *Roman*, this is perhaps most explicit. Before casting Lucky McKee as the title character, Bettis herself—primarily an actor—had starred as May in McKee's cult 2002 horror film of the same name. Swapping the director/actor role between McKee and Bettis and shifting the focus of the story from a mentally unstable young woman who kills to a mentally unstable man who kills, it is unsurprising that *Roman* went by the working title *May 2: The Story of Roman*.

Just as Bettis's *May* struggled to adapt socially and found a potential romantic encounter pushed her over the edge into murder, McKee's *Roman* follows a similarly doomed trajectory. Beginning with a clumsy meet-cute between Roman and his unnamed neighbor (played by Kristen Bell), a misreading of the signs being sent sees Roman overwhelmed with violence, murdering her before he realizes he is doing so. Storing her body in his bathtub with bags of ice, he spends one day each week cutting off a body part and then taking it on a farewell "date," saying good-bye before he sends it off into a picturesque lake where "they" have been picnicking. Alongside what Roman sees as his deepening, developing relationship with the dead woman, he also begins a relationship with a new neighbor, Eva (Nectar Rose), who clearly has psychological issues of her own.

In this perverse coming-of-age horror-romance about a stunted, violent man-child, Bettis flips McKee's examination of the perils of living up to idealized femininity and the violence that can result when those messages are misinterpreted by someone living with mental health issues and applies the same ideas to an equally troubled male character. What marks both films is that while they never seek to downplay May and Roman's unambiguously disturbing behavior, each director grants their character nothing less than an almost total commitment to their subjective experiences. *May* and *Roman* are effective individually because they are compelling tragedies about the failures to live up to gendered norms, but by swapping the actor/director roles between Bettis and McKee, when we look at the films as a set, the power dynamics that typically govern the gendered roles behind and in front of the camera are subverted by becoming exchangeable. Each film in itself is an impressive exercise in collaboration, but when considered together, what McKee and Bettis achieve is an extraordinary creative process that fundamentally hinges on equality.

Written by her husband, Phil Hay, and his cowriting partner, Matt Manfredi, Karyn Kusama's *The Invitation* also offers a rich example of how horror cinema can act as a forum to open up how we think of gender and authorship in the genre through its very deliberate placement of a male character at the heart of its story. The always eloquent Kusama has addressed precisely these issues head on, stating, "I am the director, and I believe that's clear watching the film. But I'm also collaborating [with] male writers and our main character is a man." She continues, "An integral part of directing this film was my attempt to step into, and live the experience of, Will, as he figures out what's happening to him. To me, that work is as feminist an act as, say, writing an interesting and complex portrait of a female character" (Gaudette 2016). Will is played by Logan Marshall-Green, a man who attends a reunion of sorts with his old friends at a dinner party at the house of his ex-wife, Eden (Tammy Blanchard). Divorcing after the tragic death of their son—the trauma of which is shown through flashback as Will wanders through his old home—both Will and Eden now have new partners. Will's suspicions about his ex-wife's unusual behavior is at first dismissed as emotional baggage by their friends, but it is soon apparent that Eden and her new husband have joined a terrifying cult that sees their salvation dependent upon the mass murder of their friends. While Will survives, at the end of the film, he looks out over the nearby community and realizes the horrors that have unfolded are not specific to Eden's home; the cult's mission is widespread, its scope unknown.

The Invitation explores the feminization of pain and constructs it as a notably internalized mode of suffering. This is how Will experiences his grief, a character who is not just feminized by his way of dealing with pain according to the film's internal logic, but also—perhaps uncoincidentally—he has long hair. In terms of what makes this film so effective and meaningful, it cannot be underplayed that the central focus of the film is Will confronting the ritualized violence that the male-dominated cult represents as an alternate way to deal with pain. Will is hardly a nonviolent figure, but he enacts violence only to survive; what is so central to the film by its conclusion is that he has learned to mourn by the end of the film in a way that doesn't, like the male-dominated cult, produce violence. The final shot of Will and his girlfriend holding hands is tantalizing; on one hand, as they look toward the other houses going through what they have, the scale of this ritualized male violence is terrifying. But their solidarity is also a sign of resistance and survival, the product of them rejecting the logic of ritualized male violence.

To reiterate a point made earlier in this chapter, these are far from the only women-directed horror films centering around male characters, and the 1970s and 1980s are notable omissions here, particularly in regard to forementioned examples such as *Blood Sabbath* and *Cold Light of Day*, whose exclusion—while less than ideal—is, I argue, justifiable in the context of this consciously preliminary "sounding out" of the thematic terrain here. Yet across this albeit brief exploration of six women-directed horror (or horror-adjacent) films that feature central male characters, I emphasize not just how the gender of a filmmaker when it is outside the dominant norm of "male director" guides our critical hand toward questions of gender politics, but that there is in fact as much diversity in these films in terms of content and theme as there is in women-directed cinema more generally. Emphasizing the gender of a filmmaker is a useful "reading protocol" that invites us to reframe critical reception, to bring the assumptions we bring to watching women-directed film, and, at its best, to retroactively demand a much-needed defamiliarization of the widely assumed neutrality of male-directed film. By embracing this "reading protocol" in favor of a reductive search for a singular "feminine sensibility" in these films, we may make some progress in advancing toward the ideal scenario where the label "woman director" will seem just as superfluous to their craft as that of "male director." But there is much work to be done here: like studies of women-directed cinema more broadly, we have only begun to scratch the surface. This chapter may therefore be best conceived as a rallying of the troops and a demand for this to be added to the seemingly ever-growing list of "things to do" for scholars, critics, and researchers concerned with gender, genre, and filmmaking.

NOTES

1. A term borrowed from Jeffrey Sconce's foundational essay "'Trashing' the Academy: Taste, Excess, and an Emerging Politics of Cinematic Style" (1995).

2. *The Seashell and the Clergyman* has been described as related to horror by James Robertson (2005, 38) and Ela Bittencourt (2018). In 2019, it was also programmed in the Slash Film Festival's "Female Terror" program (https://slash filmfestival.com/en/films-2019/the-seashell-and-the-clergyman/).

3. *Seashell* has been explicitly cited as an influence on Lynch; see Lawless (2015). While not widely noted, it is impossible to look at the respective ballroom dancing scenes and not identify probable influence.

4. The *bagarre coquille* has "perhaps less to do with gender than politics within the surrealist movement in Paris at the time, whom soon after rejected Artaud himself from their ranks" (Mounsef 2003, 43). Mounsef continues, "It becomes clear that all the details of the controversy around *La Coquille* point in the direction of a conspiracy orchestrated by the surrealists," who used "Dulac to settle the score with Artaud [which] is at the heart of the gendered politics involved in marginalizing women from the first avant-garde" (45).

5. I have written extensively about *Outrage* and its significance not only in women's filmmaking but in the history of representing rape trauma in cinema. See my book *Rape-Revenge Films: A Critical Study* (Jefferson, NC: McFarland, 2011) and *"Outrage* (1950): Ida Lupino's Vision of Rape Trauma," *Senses of Cinema*, October 2018, sensesofcinema.com/2018/cteq/outrage-1950-ida-lupinos-vision -of-rape-trauma/#fn-35471-1.

6. This is taken from the program entry for the film *Monkey, Ostrich, and Grave*, Representation and the Real: Russian Film Symposium 2020, University of Pittsburgh, May 4–9, 2020, https://www.rusfilm.pitt.edu/monkey-ostrich-and-grave/.

7. The IFFR website is not archived, but this is quoted in the Wikipedia entry for *The Green Elephant*, https://en.wikipedia.org/wiki/The_Green_Elephant.

BIBLIOGRAPHY

Bittencourt, Ela. "A Surrealist Filmmaker's Legacy of Feminism and Cinematic Innovation." *Hyperallergic*, August 24, 2018. https://hyperallergic.com/456906 /germaine-dulac-surrealist-filmmaker-film-society-lincoln-center/.

Clover, Carol J. *Men, Women, and Chain Saws: Gender in the Modern Horror Film*. Princeton, NJ: Princeton University Press: 2015.

de Lauretis, Teresa. "Cavani's *Night Porter*: A Woman's Film?" *Film Quarterly* 30, no. 2 (Winter 1976–1977): 35–38.

Dixon, Wheeler Winston. *Lost in the Fifties: Recovering Phantom Hollywood*. Carbondale: Southern Illinois University Press, 2005.

Dolgopolov, Greg. "Horror." In *Directory of World Cinema: RUSSIA 2*, ed. Birgit Beumers, 154–157. Bristol, UK: Intellect, 2015.

Gaudette, Emily. "'The Invitation': Director Karyn Kusama and the Emotionally Sophisticated Horror Film." *Inverse*, March 11, 2016. https://www.inverse.com/article/12689-the-invitation-director-karyn-kusama-and-the-emotionally-sophisticated-horror-film.

Harper, Jim. *Flowers From Hell: The Modern Japanese Horror Film*. Hereford, UK: Noir Publishing, 2008.

Haskell, Molly. "Are Women Directors Different?" In *Women and the Cinema: A Critical Anthology*, ed. Karyn Kay and Gerald Peary, 420–435. New York: Dutton, 1977.

———. *From Reverence to Rape: The Treatment of Women in the Movies*. Harmondsworth, UK: Penguin, 1974.

Hurd, Mary G. *Women Directors and Their Films*. Westport, CT: Praeger, 2007.

Lawless, Ciaran. "10 Movies That Had the Biggest Influences on the Films of David Lynch." *Taste of Cinema*, May 5, 2015. www.tasteofcinema.com/2015/10-movies-that-had-the-biggest-influences-on-the-films-of-david-lynch/.

Levitin, Jacqueline, Judith Plessis, and Valerie Raoul. 2003. "Introduction." In *Women Filmmakers: Refocusing*, ed. Jacqueline Levitin, Judith Plessis, and Valerie Raoul, 3–13. New York: Routledge, 2003.

Mounsef, Donia. "Women Filmmakers and the Avant-Garde: From Dulac to Duras." In *Women Filmmakers: Refocusing*, ed. Jacqueline Levitin, Judith Plessis and Valerie Raoul, 38–50. New York: Routledge, 2003.

Newland, Christina. "'Mother of All of Us': Ida Lupino and the Label of Proto-Feminism." *Mubi*, November 16, 2018. https://mubi.com/notebook/posts/mother-of-all-of-us-ida-lupino-and-the-label-of-proto-feminism.

Paszkiewicz, Katarzyna. "When the Woman Directs (a Horror Film)." In *Women Do Genre in Film and Television*, ed. Mary Harrod and Katarzyna Paszkiewicz, 42–56. London: Routledge, 2018.

Robertson, James. *The Hidden Cinema: British Film Censorship in Action 1913–1972*. London: Routledge, 2005.

Sconce, Jeffrey. "'Trashing' the Academy: Taste, Excess, and an Emerging Politics of Cinematic Style." *Screen* 36, no. 4 (Winter 1995): 371–393.

Smaill, Belinda. "The Male Sojourner, the Female Director, and Popular European Cinema: The Worlds of Susanne Bier." *Camera Obscura* 29, no. 1 (2014): 5–31.

Van Wert, William. "Germaine Dulac: First Feminist Filmmaker." In *Women and the Cinema: A Critical Anthology*, ed. Karyn Kay and Gerald Peary, 213–223. New York: Dutton, 1977.

Weiner, Debra. "Interview with Ida Lupino." In *Women and the Cinema: A Critical Anthology*, ed. Karyn Kay and Gerald Peary, 169–178. New York: Dutton, 1977.

THREE

Angela Bettis

Gender in the Space of Collaborative Horror

James Francis Jr.

Angela Bettis is most known for her performance as the title character in American writer-director Lucky McKee's *May* (2002). Later in the same year, she appeared in the made-for-television *Carrie* remake, directed by David Carson. These two roles gave Bettis the opportunity to showcase her talent in taking on the role of a woman as an outsider who becomes both savior and destroyer of her own existence. In each title role, Bettis simultaneously channels delicacy and intimacy with rage, provoking sympathy from the viewing audience for characters whose obsessive behavior results in murder. While relatively unknown outside of independent horror circles, Bettis's remarkably nuanced performances are time and again hailed as iconic due to her ability to portray disturbed anti-heroes as ferociously villainous and yet at the same time exceeding vulnerable, therefore adding to the character development and narrative complexity on screen.

Bettis's professional acting career spans back to the 1990s with TV series and dramatic work in films such as *Girl, Interrupted* (1999), in which she plays an anorexic patient inhabiting a mental asylum, and *Bless the Child* (2000), in which she plays a heroin addict and mother of a child with supernatural abilities, representing her first appearance in a horror film. Roles offered to Bettis are typically rich with neuroses and psychoses. Indeed, she is known for starring in horror films that feel deep, disturbing, and oddly moving. It came as little surprise then when Bettis was announced as the first-time director of low-budget independent horror film *Roman* (2006), which revolves around the obsessive traits of a lonely recluse who's frenzied desperation to find love leads to murder. In *Roman*, Bettis directs Lucky McKee as the title character, a role reversal of their collaboration in *May*, in which McKee directs Bettis in a breakthrough role that led to her landing the lead role in *Carrie*.

What makes Bettis an especially important contributor to independent horror filmmaking is the approach she takes to characters who live on the periphery of stereotypically normalized societal constructions and the vision she incorporates into directing said character type. In this chapter, I closely interrogate Bettis's performance in *May* and her directorial approach in *Roman* to examine the myriad of ways in which Bettis makes an original contribution to contemporary horror, especially in her shaping (and sharpening) of narratives that focus on social outcasts as realistic and nuanced characters. By analyzing Bettis's approach to performance in McKee's *May*, and to directing McKee in her own film *Roman*, this chapter celebrates the genuinely original and riveting contributions Bettis has made to low-budget independent horror.

ANALYSIS OF ANGELA BETTIS'S PERFORMANCE IN *MAY* (LUCKY MCKEE, 2002)

In McKee's horror film *May*, a shy, introverted woman, played by Bettis, makes increasingly desperate attempts to connect with the people around her, while becoming obsessed with their body parts. The horror of the narrative comes from May's eventual dismemberment of her victims and her harvesting of their body parts to build a life-sized patchwork doll to fill the empty void in her life. Born with amblyopia (a lazy eye), May is an outcast among her childhood peers with a mother who convinces her, "If you can't find a friend, make one." The film establishes early on a life of loneliness, self-consciousness, childhood trauma, toxic perfectionism, and insecurity. Bettis portrays the character in an endearing manner, as we witness a life characterized by disrupted development due to parental neglect and excessive solitude. May's conversations with a glass-encased doll called Suzie foreshadow a dearth of friends and a deep note of isolation. As the plot progresses, it becomes disconcertingly straightforward to identify with May, due to the relatability of her dismal circumstances, which center on the character's alienation and trauma.

May represents the kind of horror stories that Bettis is deeply invested in exploring. As Bettis explains, "I think anybody who's human has got to know that feeling. Anybody who is human has got to understand loneliness on some level" (Vespe 2003). As Bettis indicates, *May* is highly relatable, yet there are scenes here of such close observation, of such control of body language, voice, and behavior, that it is not just the humanity of the story that guides the audience's response to May but Bettis's quiet tour de force as the title character.

While *May* adds to critical analysis of female characters in horror, Bettis's unique portrayal of the lead protagonist makes May's plight all the more accessible to the audience. Bettis's performance of May is carefully crafted to encourage us to root for the awkward and depraved character, despite witnessing her evolution from seeming victim to ferocious villain. While this has much to do with director McKee's artistic pull, this also has a great deal to do with Bettis's careful and nuanced performance of May: her presence on screen, the intentional movement of her wide eyes and petite frame, and the purposeful and reflective use of her voice. This represents a connective thread in Bettis's body of work, such as her performances in *The Woman* (2011) and *Carrie,* as she so often transfigures what could be read as a cliched outsider (with which the horror genre is teeming) into complex, layered constructions of humanity.

In *The Woman,* also directed by McKee, Bettis takes on the role of Belle Cleek, the matriarch of a family led by an abusive and sadistic father figure. Although she is not directly responsible for the vile atrocities that take place at the Cleek family household (including animal abuse, incest, physical assault, abduction, and torture), she quietly allows the behavior to continue. Belle's involuntary participation is very clearly depicted as villainous in the film; however, as audience we simultaneously empathize with the horrid circumstances that Belle finds herself in—a precarious and yet banal life in which she serves as a captive. Belle's slow burning demise in *The Woman* seems fitting and yet at the same time undeserved as Bettis's performance makes focal point of her implicit desire to end the cycle of violence transpiring within her own home.

Connecting fictional characterizations to real life, Bettis details what makes her characters so famously disconcerting: "Their complexity is both beautiful and frightening. Their inability to truly see and understand themselves is beautiful and frightening" (Beggs 2013). Both memorable title characters (May and Belle) played by Bettis struggle with identity. Within the diegesis of each film, Bettis's characters recognize that they are operating outside of the normative structures that they so desire to belong to, and soon come to regard themselves as monsters who have no control over their own actions. Due to the authenticity and complexity of Bettis's performance, however, we as audience come to recognize that the character's monstrous actions are the likely result of a steady stream of damaging human interactions, especially with those deemed normative within the films' narratives. This is achieved through Bettis's intricate construction of each performance as she transforms would-be stock characters into fully developed human figures due to her ability to assimilate a psychological technique of living a part. This technique, which Bettis has become renowned for, is typically expressed via her drawing out withdrawn movements in the scene, her forlorn expressions of existential sadness, and facial expressions that embody unpredictable transitions (indeed we never quite know how a character played by Bettis is going to respond next).

Of course, humanity has always dealt with concerns of physicality to determine what makes one person a better specimen or representation of the ideal body than another. The desire for friendship, companionship, and an outward alluring appearance are fundamental human concerns. McKee's *May* centers on these collective human anxieties, and thus we relate to May's struggle, her desire to be recognized, validated, and loved, through Bettis's performance in which she skillfully integrates empathic processes. The foundational narrative theme here is that of the individual vs. society. As an outsider, May is symbolically new to the world around her and positioned against its established social norms; Bettis portrays the character as stilted in her childhood mentality, unsure of how to relate to "normal" people, judged for her peculiar behavior, and destined to live a life of solitude.

Under McKee's masterful direction, the camera captures and reinforces Bettis's embodiment of social isolation as we watch her companionless body seated alone in the park observing children play, deserted on a sidewalk bench observing passersby, and shuffling uncomfortably across a crowded street to interact with a person she's attracted to. The cinematography consistently positions May on the outside looking in—as the focal length is carefully selected to compress the background, further isolating Bettis's character. May is often skewed from the center of the frame in symbolic relation to her own vision of the world around her, which becomes increasingly erratic when other characters disrupt her personal space. Ultimately, May finds herself dangerously incapable of relating to others, while at the same time Bettis renders her utterly relatable, just like the other unique and iconic women the actress and filmmaker has become renowned for portraying, particularly within McKee's body of work.

In McKee's "Sick Girl" (2006), part of the *Masters of Horror* anthology series, Bettis stars as lesbian entomologist Ida Teeter. The character is intellectually brilliant regarding her field of study; however, her romantic interactions with other women in the film prove excruciating as she frets about the nature of her work (studying insects) scaring them away. Bettis carefully portrays the anxious nature of Teeter through physicality and stilted conversation as she stumbles over her own feet and flubs her words while trying to talk to potential love interest Misty (Erin Brown). Close-up shots hone in on Bettis's unique performative facial tics and darting eyes while medium and long shots enable the audience to focus on her disjointed movements as she continuously attempts to escape each uncomfortable encounter. Likewise, in *The Woman*, Bettis's character, Belle, a tightly wound wife simmering with rage, clearly wills the ground to swallow her when she meets a fellow neighbor in the aisle of a local grocery store. When Belle returns home to find that her husband is still holding a mysterious woman captive in their cellar, Bettis playing Belle immediately shies away from her, dropping her head and averting her gaze, to convey a doubled sense of immorality in recognizing the captivity and coming to terms with her own passive participation in the abduction.

When we interrogate Bettis's body of work, especially in collaboration with McKee, we come to understand that the women at the center of these narratives are not able to fully realize their potential for fulfilling lives due to socially restrictive constructions that force them to occupy the margins of society. Furthermore, these characters are incapable of connecting to other people in platonic, familial, or romantic relationships because they ultimately refuse to live a life that others prescribe for them, which often causes the horror to transpire. Such complex portrayals of dangerous and yet nuanced outsiders feel remarkably fresh when viewed against the muscle-bound monsters, masked murderers, and deranged psychopaths of much mainstream studio horror, as Bettis renders these characters realistic, thought-provoking, complex, and terrifying.

In *May*, an introverted persona becomes extroverted in response to rejection, and the innocence of her obsessions becomes corrupted toward murder. May is driven to create a friend from scratch out of the many different body parts that she fixates on, in the hope of forming a connection with someone who fully and finally understands her—a Frankensteinian goal that, of course, ends in deep tragedy. Bettis's performance is especially memorable during May's interactions with her soon-to-be dismembered victims; she shyly fixates on the hands of a local mechanic named Adam (Jeremy Sisto); she gently admires the neck of her coworker Polly (Anna Faris); and she softly remarks that she thinks Polly's girlfriend, Ambrosia (Nichole Hiltz), has "nice gams" (legs). Time and again, Bettis's performance depicts obsession as a relatable state of being that translates on screen as more innocent than it does villainized; something that becomes especially recognizable to the audience in May's interactions with characters that she becomes intimate with. The theme of obsession in *May* is further tempered by Bettis's nuanced performance as she gently caresses Adam's hands and traces Polly's neck with her fingers, clearly in awe of the beauty of the human form.

Of course, May soon kills Polly with a double-edged scalpel at the base of the neck and eventually stabs Adam in the stomach. She then cleans, sews, and stitches the victims' body parts together, naming her creation "Amy" by rearranging the letters of her own name. On realizing Amy is yet to possess a face, May violently plucks out her own eye with a pair of scissors, placing it into a makeshift socket for Amy. And yet May is still not undone by any sense of innate evil or villainy; Bettis depicts this violent act as the work of a loving outsider, misunderstood and overlooked by society. This allows the audience to omit May's murderous "misdemeanors" due to Bettis's layered presentation of the character, which allows for real depth, thus revoking the audience's likely revulsion to her killings. Unlike Mrs. Voorhees in *Friday the 13th* (1980) and Mrs. Loomis/Debbie Salt in *Scream 2* (1997), who gratuitously victimize innocent people in the interest of red-blooded revenge; Baby Firefly in *House of 1000 Corpses* (2003) and Lola Stone in *The Loved Ones* (2009), who torture for fun through mental instability; or Samara Morgan in *The Ring* (2002), who kills from a supernatural space as an innate evil, *May* offers an atypical undertaking for the presentation of a female villain in horror due to Bettis's nuanced and novel approach to the theme of obsession regarding women in horror. The dynamics of the character represent an ongoing push for women in the genre (in front of the camera and behind it) to present a fuller realization of womanhood instead of one-note characterizations. Filmmaker Aislínn Clarke (Mr. Bones 2018) details:

> Complex female characters are not always strong, nor should they be. I want to see the full range of female experience on screen, including vulnerability, including weakness if it serves the character. Women are not always empowered in real life, so we should not seek to place only empowered female characters on screen. Women need to see ourselves fully represented within our culture, the good, the bad, and the ugly. That's what I hope to see more of in the future—the full range of female human experience, not just the ideal. That will mean better films and a better cultural conversation for all of us, not just for women.

Although Bettis embodies a dynamic range of personality and character traits beneficial to presenting May's female experience to the audience, it is vital to remember, as Clarke posits, that female stories "can and should be seen as human stories, rather than niche" (Mr. Bones 2018). Bettis's portrayal of May thus serves as an important examination of gender in performance and simultaneously demonstrates the way in which horror narratives about women can offer broader commentary on humanity at large. Additionally, Bettis's working relationship with McKee demonstrates that male directors of horror can too break away from a tradition of showcasing underdeveloped female antagonists, thereby allowing actors the freedom to portray such characters with humanity, as opposed to empty vessels hell-bent on killing for the sake of it.

ANALYSIS OF LUCKY MCKEE'S PERFORMANCE IN *ROMAN* (ANGELA BETTIS, 2006)

In an interesting role reversal, Angela Bettis's debut as a director—*Roman*—features Lucky McKee as the title character in a film about an outsider figure, playing a socially awkward man, whose obsession over a neighbor leads to an accidental murder that unravels him. How Bettis and McKee reversed their actor-director roles from *May* is a story best told by McKee, the writer of both films, in an exclusive interview for this chapter:

I was not cast as Roman from the start. I wrote the screenplay my senior year of college over a feverish weekend. One of those stories that just popped into my head and fell out onto the page. The original concept was for it to be a low budget feature that I could shoot on black and white Hi-8 videotape with friends for very little money. Almost like a practice feature that might help me get *May* made. I was actively trying to make the film, with an actor named Jesse Hlubik in the lead role, around the time I got the call to develop *May* as a feature in Los Angeles. Once I'd made *May*, I didn't want to make *Roman* anymore. Then one night, hanging with Angela, we hatched the idea of her directing and me playing the lead. Once that was decided we made the movie on videotape with a small group of friends for very little money! I wanted to rewrite the script before shooting but Angela was insistent that we preserve what was on the page. She had a clear idea of what she wanted to do with it. It was a fantastic creative experience all around. (E-mail correspondence to author, May 14, 2020)

Although Bettis and McKee switched their respective actor and director roles from *May*, they managed to create a film that once again undercuts expectations for the horror genre. In a narrative that could easily be construed to elicit disdain for McKee's character, akin to what someone might expect from *May* by reading the film's synopsis, Bettis guides a performance from McKee that wrenches empathy from the viewer, and her use of carefully calibrated cinematography enhances this reception and response from the audience.

In *Roman*, the title character's position in society is somewhat similar to May's existence in that he is deeply isolated, has a job but keeps to himself, and obsesses over a potential love interest. We immediately recognize the character as an outsider, when his welder coworkers ridicule him for being a "weirdo." Bettis follows this sequence with shots of Roman sitting alone in an apartment with no apparent acquaintances. After routinely observing his neighbor (Kristen Bell) pass by to collect her mail, Roman engineers a chance encounter, which leads to conversation and subsequent courting. Initially, Roman's actions resemble stalking, but thanks to McKee's nuanced performance under the direction of Bettis (he rarely, if ever, acts in film), he sensitively delivers lines while showcasing his physicality to reveal a painfully shy and insecure individual who is desperate to connect with someone, thus becoming a normalized figure of humanity in the film. McKee's performance appears carefully calibrated in line with Bettis's expertise, as we are quick to dismiss our judgment of Roman when his overwhelming desire for his neighbor's company eventually leads to him inadvertently suffocating her to death. The childlike innocence we witness in Bettis's portrayal in *May* thus returns in *Roman* as the audience is presented with a character whose timorous mannerisms morph into a malevolence that's at once relatable and extremely shocking all at the same time.

Bettis directs McKee's script and his performance to provoke viewer empathy for a story whose outward appearance signals the very opposite. She opens the film with a welding sequence, which informs us not only about Roman's employment but more significantly about the character's precarious masculinity. Bettis furthers this notion as she continually positions Roman among the other men at work, as they converse about boxing, car accidents, and masturbation, yet he consistently occupies the margins of the frame unlike his peers. Roman's desperate attempts to become "one of the guys" do see him, at times, become more integrated into the middle of the frame (the symbolic homosocial center of things), yet Bettis continues to make Roman's social concern for masculinity and (its instability) apparent throughout the film by way of cinematography and character positioning, among a myriad of other techniques.

Bettis's direction of the film's cinematography and McKee's performance contribute to our understanding of Roman as deeply relatable. Bettis establishes Roman's loneliness with repeated wide shots of the character seated on his sofa alone, gazing through a window to nowhere. His behavior could easily be construed as menacing, but from the vantage point of Bettis's camera—behind the sofa in the recesses of the darkness— the audience is forced to engage with the stillness of his home environment: no television, no radio, not even the sound of a ticking clock. Bettis positions her audience behind Roman as we watch each uneventful day bleed into the next without so much as an interaction. During these painful moments of social isolation, we do not imagine for a second that Roman is plotting to viciously murder his neighbor; we are encouraged by Bettis to imagine quite the opposite as we recognize a damaged man desperate for his life to commence. Bettis's careful depiction of this nuanced male character is significant and is a shared concept among other women directors of horror. Jennifer Kent, director of *The Babadook* (2014), details:

> I don't judge my characters. As a person, I tend to have, I've been told, a lot of empathy for people. So even if people have done horrible things, I'm not going to judge them. I'm going to ask, "Why?" My aim . . . for my characters, was to show their brokenness, and to show the complexity of humans. They're not heroes in the traditional way. The vehicle of horror allows characters to be broken. (quoted in O'Sullivan 2014)

All too often, characters in the horror genre mirror and perpetuate well-established stereotypes. Yet with more women coming to the fore in independent horror filmmaking—writers and directors who know a thing or two about being depicted as caricatures themselves—we are beginning to witness an important body of directors break away from tired clichés in the interest of creating complex, compelling characters who participate in dynamic interactions with one another—their stories influencing, and being influenced by, the motives of other characters.

In Bettis's *Roman*, McKee is repeatedly captured in close-ups that reveal Roman's nervous mannerisms. We see McKee performatively shirk and shy away from his coworkers' comments, pull back from potentially fulfilling interactions, and evade face-to-face contact. Roman's reticent nature is revealed in these moments of camera proximity, and we—in that closeness—get to experience his skittish temperament. Something similar transpires in *May* when McKee repeatedly offers deep and intimate close-ups of the protagonist as she interacts with her love interests, Adam and Polly, allowing the audience to identify with her palpable nervousness, expressed through her quirky facial expressions and unpredictable physicality. Filmed in extremes, which border on parody, the characterizations of May and Roman employ, and make focal point of, minute details to humanize the outsider character type. In both memorable films, we get a glimpse at the harmony between Bettis and McKee as collaborators, creatives in acting and directing, and, more importantly, friends. Overall, Bettis's approach as an actor and director allows a window for the audience to witness her fresh perspective as a woman innovating with long-established character types to the benefit of the horror genre.

In *Roman*, McKee's performance combines with cinematic experimentation and narrative technique to round out the significance of Bettis's directorial debut. Throughout the film, we bear witness to Roman's uncertainty of self, always desperate to fit in and yet at the same time desperately keen to remain alone. The climax of McKee's performance proves the most insightful as Bettis captures Roman discovering his eventual love interest Eva's dead body. Bettis's camera focuses in on a grief-stricken, tearful Roman as he wrenches out, "I killed her! I killed her." Bettis's thoughtful selection of the shot allows us to observe McKee's tall frame shrink and close in upon itself, symbolically indicating a backward, crumbling trajectory of the progress he made by stepping out into society. It is clear, from this moment onward, that Eva's death will cause Roman to slide back into an isolationist state, reclusive from the outside world, just as May finds herself at the end of her own story. McKee openly credits his powerful performance in *Roman* to Bettis's process as a director, stating:

As a director, Angela was much more precious about the words on the page than I was [and she] is also a more intellectual type of director than I am. She could discuss and pull feelings out of me with just the right few words. My approach is, more often than not, to get in the same mood as the actors and/ or antagonize them in a game-like, non-malicious way. For me, it's all about pretend and creating a convincing illusion of a character's beliefs. Angela's approach was more therapeutic and studious in nature. (Twitter message to author, March 25, 2020)

Furthermore, and to McKee's credit, it is the "therapeutic and studious" nature of Bettis's direction that insists and persists throughout *Roman*, particularly at the end of the film, during the character's confession of guilt. Bettis's use of the cinematic apparatus is deftly applied to construct an intricate and orchestrated presentation of an obsessive outsider figure in which the subject matter is not treated as an absolute of evil.

CONCLUSION

In the DVD commentary for *Roman*, Bettis articulates the vision behind her directorial debut of McKee's script in *Roman*:

I think it was pretty important to him to see it not be his vision; he wanted to see somebody . . . take his writing and make their own vision out of it, which is what I tried to do and he actually did give me plenty of space to do that, at the same time . . . tutoring me on . . . [the] process of being a director and all the steps in filmmaking. (Bettis 2006)

With the independent horror film, a space generally regarded as more collaborative and inclusive than mainstream and/or big-budget genre cinema, Bettis was able to maximize her potential as a storyteller through a series of important collaborations with McKee. What is especially encouraging to see is that McKee made a particular effort not to intrude on Bettis's directorial debut. He recalls how Bettis was fully in control of the project from the initial concept: "I begged her to let me rewrite the script before filming, but she wouldn't let me! When I'm shooting anything, I tinker constantly, tweaking and cutting the dialogue and action, etc." (Twitter message to author, March 25, 2020). McKee also recalls the synergetic and supportive nature of Bettis's approach to directing *Roman*: "It was effortless and enlightening. . . . It was an invaluable learning experience as a director to take on a lead role and have the goods in front of the camera. Angela held my hand. Big time" (quoted in Wilkins 2011).

In the recent volume *Women Make Horror: Filmmaking, Feminism, Genre*, Alison Peirse inquires, "What makes a horror film a feminist film?" This is a remarkably complex question as some horror films made by women should not be labeled feminist, just as some horror films made by men should. Furthermore, a feminist horror film might be categorized as such due to the writer's or director's attributes, elements found in the work, and/or how the film is read (Peirse 2020, 11). Caution must be taken when assigning such an identifier to directors like Angela Bettis. Sally Robinson's *Engendering the Subject: Gender and Self-Representation in Contemporary Women's Fiction* offers a poignant reflection about women writers that we can apply to women directors:

> "Women's writing" is a construct that is both useful and risky, in the same way that the categories of Woman and women are. It is useful in that it specifies a difference that feminist literary study cannot do without, just as feminist theory cannot do without the category of women. . . . The construct is risky, however, in that it can imply a monolithic object of study, as if all women's writing could be represented as homogeneous. If the category of women is multiple, then, surely, the category of women's writing must be more so. The danger in adhering to the notion of a specificity of women's writing is that, first, such adherence threatens to erase differences between and within writing produced by women from different cultural locations; and, second, homogenization of such a diverse field of cultural production can lead to recuperation. (Robinson 1991, 10)

When we consider Robinson's argument toward an understanding of women directors of horror, it becomes apparent that viewing the work and examining the directing process through a gendered lens is helpful to form critical discourse about how women directors produce their films. Simultaneously, however, by applying the label of "woman director," we risk inadvertently creating assumptions that pigeonhole women who direct, characterizing their films as indistinguishable and minimizing their diverse individual efforts. While some filmmakers, such as Jennifer Kent and Alice Lowe, appear to channel their female identify into their work, with films such as *The Babadook* and *Prevenge*, which explore the gendered subject matter of motherhood, not all women directors focus on the female experience or want to be associated with such a label.

As highlighted in the introduction, Kathryn Bigelow, who became the first woman to win an Academy Award for Best Director, rejects the "feminist" tag; she also consistently resists any attempt to categorize her as a "female" director, "whether in relation to her films, her position in the industry, or audiences" (Paszkiewicz 2015, 167). Iranian American horror director Ana Lily Amirpour shares a similar viewpoint, claiming, "I really don't think race, gender, and this stuff is as big a factor as people want it to be" (Reilly 2016). From Lowe and Kent to Bigelow and Amirpour, these film directors validate Robinson's position concerning the risk of homogenization, as no woman director is the same as another. As this volume demonstrates, women directors of horror represent a vast and dynamic spectrum; furthermore, the filmmakers' work, directing practices, and views on what it means to be a woman directing horror are equally varied.

Whether or not we can deem Bettis's directing sensibilities as specifically correlated to gender is subjective. What is clear though is that Bettis's approach to *Roman* was taken in the interest of playing to individual strengths to form a collective work environment conducive to innovation, productivity, and growth. Interestingly, Bettis herself was surprised by the collaborative and successful work environment that transpired because of her leadership on the set of *Roman*, which also speaks to the collaborative, trusting production network that tends to be associated with independent filmmaking:

> I was pretty amazed by how willing people were to help for nothing and also what beautiful work they all did. Like if anything, my dream for this thing is that all those people that contributed all these beautiful elements to it can use this thing as a calling card and perhaps get more work and are proud of what they did in it because . . . I tried to give those people control of their particular thing that they were working on. And I hope in the end they're proud of those things and they came out exactly as they envisioned. (Bettis 2006)

Bettis's work ethic mirrors, in some part, the culture of horror filmmaking itself: the genre that has been marginalized and undermined for most of its existence has become recognized as a key creative site for women to develop careers beyond, but not disregarding, acting. As Melbourne-based filmmaker Donna McRae, director of *Johnny Ghost* (2011), reminds us:

> [Horror] is a genre [in which] you can explore a host of ideas more freely than if you were to do it at face value and there is a market for it. Also, the community that has emerged is very supportive, which makes it easier to exchange ideas and feel that you are not isolated in what could be seen as a male-dominated working space. (quoted in Kidd 2012)

Still, it took a good deal of time for Bettis to envision a pathway to directing film, despite possessing something of a cult following among horror fans and financiers. She admits:

> I never thought that I could be [a director]. The guys that I really admire are the guys that are writer/filmmakers that bear a concept and have this baby and see it through beginning to end with a higher vision. I'm kind of not one of those. I don't have these concepts that haunt me that I have to extract until they're gone. . . . My love is for storytelling, all kinds. I'm not really devoted or specified towards any specific genre at all. I really like it all. There's good storytelling in all the genres, you know. I just want to tell good stories and do good work. (Topel 2012)

On the recent release of *The ABCs of Death* (2012), an American anthology horror comedy in which Bettis directs a segment, the filmmaker was asked, "You're the only female director. . . . Is that important to you, being the only female director, or should we not even point it out?" Bettis responds, "It's not important to me. It really isn't." Yet she continues to champion other women to get involved in horror filmmaking specifically as directors, actors, and other creative and technical positions, emphatically urging, "Go, females, go! I don't know if I feel a responsibility to encourage women; I just do! . . . In whatever way that inspiration comes, we should shine!" (quoted in Beggs 2013). Bettis does not omit men from the picture either. She continues, "Honestly, I feel the same way about men. I find human beings to be so complex and full of beauty. Creativity is our way to express and challenge and flow" (Beggs 2013). One of those men, McKee, supports Bettis's call to action but also acknowledges the hardships women face in the film industry in general when admitting:

> The biggest distinction between men and women when making a film is that women have to battle with a lot more ingrained sexism. In my experience, they aren't listened to in the same way as men. They aren't trusted in the same way. It's absurd and frustrating. (Twitter message to author, March 25, 2020)

The working relationship between Bettis and McKee breaks this cycle, and the result is two iconic independent horror films (*May* and *Roman*) that function as intricate commentaries on obsession and the outsider character, each providing different but complementary gendered perspectives. McKee further laments, "It's sad there hasn't been an equal amount [of] female directors up to this point," but he is hopeful that we are in an upsweep of recognition so that "as time goes on, their voices will become more amplified" (Twitter message to author, March 25, 2020). It is clear to see why Bettis and McKee work so well together as horror filmmakers; they share compatible viewpoints that focus on equality for access and inclusion. As McKee indicates:

> The best thing about film is that it's about sharing individual and collective points of view of creative and emotionally expressive people. We all find comfort in art. Hopefully women, and really every person, will feel more and more represented and find more and more comfort as people improve and evolve all art forms. (Twitter message to author, March 25, 2020)

Bettis and McKee present a positive outlook for women in horror and the development of the genre. For Bettis, the work comes first; she operates from a point of collaborative efforts and celebrates the creativity of others who contribute to the field, gender notwithstanding. Bettis's goal for directing is simple: "I just hope I get to do it more" (Topel 2012). As she is a progressive voice for women in horror, creating dynamic characters and directing with innovation, we do, too.[1]

NOTE

1. In an effort to continue Bettis's philosophy of shared access and opportunity, and to continue the conversation about women in horror and better understand their roles as directors, writers, actors, producers, and more, see *Darlin'* (Pollyanna McIntosh, 2019); *Tales from the Lodge* (Abigail Blackmore, 2019); and *Body at Brighton Rock* (Roxanne Benjamin, 2019) as they discuss their feature-length directorial debuts at South by Southwest (SXSW) in an enlightening group interview regarding the engendered space of filmmaking for the genre.

BIBLIOGRAPHY

Beggs, Scott. "*ABCs of Death* Director Angela Bettis Talks Fake Blood, Spiders and the Scariest Thing About Human Beings." *Film School Rejects*, last modified January 31, 2013. https://www.filmschoolrejects.com/abcs-of-death-director -angela-bettis-talks-fake-blood-spiders-and-the-scariest-thing-about-human -6556277140dc/.
Bettis, Angela. "DVD Commentary." *Roman*. DVD. Directed by Angela Bettis. La Crosse, WI: Echo Bridge Home Entertainment, 2006.
Kidd, Briony. "Scream Time: Women Take Power over Horror." *Metro*, Winter 2012.
McKee, Lucky. Interview by James Francis. May 14, 2020. E-mail.
Mr. Bones. "Horror's Scream Queens and Rising Talent: Six Questions for Aislinn Clarke." *Morbidly Beautiful*, last modified February 18, 2018. https://morbidly beautiful.com/deadly-beauty-aislinn-clarke.
O'Sullivan, Michael. "*Babadook* Director Kent Talks about Women Making Horror Movies." *Washington Post*, last modified December 12, 2014. https://www .washingtonpost.com/lifestyle/style/babadook-director-jennifer-kent-talks -about-women-making-horror-movies/2014/12/12/11dba89a-8082-11e4-9f38 -95a187e4c1f7_story.html.
Paszkiewicz, Katarzyna. "Hollywood Transgressor or Hollywood Transvestite? The Reception of Kathryn Bigelow's *The Hurt Locker*." In *Doing Women's Film History: Reframing Cinemas, Past and Future*, ed. Christine Gledhill and Julia Knight. Urbana: University of Illinois Press, 2015.
Peirse, Alison. *Women Make Horror: Filmmaking, Feminism, Genre*. New Brunswick, NJ: Rutgers University Press, 2020.
Reilly, Phoebe. "From 'Babadook' to 'Raw': The Rise of the Modern Female Horror Filmmaker." *Rolling Stone*, October 26, 2016. https://www.rollingstone .com/movies/movie-features/from-babadook-to-raw-the-rise-of-the-modern -female-horror-filmmaker-120169/.

Robinson, Sally. *Engendering the Subject: Gender and Self-Representation in Contemporary Women's Fiction*. Albany: State University of New York Press, 1991.

Topel, Fred. "Exclusive Interview: Angela Bettis on *The ABCs of Death*." *Mandatory*, last Modified October 2, 2012. https://www.mandatory.com/fun/197089 -exclusive-interview-angela-bettis-on-the-abcs-of-death.

Vespe, Eric. "Quint Interviews The Star of the Great Horror Film, *MAY*, here'sssss Angela Bettis!" *Ain't It Cool*, last Modified February 3, 2003. https://www .legacy.aintitcool.com/node/14366.

Wilkins, Budd. "Interview: Lucky McKee Talks *The Woman*." *Slant*, last Modified October 20, 2011. https://www.slantmagazine.com/film/interview-lucky -mckee/.

FOUR

Stitches, Screams, and Female Beauty

Canadian Women Horror Film

Shelby Shukaliak, Eve O'Dea, and Ernest Mathijs

Cinema is never only regional. Canadian horror films by women are no exception. If one looks at how Canada as a society, and Canadian film as an assembly of aesthetics, politics, and production, and distribution realities, functions, an international frame of reference in its cinema seems, in fact, inevitable.[1]

This chapter offers an overview of the most prominent themes and voices in Canadian women horror film by making sidesteps and comparisons, and thus framing a context of references, with feminist horror film from inside as well as outside Canada. The themes this context dictates are threefold: a felt internationalism, exuberance, and beauty. Together, these three themes emphasize a context of aesthetics of "looks" for the feminism in Canadian women horror film. The felt internationalism, or the way in which these films look beyond narrow borders of nationhood (as received through ideological frameworks), sets the stage, if you want, for the presentation of "outside" identities as they are explored in Canadian women horror film. Together with its ally, feminism, this intent to "look outside" also provokes (one could say it necessitates) a hyperbolic assembly of styles, glances, and gestures that make the act of "how to look" (how to attract and direct one's gaze) an essential part of the films—thereby firmly interrogating the very concept of "looks" and its affiliation with beauty and exuberance. To use one pars pro toto: in *Ginger Snaps 2: Unleashed* (2003), there is a scene in which Ghost (Tatiana Maslany) regards with curiosity her mom, a burn victim completely covered in stitched medical gauze. Only the mother's eyes peek out. We think they look as if she's in pain, suffering as she realizes her looks will be gone forever. Only later do we get to see the look is not about beauty but about fear. Only Brigitte (Emily Perkins, herself a survivor of her sister's werewolf infection), looking in from the outside as a foreigner to Ghost's imaginary framework, questions the situation and realizes the ambiguity. But, trusting Ghost, she moves on. Looks deceive.

The case studies for this overview are from contemporary horror cinema, with emphasis on the *Ginger Snaps* trilogy (Fawcett/Sullivan/Harvey, 2000–2004), *American Mary* (The Soska Sisters, 2012), and *Rabid* (The Soska Sisters, 2019), and with international coproduction *Daughters of Darkness* (Kümel, 1971) and American *Jennifer's Body* (Kusama, 2009) and *The Love Witch* (Biller, 2016) (one industry-processed film, one indie production) as checkpoints. Methodologically, then, this chapter relies on production analysis using direct sources, aesthetic analysis, and some reception analysis (mostly public reception materials) to "stitch"[2] together notions of feminist intervention, radical aesthetics, and hyperbolically applied genre conventions—exactly as in the pars pro toto of *Ginger Snaps 2*. Together, this constellation creates an insight into how Canadian female horror film moves inside and outside its own territory, screams and all.

CANADA'S "FELT" INTERNATIONALISM AND GENDER

Discussions of Canadian cinema often highlight its "difference" from other territories, most notably American (Hollywood) studio productions and European art-house productions—even if the same sources that point to those differences equally often note just how much Canadian film employs aesthetic and production strategies from those spheres of influence. George Melnyk (2004) and Jim Leach (2006) make that connection explicitly in their analyses of Canadian film at large. Will Straw (1998) notes that tropes often associated with "Canadian-ness" such as "survival" (Margaret Atwood) and "adolescence" (Peter Harcourt) preference volatility and dependency, and they stress how Canadian film always already exists "in comparison to" other territories (White 2006 is one exception). With regard to genre film and horror in particular, this is even more the case. Andrew Dowler (1985) called horror so much as adventitious to Canadian film, and Geoff Pevere (2000) tellingly stated:

> It's probably a good thing that most people don't draw conclusions about the national character from the concentrated viewing of new Canadian movies. Should the world find out the truth—that we're actually a race of alienated mother-hating suicidal teenage werewolf junkies—we'd finally have a reason to feel lonely and misunderstood.

Pevere makes this comment tongue-in-cheek, of course, but not all critics weave wit around the suggestion (see, for instance, Pratley 2003). In the conclusion of their overview of Canadian horror film, André Loiselle and Gina Freitag (2016) consider the notion of a "Canadian" horror a "mental case" (270).

Beyond considerations of Canada as "only" Hollywood-North, the entanglement or obsession with "the outside" works through in analyses of production and exhibition industries, most often as variations on the question: "Where in the world is *Orphan Black*?" (Levine 2009; Sinic 2009), or, as Brenda Longfellow mentions, in the inverse emphasis on films shot in Canadian cities that become distinct because they try so hard to focus on the fact that these Canadian cities are supposed to be American (Longfellow 1996). This situation has led Charles Acland (2003) to propose "felt internationalism," a form of imagined cosmopolitanism, as a key lens through which one *needs* to approach Canadian cinema, from production circumstances to audience reactions. Canada's self-declared internationalism in terms of the political rhetoric it applies to foreign policy and diplomacy, and in terms of its hosting of a society of multicultural diversities, add to that profile to the point one can argue looking anxiously past its borders for an affirmation of its own identity makes up part of Canada's cultural imagination at large.

The horror genre itself is moreover constituent of an *international* neighborhood. In spite of numerous works attempting to carve out "nation-specific" horror cinema identities (see Schneider and Williams 2005), the prevailing view is that horror crosses borders—one could even go so far as to say that the genre's affinity with liminality, transgression, and "otherness" dictates that (see, for instance, Cherry 2008; Mathijs and Sexton 2011; Benshoff 2016; Mathijs 2020). David Cronenberg is an obvious case in point. As Mathijs (2013) has shown, for instance, the reception of the *Ginger Snaps* films is internationalist *before* it is Canadian. Vincenzo Natali's *Cube* (1997) and *Splice* (2010) too had a distinct international recognition that fed into its Canadian reception (see Christopher 2019). A quick look at the reception of Don McKellar's *Last Night* (1998) shows an intimate relationship between a "typical" Canadian theme, international genre prestige (fueled by numerous references to internationally acknowledged horror iconography—David Cronenberg's acting performance key among them), and local recognition (Mathijs 2008; 2012).[3] This dual bind between local and international receptions for the horror genre is not unique to Canada. The receptions of the Giallo film or of Asia-Extreme horror are other examples (Hunter 2010; Macias 2001). Indeed, in the introduction of her interview book with Canadian filmmakers such as Natali, Cronenberg, and James Cameron, Angela Baldassarre (2003) argues that "Canadian filmmaking has been a misunderstood beast in the jungle of international filmmaking," in which "writing about 'our' style" acts as an affirmative balancing act, aimed at evening up the odds (8). In general, if one looks at the dominant networks of exchange and access within which the horror genre operates (such as festivals, subcultural arrangements, key venues, and audience debates), the frame of reference of internationalism seems the default.

If one looks at feminist writing on horror film, both as a political perspective on and as an aesthetic intervention into filmmaking, internationalism again prevails. Gender is, of course, not a "national" issue. Much the same way radical, progressive movements see "national" borders as obstacles to change, the work of feminist film scholars from Molly Haskell and Laura Mulvey to Carol Clover, Linda Williams, Kate Egan, and Alexandra Heller-Nicholas stresses how the anxieties of gender representation apply internationally (for an overview, see Austin-Smith 2019). Bonnie Zimmerman's discussion of the feminist lesbian vampire film *Daughters of Darkness* is an excellent exemplar—and one to which we return further on in this chapter (Zimmerman 1981). Mathijs and Sexton (2011) include gender as part of their overview of significant anxieties that fuel cult receptions, and horror films are a prime example in their argumentation.

STITCHING THE SCENE AESTHETICALLY

The term "felt," as used by Acland, is narrow in its understandings. It stands for "proxy" (a "sort of kind of"). In the case of feminist horror, however, it has the power to expand into an operative term, a direction. It is in this sense that this chapter aims to approach the felt internationalism of feminist Canadian horror film. Loiselle and Freitag observe how in Canadian horror film, particularly in the subgenre of the body horror film (which is where our examples are primarily located), "the female gender takes on the power of the 'locus of identification'" (2016, 273). At the same time, they note, there is a "slippage" that renders characters unstable: "unsettled" (as in a nation both settled and unsettled—a comparison they make), continually uprooted, and impossible to "refine" in terms of its identity. Felt as explored by Loiselle and Freitag, then, is an undirected aim.

Our chapter explores this gendered felt internationalism by stitching together elements of radical aesthetics (emphasizing ugliness and beauty) and of the subjectivity of its female characters (and, in a way, of its female creators). The term "stitching" is operationalized here as an aesthetic tool: one that can sew together wounds or worn and torn types of fabric, and that can do so brutally and with scars or elegantly blended—seamless. By emphasizing autonomy and female beauty (or efforts toward that), this chapters acknowledges how Canadian women horror is at once "felt" (as in "understood") to be a challenge to normative filmmaking (and therefore, international, unbound by Canada as a nation) and equally "felt" (as in referencing a tactile, embodied impression) as an identifier for the experience of belonging.

Before we move fully into the case studies, it is necessary to sketch (indeed *stitch*) some examples of films that inform the group of films that make up our frame of reference. Canadian scholarship on gender, often adverse to discussions of genre, generally shies away from making claims about the international scope of Canadian women horror filmmaking (Austin-Smith and Melnyk 2010). That said, there are notable exceptions, and they are foregrounded because of the interests that discussions of them put on aesthetics. The work of women filmmakers such as Joyce Wieland, Holly Dale, or Jovanka Vuckovic, whose frame of reference includes horror (incidentally and/or intentionally), is occasionally listed alongside international horror film fare. To name four examples: Wieland's *The Far Shore* (1976) and *Rat Life and Diet in North America* (1968) appear alongside Anna Biller's *Three Examples of Myself as Queen Bee* (1994) and *Viva* (2006) on lists that stress genre-inspired aesthetics (Sloan 2010). Tangential as this stitch appears, it speaks volumes about what critics and commentators accept as valid points of reference. Holly Dale's *Blood and Donuts* (1995) is regularly mentioned as an effort in women filmmaking that engages with the horror genre fully—its hyperbole makes it almost a send-up of horror genre tropes. Assumedly solid masculine genre tropes are presented in such an aesthetically overt fashion that they become comments on the genre (the fact that *Blood and Donuts* fits perfectly a wave of highly self-reflexive horror films saturated in intertextual aesthetics, such as the final installments of the *Nightmare on Elm Street* franchise, 1994, or the first *Scream*, 1996, film, even makes it a symptomatic example). Central to that aesthetic are the use of expressive lighting and color, the many comments on beauty and ugliness in the film, and, almost totemic, the performance of David Cronenberg as a gangster kingpin who gets killed by a vampire. "Your shoes make a smudge," Cronenberg says to Frank Moore's character (the same Frank Moore as in *Rabid*, 1977, and Wieland's *The Far Shore*) as he compares the aesthetic quality and durability of their respective footwear, to which he adds: "Mine make a mark" (see Mathijs 2012). One critic in *Take One* called the performance "a comeuppance" (1994). The visibility of *Blood and Donuts* also brings into the frame Dale's earlier work, with Janis Cole, such as her street documentary *Hookers on Davie Street* (1984) and the documentary about women in prison *P4W* (1981)—two films that have since been connected to the contemporary horror genre's preoccupation with styles and aesthetics of exploitation cinema as well as documentary modes of delivery as it continues to explore thin lines between *vérité* and sensationalism. In the case of Vuckovic, her book on zombies, published when she was editor of the genre magazine *Rue Morgue*, stresses the international scope of this type of film while limiting its attention on Canadian film to the aesthetics of George Romero's collaboration with *Ginger Snaps'* coproducer Paula Devonshire (*Diary of the Dead*, 2007, and *Survival of the Dead*, 2009) (see Vuckovic 2011).[4] *Ginger Snaps'* writer Karen Walton's work on, for instance, *Orphan Black* (2013–) shows the same "felt" internationalism in its horror genre aesthetics and feminist overtones. One only needs to look at the presentation of Tatiana Maslany's character(s) in the opening scenes to note the curious sense of location, dislocation, and self that prompted Serra Tinic to ask, "Where in the world is *Orphan Black*?" (2015). Similarly, Julia Mendenhall's book on *I've Heard Mermaids Singing* (Patricia Rozema, 1987) stresses genre-inspired aesthetics. In other words, any link between gender and horror in the case of Canadian filmmaking seems to go via appreciations of radical aesthetics (and their political uses) rather than via ideological and programmatic avenues (Mendenhall 2014).

The "felt" internationalism triangle of women's horror film in Canada is further exemplified by the work of Gigi Saul Guerrero, whose short films on the immigrant experiences of Mexican workers and families in the United States and Canada are firmly rooted in production cultures of coproduction established alongside North America's cross-national Pacific coastline: from Baja to the Bay Area to the North Shores of Vancouver, where Guerrero's Luchagore Productions is based. Films such as *The Cull* (2018) and *Culture Shock* (2019) are indicative of feminist sensitivities amid international inspirations. Through efforts from filmmakers such as Danis Goulet (*Wakening*, 2014) and Nyla Innuksuk (*Kajutaijuq*, 2015), this sensitivity finds further expression, anchoring it.

FOREIGN LOOKS

One of the consequences of Canadian women horror film's "felt internationalism," and indeed one of the key ways in which these films connect with larger discourses (and myths) about Canada as a self-declared multicultural nation, is the felt desire toward inclusiveness. It means that it is challenging to pinpoint traditional "foreigners" in Canadian women horror films because everyone is always already "one of us." If one exempts the allowance of mild stabs at Americans, perhaps, monsters in Canadian women horror films are homegrown or home-trained. There are some exceptions. A film such as *Octavio Is Dead!* (Sook-Yin Lee, 2018) takes the theme of the foreign "other" into the realm of the supernatural (a faint patriarchic ghost) as part of the search for the Latin American father (Octavio) of bisexual and androgynous Tyler Kent (Sarah Gadon). But by and large, cultural, ethnic, and linguistic foreigners are not explicitly or directly incriminated.

The result is twofold. On the one hand, the inclusive attitude of Canadian women horror films means that the threat that the horror genre demands, as part of its template, has to come from inside the community, in the shape of key characters' lack of belonging. This trope is explored to the fullest, as our case studies below show. On the other hand, it means that if the horror genre's "other" cannot be signaled through language, skin color, or cultural and heritage affection and location, then it needs to be motioned at through different aesthetic means: through the aesthetics of "beauty" and as a play on the standards and norms of what it means to be beautiful. This is fertile ground for female horror filmmakers, as it offers the opportunity to play with visualizations and allegories of what are known as female beauty duties and routines. It also highlights the importance of age as a factor in beauty. Every single one of our case studies singles out "young woman" as volatile, potentially monstrous; the cases equally point to maturity as a means of overcoming that volatility. The connection of age to beauty, in turn, translates into an emphasis on aesthetics of fashion, self-decoration, beautification and hyperbolic *cutification*, and, ultimately, on "looks."

This emphasis is an innovation for national Canadian cinema, into which it injects an often-ignored motive of refinement and exuberance of fashion. Even though it may appear a gross generalization—with the exception of isolated examples, such as the carnivalesque setting of beautiful lesbian "fairy tales" *When Night is Falling* (Patricia Rozema, 1995) or *Better Than Chocolate* (Anne Wheeler, 1999), Guy Maddin's hyperbolic imaginations (*Dracula: Pages from a Virgin's Diary*, 2002), or the seniors fashion show at the center of *Incident at Elysian Fields* (Judy Holm/Michael MacNamara, 2017; it features Art Hindle, veteran from David Cronenberg's *The Brood* and Bob Clarke's *Black Christmas*)—Canadian cinema has avoided the kind of exuberance that has colored international film, at least where it concerns aestheticizing "otherness." Canadian women horror film's attention to this, then, is not only welcome but also complicated. One could argue, perhaps, that this innovative attention to exuberance and refinement is a form of criticism (a pastiche even) of the American Dream's obsession with capitalist grandeur and upward class mobility, from a slightly more socialist Canadian point of view. If that is the case, it would qualify Loiselle and Freitag's observation that Canadian horror based in America comes from a place of insecurity in not being American.

THE *GINGER SNAPS* TRILOGY

The first of our case studies, the *Ginger Snaps* trilogy, exemplifies best this exuberance.[5] Felt internationalism is dealt with upfront in the first film, in the opening scenes, and referenced throughout, all the way to right before the tragic end, when, in one last desperate attempt to save her daughters, Brigitte and Ginger (Emily Perkins and Katherine Isabelle), mother Pam Fitzgerald (Mimi Rogers) urges the younger of the two sisters, Brigitte, to run "away from here," to "just go." Pam's exclamation (it is also a lament) is the logical result of a tone set early on in the film in which street hockey, as a staple of Canadian everyday life, is briefly foregrounded to set the story apart from, away from, the United States, all the while (and indeed simultaneously) flirting with American stereotypes of high school, suburbia, and nuclear family routines (some of which neatly stress home beauty accents—again encapsulated perfectly by sweet, gentle, and domesticated but also slightly kooky stay-at-home mom Pam). The tension between "here" and "there" in *Ginger Snaps* is further achieved through the mystery that hangs over the origin of the werewolf curse that infects Ginger. It is not identified as foreign, but it is also not from around. Brigitte looks for its origin in old movies, which, in a montage, are shown to be an international mix of Lon Chaney Jr. and Paul Naschy, but she does not get very far. The one person Brigitte can rely on in her quest to help her sister, Sam (Kris Lemche), seeks for cures wherever he can, but he too does not get further than suggesting first a silver ring and then the herb monkshood (it is worth noting Sam deals soft drugs to the high school of the Fitzgerald sisters, and the link between monkshood as cure and monkshood as "weed" is not lost on viewers), thereby illustrating the multiplicity of origins of the werewolf myth. Both, screenwriter Karen Walton has mentioned, are equally Canadian and non-Canadian in that they are "not a gun" and "not exotic" but still present themselves as somewhat exotic. They are also, of course, tools for beautification. The pierced silver ring in Ginger's belly button is arguably more convincingly such a tool than the monkshood "weed," which is more a tool to improve self-impressions and "imaginations" (weed hazes) of beauty than one to actually achieve it. But deceptions count too.

The second *Ginger Snaps* film, which sidelines Ginger in favor of an examination of how the werewolf curse affects Brigitte as she is interned in a recovery clinic, continues the ambiguity of felt internationalism, this time through the tropes of comic book imaginations and serial killer motives, embodied by Ghost (Tatiana Maslany). Tiny details, such as clothing particulars (zippers, hair clips) or a tattoo (the Def Leppard tattoo of a case worker), remind viewers continually of how accentuations of beauty place women in a spotlight, sometimes exuberantly, and how they stress the "in-betweenness" of homeliness, both domestic and outer-worldly. In the third of the *Ginger Snaps* films, *Ginger Snaps Back*, the felt internationalism finds perhaps its most accomplished expression, with the setting of a frontier trader fort in the early nineteenth century (the film is a "prequel" in that it imagines the blood curse of the sisters back to earlier times). The setting allows explorations of foreignness, in particular by juxtaposing settlers, traders, hunters, First Nation people and tribes, Puritans, homesteaders, and militia as small, unique groupings before they would become one heterogenic Canadian. *Ginger Snaps Back* has often been described as the best-looking of the trilogy, and its exuberant display of tokens, jewelry, accouterments, and ornate clothing (in particular the dresses of the sisters) forms a smorgasbord of signs of felt internationalism (see Mathijs 2013 for detailed discussions of the sequel and prequel).

With felt internationalism in place and beauty signaled as its vehicle, the *Ginger Snaps* films show a feminist queering of the tropes they introduce. Rather than confirming their significance, it is as if the films undermine their cohesiveness—as if beauty once presented needs to be deconstructed. After the opening credits, which give an overview of horror genre templates (everything from a chainsaw to clowns, from poison to guts, and from maniacal laughter to Goth suicide pacts), Brigitte and Ginger, teens, decide to resist the regimentations of beautification (and the objectification that comes with it) they observe around them in high school. High school, according to the sisters, is a "hormonal toilet," and they privately pick on the good-looking girls—such as Trina (Danielle Hampton), whose ideal death they imagine to be "D.O.A. at the hair dye aisle. Perished while seeking matching barrettes on nothing but diet pills and laxatives." The attitude of the Fitzgerald sisters is one of ostensive disdain for formats of beauty. When Ginger says, "A girl can only be a slut, bitch, tease, or the virgin next door," she refers not only to gender roles accorded/directed at girls in high school vernacular masculine parlance (and, perhaps, in society at large), but she is also, and importantly, addressing the kinds of beautification and aesthetics that are associated with femininity, refinement, appropriate displays of fashion and exuberance, and carrying oneself into adulthood with style. The theme of sexualization is addressed multiple times in *Ginger Snaps* (less so in the sequel and prequel). But in each case that form of fetishization is brought back to a matter of looks, of exuberance and fashion. For instance, when Ginger explains how she distrusts the school's janitor (a man of Asian American appearance), she first mentions, bitingly, how he would stare down Brigitte's shirt, and later on, after she has turned almost fully into a spectacle and she has disposed of him, she comments on how he tastes— as if it is a matter of aesthetic taste, not bloodlust. Perhaps visually the most poignant example of the emphasis on beauty and its deconstruction in *Ginger Snaps* lies in the attire of the sisters. Mathijs (2013) has analyzed the costume design and art direction of the Fitzgerald sisters, and in linking it with the contemporary international examples (or foreign looks) of *Sister My Sister* (Nancy Meckler, 1994), *Heavenly Creatures* (Peter Jackson, 1995), and *Girl Interrupted* (James Mangold, 1999), he finds that the Fitzgerald Sisters are equally *without* a style (at the beginning of the film) and exuberantly embody *all* styles—hyperbolic and nondenominative at the same time—near the end of the film (Mathijs 2013, 32–38). Ultimately the double emphasis on and against beauty of *Ginger Snaps* is reflected in Ginger's transformation, from silver-streak-haired beauty to monstrous creature of beauty. After Ginger is bitten by a werewolf, her rage intensifies, and its direction is firmly toward demolishing ideals of beauty. First Trina's dog, then Trina herself become her victims, then everyone else. Yet, at the same time, new beauty emerges. As Ginger courts (well, overpowers) Jason (Jesse Moss) and as she prepares her "entry" at the Halloween party, she dresses up, first just making sure she's attractive by trying to use traditional beauty routines ("I cannot have a hairy chest, Bee," she says; "it's fucked up") and eventually by proudly flaunting her newly found curves, including her werewolf mammary system under a revealing shirt. In doing so, Ginger actually not only deconstructs beauty; she also refashions it, makes it hers, confronting instead of confirming to ideals of fashion.

AMERICAN MARY, RABID, AND JENNIFER'S BODY

A perfect follow-up to the frame of reference stitched together by *Ginger Snaps* above is offered by a comparison of *American Mary* (Soska Sisters 2012), *Rabid* (Soska Sisters, 2019), and *Jennifer's Body* (Kusama, 2009), female-directed, feminist-inspired horror films with strong ties to Canada's "felt" international landscape. *American Mary* is Canadian, and *Jennifer's Body* is clearly heavily influenced by Canada's *Ginger Snaps*, aesthetically and in terms of production culture, and by the decidedly "felt international" *Juno* (2007), written by Diablo Cody and directed by Jason Reitman.[6] Any comparison of these films must acknowledge that in this felt internationalism, Canada is often postured as a younger sibling to the United States without a definitive culture of its own, which results in a national need to project distaste upon that which is distinctly Canadian. More, Andre Loiselle argues that Canadian horror that distinctly refers to itself as American is situated in a "typically Canadian" hypocrisy, where Canadians project their own fears of becoming too much like the United States onto the United States (Loiselle 2013, 124). There is no easy way out of this, except through an emphasis on aesthetics that reflect a lack of distinct identity (or, better, conformity to prescribed types and norms) as a power tool. Exactly such a lack of distinct identity directly informs the feminist themes in *American Mary* (2012) and *Rabid* (2019), namely that female autonomy in Canadian horror—both diegetically and in the filmmaker space—goes hand-in-hand with a reclamation of power and agency through the presentation of protagonists and antagonists, through self-reflexivity, and by considering the shift from one, certain national identity, via altering the male gaze, to an identity decidedly more female, acceptant of, and celebrating exuberantly noncertainty.

Let us start with *Jennifer's Body*, American body-horror film that—despite its similar themes exploring autonomy and power—does not need to posit itself as distinctly American and appears to have full confidence in its own identity. Much has been written about *Jennifer's Body*'s ability to position, like *Ginger Snaps*, its protagonist Jennifer Check (Megan Fox), together with a "sister" (Needy, Amanda Seyfried), as a revenge against beauty dictates as circulated through the circuit of high school (Paszkiewiz 2018; Vena 2018).[7] The story takes place in small-town America without shoving its Americana (pardon the pun) down our throats. Best friends Jennifer and Needy are two sexually empowered young women—Jennifer through her uncompromising promiscuity, and Needy through a monogamous relationship—whose lives are upturned when Jennifer is possessed by an evil spirit that survives on human flesh. Jennifer's possession happens as a result of a Satanic band believing she's a virgin based on the singer's misogynistic assumption that young women who present as sexually forward and empowered are *falsely* doing so to mask insecurity. Jennifer's promiscuity (arguably) saves her life and spells out the doom of the band who attempted to sacrifice her for their own gain. Screenwriter and producer Diablo Cody has spoken publicly about having enjoyed her past work as an exotic dancer and about the sex-positive stance taken by the film. Much like the characters in *Ginger Snaps, Rabid,* and *American Mary,* Jennifer presents as stylish and attractive when in an empowered position; she looks healthier and is physically stronger when she has recently fed on a human. On the flip side, Needy is empowered by the desire to save her best friend—a motivation that morphs from an attempt to cure her of her possession to killing Jennifer to preserve her in her memory. The films ends with Needy taking on some of Jennifer's supernatural powers through a bite and killing the band whose actions began the whole ordeal. There is room left by the filmmakers for this to be a silly horror—it does not have to try to be American because it simply is.

Jennifer's Body wears its obsession with protocols of embellishment and exuberance on its sleeve, all the way to hyperbolic language, size- and color-fixated body makeup, and references to *The Rocky Horror Picture Show* screenings at the Bijou (you can't really get much more over the top than that). For much of its running time, *Jennifer's Body* copies *Ginger Snaps* and cranks it up a few notches—Americana-ized it, one could say.

Copycat concerns aside, what *Jennifer's Body* succeeds in doing is to offer a not-to-be-misunderstood overtone of self-reflexive feminist criticism of beauty regimentation—a bleeding obviousness that drives home the message that "pretty" is a stale convention. The film does this on all fronts. The characters names are cartoonish. Check and Needy are indeed what they signal: Jennifer Check plays being "checked out"—a term Ginger uses at the beginning of *Ginger Snaps*, right before she assaults pretty Tina and starts her crusade against normative beauty. And Needy is "needy" (Rafferty 2009). Laxatives in *Jennifer's Body* are uniquely fashion-and-glamour instruments, not medication to be administered under supervision. The stereotypical "hallway walk" of a character with newly found confidence in *Jennifer's Body* is even more a red-carpet parade than it was in *Ginger Snaps* (the slow-motion hammering it in as a sharpened nail). In its singularity, *Jennifer's Body* is a success: it puts the query of beauty and the need of its deconstruction front stage without looking back.

What *Jennifer's Body* lacks is what makes Canadian women horror unique: insecurity and absence of confidence. For some commentators, *Jennifer's Body*'s overly cheeky use of hyperbole and exuberance makes it a "dodgy hipster film" (Sragow, see Vena 2018). For others, it is a repository of slang and euphemisms, directing meaning by inferring it (Siska 2010). It is certainly sillier in its singularity. That very silliness is missing from Canadian women horror films. One could argue that there is a fear in the tone of Canadian films that they will not be taken seriously unless they take themselves seriously. Often, such a desire backfires. It makes films look less committed, gives less of a sense of conviction. Taken one step further, this makes it possible that the underrepresentation of Canadian horror in international cinema aligns with the underrepresentation of female-led horror. The old adage that women must be twice as good to be taken half as seriously could be applied to the idea of Canadian genre filmmaking.

American Mary (2012) and *Rabid* (2019) contradict that adage, and this fear, to a large extent. Directed by the Soska Sisters, who had previously delivered a radical aesthetic statement with exploitation exercise *Dead Hooker in a Trunk* (2008), both films make it a point to declare their affiliation with alternative aesthetics and feminist deconstructions of genre formulas. The setting of both films highlights how central the commodification and beautification of female body is to the stories. *American Mary* tells the story of medical student Mary (Katharine Isabelle, who was cast because of her earlier role as Ginger), who uses her skills and talent to "earn" her way through medical school as she "performs" surgery on members of the body-modification community. The quotation marks around "earning" and "performing" in relation to beauty essentially deliver the message of the Soska Sisters: beauty is a business, and a woman's body is a battlefield both aesthetically and, necessarily, economically. Mary avenges herself on a doctor who assaulted her, and the police chase her. Unable to perform self-surgery successfully, Mary dies. *Rabid*, a reimagination of David Cronenberg's film from 1977, tells the story of Rose (Laura Vandervoort), a seamstress who quickly rises to prominence in a fashion designer's company when she emerges from reconstructive surgery a "belle." Rose's new but hesitant confidence, and her beauty, come at a price: she has to consume human blood to survive and thrive. The fear of firm confidence is obvious in both films, as they pitch a localized (sometimes body-located) identity against the more cosmopolitan self-assurance of the industries in which the stories are set: the medical world and the fashion world. Both worlds deal in the promise of making ugly pretty and sickly healthy—and both worlds are governed by men. Much like the high schools in *Ginger Snaps* (and the rehab institution in *Ginger Snaps Unleashed*) and *Jennifer's Body*, the premises where transformation is triggered, suffered, and celebrated are liminal: the dressing rooms and night clubs of the fashion circuit in *Rabid* and the surgery theaters in *American Mary* (and also, to some extent, in *Rabid*). But in the aesthetics of the Soska Sisters, these locales do not promise certainty the way a graduation promises maturity or recovery promises reentrance into society. Instead, they lead to further chains of insecurity, ending with the demise of the protagonists. Or, put differently, the consumption does not end until Mary and Rose self-cannibalize.

This fear, of the ultimate self-destruction, is referenced explicitly in *Rabid*, with Rose aware of what she is becoming yet fearing it within herself. *American Mary* projects this in a more explicit way, by using the national signifier in its title and becoming almost a mockery of the "American Dream." In both films, the inciting incident is either an explicit or implicit rape, leading to a period of insecurity, then empowerment through revenge of the action, then finally their downfall. *American Mary* sees promising surgical student Mary drop out of med school following a harrowing depiction of being drugged and raped by one of her professors and start her own underground surgical practice that gains fame and notoriety in the "body mod" world. Her plight is initially presented with a relatable hopelessness that mirrors problematic societal realities for women: financial instability, sexuality as a currency, and abuse of power by male superiors. The establishment of her body mod practice answers all of these issues by offering her a steady and impressive (if not morally questionable) source of income in a historically male-dominated field that both puts her in a physical position of power over her patients and gives her the tools to exact revenge upon her rapist.

The insecurity and fear are negotiated through exuberance, as simultaneously ostensive confirmation of beauty (as traditionally perceived), renegotiation of beauty (through hyperbole as style), and reclamation of beauty (on its own, feminist, terms). Throughout *American Mary*, Mary maintains an extremely stylish appearance, seen in her sharp high heels, edgy corsets, and sleek, dark hair, which comes across as an appreciation by the filmmakers for high fashion and as a representation of power, rather than the sexual objectification of the female protagonist. According to an interview with the Soska Sisters, they were worried Isabelle would react hesitantly to the costume choice. Instead, she strutted in the outfit, declaring, "Ain't it hot"?[8] This duality is similarly (and more explicitly) seen in *Rabid*, where Rose the-fashion-designer only functions because of the vampiric infection that pushes her to create and wear harsher and edgier styles that finally catch the eye of her demanding boss. As the film progresses, it matters less that Rose's need for human flesh is the result of an experimental cosmetic surgery after a horrific accident that disfigured her face, and this is a violation that she attempts to correct as the infection takes a stronger hold of her faculties. Beauty becomes a pursuit in its own end, inconsequential of the needs. Rose's case is presented particularly self-reflexively by the Soska Sisters, who incorporate referentiality by way of dialogue, aesthetics, and an inversion of the male authority present in the original. The first words in the film are about "remaking old trends"—referring not only to Rose's job as a designer but to the original David Cronenberg film (in that sense, the opening resembles the opening montage of *Ginger Snaps* in its nods to the history of the horror genre).

Aesthetically, *American Mary* and *Rabid* go full out, meeting the brazenness of *Jennifer's Body*, textually and in palette. *American Mary* is bathed in black and red. *Rabid* references the color scheme in the original by using white and neutral and then setting it directly against bright reds and bold lighting. The juxtaposition implicitly references virginity and womanhood and explicitly her humanity and her vampiric desire for human flesh. In an even more elaborate aesthetic stitch, the scene in which Rose is operated upon also explicitly winks at *American Mary*, as the surgeons performing the macabre procedures in both films are wearing blood red scrubs and surgical gear—itself a nudge to Cronenberg's surgery scenes in *Dead Ringers* (1988), a film about twin gynecologists. It is a powerful choice by the Soska Sisters to position themselves with a body of work robust enough to warrant referentiality. It is revealing of the Canadian felt internationalism, however, that *Rabid*, whose source material takes place in Montreal, does not appear to take place in a Canadian city. Instead, it maintains an internationality, with foreign characters in positions of power, especially in the German fashion designer Gunter (Mackenzie Gray), whom Rose spends the film trying to impress, and in the figure of Dr. Burroughs (Ted Atherton), whose clinic Rose attends (Dr. Burroughs's full name is William Burroughs). In all three films, the protagonist ends up either dead or imprisoned—perhaps a critique of the perceived futility of upheaving a deeply entrenched patriarchy and the America-centric film industry.

INTERNATIONAL CHECKPOINT: *DAUGHTERS OF DARKNESS* AND *THE LOVE WITCH*

The connection between a felt internationalism and innovative, exuberant aesthetics of beauty stitched from the remnants of "old" conventions, expressed in women-led horror films from Canada, is not a unique "Canadian thing." But they put Canada on an international map, alongside other checkpoints. In his enlightening comparison of *American Mary* with *American Psycho* and *American Nightmare*, Loiselle (2013) points to the problem of studying bodies of work about bodies of people as bodies of national identity. The corporeality of the bodies in films such as *American Mary*, Loiselle argues, both confirms their anchorage within a national(ized) context and the accident or fortuitousness of cultural projection. To end our examination of Canadian women horror, we present a few of these checkpoints, to offer a broader picture of the aesthetics of stitching together felt internationalism via aesthetics of exuberance and beauty.

Of the many openings, Jean Cocteau's *La Belle et la Bête* (1946) offers a useful one. An exuberant, stylish interpretation of the original French story of 1740 (originally published in a collection tellingly called *La jeune Américaine et les contes marins*), Cocteau's film follows the classic eighteenth-century fairy tale, forging a cast of beastly creatures who turn into beautiful, anthropomorphic talking furniture, and musical numbers. Cocteau's beast's fur required hours of makeup, the appearance of the film is gauzy, the costumes are ornate, the gardens lush. Aesthetically, *La Belle et la Bête* is a triumph of exuberance, sexual finesse, and *raffinement* intact. The frame is filled with objects that serve no purpose beyond their tangible meaning—beyond, that is, the fact that they are worthy of our looking at them. Everything is made to look artificial, like a set piece. The aesthetics of *La Belle et la Bête* have been applied particularly in horror films with a sense of style designed to provoke horror (revulsion from ugliness and monstrosity, rejection of "the other") while retaining admiration for beauty reclaimed on its own terms (or, at least, terms agreed upon by both beast and beauty). *Daughters of Darkness* and *The Love Witch* are two cases in point that have linked that aesthetic attitude to feminist critiques of beauty as well as interrogations of national identity. As Mathijs (2005) points out, *Daughters of Darkness* has struggled to achieve any territorial identity, save that of being a beacon of international style when it comes to vampire movies. Similarly, *The Love Witch* is not an American sexploitation film as much as it is a reflection on the transnationalism of exploitation cinema's styles (see O'Meara 2019). Any cultural projections aimed at isolating a national identity of the films is bound to fail the same way attempts to point at the "Frenchness" of *La belle et la bête* only end up ridiculing the one who makes the comment.

In terms of applying shell-like visual quality, acting, movement and gesture, production design, color, costuming, and art direction, *Daughters of Darkness* and *The Love Witch* show off a "smart style": they are films, like *La Belle et la Bête*, that are self-aware of their cleverness; they use it to stitch together self-reflexively new modes of beauty. In the words of Countess Bathory (Delphine Seyrig) in *Daughters of Darkness*:

> Who do you think I am? Just because my name happens to be Bathory? A kind of ghoul, a vampire. . . . Oh no, my dear, . . . I am just an outmoded character, nothing more. You know, the beautiful stranger; slightly sad, slightly mysterious, that haunts one place after another.

"One after another" is indicative of a process of renewal, untainted yet by new conventions. Canadian women horror films share that attitude in how they approach, subvert, explode, and stitch together what it means to be considered beautiful while being "most horrible," to paraphrase cute Tootie (Margaret O'Brien) in *Meet Me in St. Louis* (Vincente Minelli, 1944) as she returns from her first Halloween "kill." *Daughters of Darkness* presents the old vampire queen in a new light, reinventing her, and passing on the beauty of the imagery to the next generation—quite fittingly it passes to Valerie (Danielle Ouimet, fresh from the groundbreaking Canadian/Quebec sexploitation film *Valerie*, 1970). The ambiguity of the body, or the body in transformation from a prescribed beauty routine to a liberated one, is made part of that renewal. The vampires of *Daughters of Darkness* drink blood, as do most vampires in fiction, but these ones bleed as well—they bleed like women. The bodies also become more feminist. Cocteau's convictions did that for *La Belle et la Bête*. Seyrig's performance and her intimate collaboration with Kümel ensured that for *Daughters of Darkness*. Biller's principles as a feminist guaranteed that for *The Love Witch*. Similarly, Karen Walton, the Soska Sisters, and Diablo Cody/ Jason Reitman did that for the films discussed in this chapter.[9] As these bodies become more critical of their prescribed normativity, they become more attractive and alluring, yet not particularly sexual. In *Daughters of Darkness*, Seyrig's feminine presentation is such that she seems to defy any boundary of sex or gender. Ditto for *The Love Witch*. Anna Biller uses reflections on the genre of exploitation cinema as her point of departure to reinvent it. Biller relies heavily on high-femme presentation and staging to achieve that. Her debut, *Three Examples of Myself as Queen* (1994), is nauseatingly pink, luscious, and plush. Its unnaturalness coupled with her actors' matter-of-fact reaction to situations present a feeling of unease and of artifice. *The Love Witch* perfects this sort of hyper-femininity tied with B-film-inspired acting style, mise-en-scene, staging, and lighting (all high-drama elements of film). Together, this exuberance allows the viewer to question if *they're* the crazy one. *The Love Witch* comments on the physical limits of the body. The lead character, Elaine (Samantha Robinson), makes a "Witch Bottle" out of various bodily fluids and herbs, triumphantly declaring, "Tampons aren't gross." She does so in the light of day, in highly saturated sets. *Daughters of Darkness* and *The Love Witch* show horror and other oddities taking place in brightly lit, purposely artificial environments, giving the terror nowhere to hide. It is no longer enough to merely stay out of the shadows. Exuberance and beauty reinvented demand their own light.

CONCLUSION

Neither *The Love Witch* nor *Daughters of Darkness* claim to be anything else than films, and they do not hide their plots or shroud them in pseudo-detective detours. As made-up stories and films of artifice, they are, however, engaged and enrolled in seeking new ways for a genre often considered unable to reinvent itself for more than the duration of a cycle. The visual style that ensues, and that is activated along the way, is smart. Smart means insecure, in that it allows for inclusivity even if that means incoherence, and especially when it gives an impression of balance, refinement, and attention to occasionally contradictory details and to precision in favor of overgeneralization or spectacle. Canadian women horror films more than fit these attitudes and contexts; they move alongside them and even captain the flow. This does not mean Canadian women horror film is felt international more than it is national. It does mean that the films' interventions in the genre are effective challenges to staled formulas. Canadian women horror films act as innovations of radical, sometimes hyperbolic aesthetics, critiques of beauty, *and* exercises in exuberance. As such, they exist in an atmosphere of their own, where their name tag and address happens to include Canada, a nation from which they borrow a heritage of debates about cultural insecurity, a territory with which they share a penchant for daring, feminist aesthetics, *and* equally a place where their tags include the kinds of aesthetics that encourage viewers and critics to rank them *with* their international companions. Recent films such as *Trim* (Mayumi Yoshida 2019), a decidedly felt international women-led horror short from

Vancouver, run with this as they claim to be beautiful about beauty, with a twist. The short screenplay for *Trim* follows this chapter.

NOTES

1. This chapter has benefited from a series of in-person and online conversations with Anna Biller, Paula Devonshire, Gigi Saul Guerrero, Steven Hoban, Katharine Isabelle, Harry Kümel, Jennifer Morden, Sylvia and Jen Soska, and Karen Walton. The conversations are documented as part of the AURA project "Queen Bee" (FAS # F18-05788) and are archived at the Visual Resources Centre of the University of British Columbia (contact: ernest.mathijs@ubc.ca).

2. The connection with the poststructuralist theoretical notion of "suture" in film theory (Heath 1977; Oudart 1969) is not lost on us. We avoid elaboration here for reasons of space. It will be expanded on in a separate publication from this project.

3. There are also McKellar's signature reflexivity and intra-intertextuality (for instance in the way the film harks back to Speaking Parts) and McKellar's cultural "place of belonging" in the Toronto New Wave and its near-anarchist affinities (see Christopher 2019).

4. Vuckovic's own horror shorts have yet to attract significant attention from feminist film scholars.

5. To be clear: the *Ginger Snaps* trilogy is here presented as part of Canadian women horror. The writer is Karen Walton, main cast are Emily Perkins and Katharine Isabelle, producer is Karen Lee, and key to the production team was Paul Devonshire. Many of the crew met with and worked with director John Fawcett and producer Steven Hoban during their immersion and tenure at the Canadian Film Centre. Nose-counting, mingling, and chromosome accountability aside, the trilogy has always been celebrated as feminist.

6. In *Juno*, the scene that has two major characters compare "gross-out aesthetics" (of Hershell Gordon Lewis and Dario Argento to be precise) is a beacon of the stitching of gendered horror aesthetics, albeit parodied gently.

7. In spite of the attention *Jennifer's Body* received, it is alarming to see Canadian scholars ignore or neglect to mention its explicit borrowings. In their 2018 PhD dissertation, Dan Vena writes that *"Jennifer's Body* was set up to be a milestone in American horror cinema. Upon its release it would be one of the first times in over twenty tears that a horror film was spear-headed by two women artists, the other notable examples being *The Slumber Party Massacre* (1982) and more recently, *Twilight* (2008)."* The omission of any of the *Ginger Snaps* films (which Vena does reference, in another part of the same work) or of *Dead Hooker in a Trunk* is, to say the least, worrying (Vena 2018: 148–149).

8. Interview conducted by Ernest Mathijs, May 2019. Outtakes of the interview are available on the Blu-Ray of *Rabid*, as released by Shout Factory.

9. *Daughters of Darkness* shares that with *Donkey Skin* (Jacques Demy, 1970), again with Seyrig cementing her legacy as an iconic cinematic figure and a feminist figure of authority on how she subverts formulas.

BIBLIOGRAPHY

Acland, Charles. *Screen Traffic*. Durham, NC: Duke University Press, 2003.

Austin-Smith, Brenda. "Cult Cinema and Gender." In *The Routledge Companion to Cult Cinema*, ed. Ernest Mathijs and Jamie Sexton, 143–152. London: Routledge, 2019.

Austin-Smith, Brenda, and George Melnyk, eds. *The Gendered Screen: Canadian Women Filmmakers*. London: Wilfird Laurier University Press, 2010.

Baldassarre, Angela. *Reel Canadians: Interviews from the Canadian Film World*. Toronto: Guernica Editions, 2003.

Benshoff, Harry, ed. *A Companion to the Horror Film*. Boston: Wiley-Blackwell, 2016.

Cherry, Brigid. *Horror*, London: Routledge, 2008.

Christopher, David. *The Toronto New Wave, Post-Anarchist Cinema Theory, and the Progressive Apocalypse*. PhD Dissertation, University of Victoria (BC), 2019.

Dowler, Andrew. "Canadian Gothic, eh? A Glib Overview of Current Schlock." *Cinema Canada* 123 (October 1985): 17.

Heath, Stephen. "Dossier Suture: Notes on Suture." *Screen*, Volume 18, Issue 4, Winter 1977, Pages 48–76.

———. "On Suture." In *Questions of Cinema*, 76–112. Basingstoke, UK: MacMillan, 1981.

Hunter, Russ. "'Didn't You Used to Be Dario Argento?': The Cult Reception of Dario Argento." In *Italian Film Directors in the New Millennium*, ed. William Hope, 63–74. Cambridge: Cambridge Scholars Press, 2010.

Leach, Jim. *Film in Canada*, Oxford: Oxford University Press, 2006.

Longfellow, Brenda. "Globalization and National Identity in Canadian Film." *Canadian Journal of Film Studies* 5, no 2 (1996): 3–16.

Loiselle, André. "Canadian Horror, American Bodies: Corporeal Obsession and Cultural Projection in *American Nightmare*, *American Psycho*, and *American Mary*." *Brno Studies in English* 39, no. 2 (2013): 123–136.

Loiselle, André, and Gina Freitag, eds. *The Canadian Horror Film: Terror of the Soul*. Toronto: University of Toronto Press, 2016.

Macias, Patrick. *Tokyoscope: The Japanese Cult Companion*. San Francisco: Cadence Books, 2001.

Mathijs, Ernest. "Bad Reputations: The Reception of Trash Cinema." *Screen* 46, no. 4 (2005): 451–472.

———. "Cronenberg Connected: Cameo Acting, Cult Stardom, and Supertexts." In *Cult Film Stardom: Offbeat Attractions and Processes of Cultification*, ed. Kate Egan and Sarah Thomas, 144–162. Basingstoke, UK: Palgrave-Macmillan, 2012.

———. *From Baron of Blood to Cultural Hero: The Cinema of David Cronenberg*. New York: Columbia University Press, 2008.

———. *John Fawcett's Ginger Snaps*. Toronto: University of Toronto Press, 2013.

———. "Women in Horror, Social Activism, and Twitter: Asia Argento, Anna Biller, and the Soska Sisters." in (Eds): In *Twitter, the Public Sphere, and the Chaos of Online Deliberation*, ed. Gwen Bouvier and Judith E. Rosenbaum. New York: Palgrave/Springer, 2020.

Mathijs, Ernest, and Jamie Sexton. *Cult Cinema*. Boston: Wiley, 2011.

Melnyk, George. *One Hundred Years of Canadian Cinema*. Toronto: Toronto University Press, 2004.

Mendenhall, Julia. *I've Heard the Mermaids Singing: A Queer Film Classic*. Vancouver: Arsenal Pulp Press, 2014.

O'Meara, Jennifer. "Anna Biller." In *The Routledge Companion to Cult Cinema*, ed. Ernest Mathijs and Jaime Sexton, 411–421. London: Routledge, 2019.

Oudart, Jean-Pierre. "La suture." *Cahiers du cinema* 211 (April 1969): 36–39, and 212 (May 1969): 50–55.

Paszkiewicz, Katarzyna. "When the Woman Directs (a Horror Film)." In *Women Do Genre in Film and Television*, ed. Mary Harrod and Katarzyna Paszkiewicz, 42–56. London: Routledge, 2018.

Pevere, Geoff. "Toronto Film Festival Canadian Reflections." *Toronto Star*, September 8, 2000.

Pratley, Gerald. *A Century of Canadian Cinema: Gerald Pratley's Feature Film Guide, 1900 to the Present*. Toronto: Lynx Images, 2003.

Rafferty, Eoin. "Jennifer's Body." *The Irish Journal of Gothic and Horror Studies* 7 (2009): 67–68.

Schneider, Steven Jay, and Tony Williams, eds. *Horror International*. Detroit: Wayne State University Press, 2005.

Siska, Resmita. "An Analysis of Semantic Change in Euphemistic Terms in the Script 'Jennifer's Body' Movie." State Islamic University Syarif Hidayatullah Jakarta, 2010.

Sloan, Johanne. *Joyce Wieland's The Far Shore*. Toronto: University of Toronto Press, 2010.

Straw, Will. "Canadian Cinema." In *The Oxford Guide to Film Studies*, ed. John Hill and Pamela Church Gibson, 523–527. Oxford: Oxford University Press, 1998.

Tinic, Serra. "Where in the World Is *Orphan Black*? Change and Continuity in Global TV Production and Distribution." *Media Industries* 1, no. 3 (2015).

Vena, Dan. *Unfinished Business: The New Wave of Women's Horror Cinema*. PhD dissertation. Queen's University, Kingston, Ontario, 2018.

Vuckovic, Jovanka. *Zombies! Illustrated History of the Undead*. New York: St. Martins Griffin, 2011.

White, Jerry, ed. *The Cinema of Canada*. London: Wallflower Press, 2006.

Zimmerman, Bonnie. "Lesbian Vampires: *Daughters of Darkness*." *Jump Cut* 24/25 (1981): 23–24.

Trim

written by

Mayumi Yoshida

EXT. PHONE BOOTH - NIGHT

A middle aged man JUWON(60), at a phone booth. Making calls.
In Korean. He makes an agreement.

                    JUWON
          Ice? Uh...Yes. Yes, I will.
          Thank you I'll make sure I have
          them by then.

                                        CUT TO BLACK

Title card. "Trim"

INT. BATHROOM - DAY

ECU of an eyeball, then a sharp object approaches the eye.

Quick cuts of a woman looking at her body. Pinching it.
Sucking it in. The eyelid caves in and makes the eyeball pop
out. Two girls KATE (28) and MAI (28) next to each other in
front of the mirror, poking into their eyelid.

                    KATE
          Fuck. How do you do this?

                    MAI
          It's hard at first but you get used
          to it.

Mai steps back and looks at herself again and pulls her shirt
up revealing her torso.

                    MAI (CONT'D)
          I'm gonna do it. Get rid of this.
          This. I met this guy at the bar who
          knows this like underground surgeon
          who does it in like 5 days. I'm
          going in tomorrow.

                    KATE
          That sounds super sketchy

                    MAI
          Yeah, but I can get it done for
          like $1000. It's dirt cheap.

                    KATE
          True. I need to get my roots
          redone. I'm so fucking broke
          though.

                    MAI

          Dude, my friend just got hers done
          super cheap at this place. Like
          $30.

                    KATE
          Woah, that's crazy. Are they even
          good?

                    MIA
          Yeah she looked so good. I think
          they're closing down or something
          though.

                    KATE
               (Starts poking her eyes
               again)
          Did you do this everyday?

                    MIA
          Yep. Since I was 15. But not in a
          week…"

Sara looks at her eyes. Looking dissatisfied. Tries to start
poking her eyelid again,

INT. SALON - NIGHT

From inside the salon, we see Kate walking down the street
and finds the salon. She enters. No one is present. Kate
notices the crazy interior of the salon. There are mannequin
heads everywhere. She walks closer to one wall as if it's
sucking her in. She is fixated on one of the faces. Kate's
expression changes. She quickly looks back.

No ones there. She looks down. A cute af dog is there with a
plushie. She looks up again, then from the corner of the
counter, KYLE(19) jumps out.

                    KYLE
          Hi, sorry! I didn't hear you come
          in!

A plushie on the counter repeats.

                    PLUSHIE
          Hi, sorry! I didn't hear you come
          in!
          Hi, sorry! I didn't hear you come
          in!
          i"That's ok…"

"That's ok…"
                    Hi, sorry! I didn't hear you come
                    in!

                              KYLE
                    Oh, sorry it randomly does that.
                    Did you have an appointment?

                              KATE
                    Uh, no i'm just...I wanted to get
                    my roots redone, and a trim.

Someone walks in the store. It's Juwon from the first phone
call scene.

                              JUWON
                           (In Korean)
                    Oh, customer?

                              KYLE
                    She wants her roots redone

They look at each other for a moment. A discomforting beat.

                              JUWON
                    Well yes, please come sit.

The old man whispers something to Kyle. Kyle leaves the salon
with the dog.

INT. SALON - CONTINUOUS

Kate sits down at the chair. The mannequins all behind her.
Watching. The old man sits behind Sara. He doesn't say
anything. Sara sits awkwardly as he touches her hair. Split
screen. Sounds of scissors in the background.

                              KATE
                    I heard you're closing.

                              JUWON
                    Yes.

                              KATE

                    Why?

                              JUWON
                    Hard to keep up. Before it was just
                    this and this.

He pulls up the scissors and razor.

Beat.

                    JUWON (CONT'D)
          Mens or womens magazine?
                    KATE
     Both.

Split screen. Sounds of scissors in the background.

Shot of Sara flipping through magazine.

Shot of Old man trimming the back of her hair.

Shot of the mannequins staring down at them.

Shot of her bangs getting trimmed. We see her eyes very
clearly.

                    JUWON
          You have beautiful eyes.

                    KATE
          I hate them. I wish I had eyes like
          these.
               (Points at a model in a
               magazine)
          I'd die for those.

                                        CUT TO BLACK

INT. SALON - CONTINUOUS

Big industrial sound. Kate is under an old big steam machine
wrapped in foil. All the mannequins are staring her down.
This time, all of the mannequins are angled so it's looking
down at her directly.

Gradually Kate starts falling asleep.

                                        CUT TO BLACK

INT. BATHROOM - HYPNOSIS - NIGHT

Kate wakes up in a bathtub filled with pink water and barbies
and floating around her. What the fuck?

There's a washed up DRAG QUEEN standing by the mirror in a
corset. Another one is dressed all in red bodysuit and has a
weird face. Magazine cut outs glued to one of her eyes and
her nose and mouth.

Split screen.

Shot of The leotard woman pulling the string to tighten his corset.

Shot of the string tightening extremely then we hear CRACK. Ribs breaking.

Shot of The drag queen laughing manicly.

Shot of The leotard woman looking into the mirror and admiring her face. There's red glitter and diamonds on her face.

Kate then realizes she's getting pulled from underneath. She screams but can't, her voice doesn't come out. She disappears in the bath tub.

INT. SALON - MOMENTS LATER

Bird's eye view of Kate's head in the shampoo bowl. Glitter running down her face from her eyes, the shampoo bowl is filled with red glitter.

Juwon drops two eye balls in a small tin bowl.

He looks frightened. Not the emotionless man we saw before.

Then he turns around to see Kare. Awake.

An uncertain beat.

                                        CUT TO BLACK

INT. SALON - CONTINUOUS

CCTV camera by the mannequins face. We see them play cat and mouse. Kate is still weak and tries to get out of this place but she can't see. We hear her begging in the background. The old man keeps chanting a word in Korean.

                        KATE
            No, please, don't kill me! No!

                        JUWON
                    (Korean)
            Please forgive me. Please. Please
            forgive me.

POV from outside of the salon, we can see Juwon strangle Kate.

INT. SALON - MOMENTS LATER

Kate lies on the couch, unconscious again. Juwon is out of breath. He looks up from the body.

Kyle and the dog are stading there. With bag full of take out food and a bag of ice.

They all stand there quietly.

Kyle with a big smile on his face.

              KYLE
    Dinner?

Kyle looks for a table and trips on some of the furniture. He isn't addressing the body that's in the room at all. They both pull chairs together, Juwon quickly takes the ice and pours it in the tin bowl with the eyeballs. They start digging into the food, throwing the plastic bags on the ground.

Juwon is exhausted and still a little shaky.

              KYLE (CONT'D)
    Here's to 30 years of running this
    place dad. I'm proud of you. Mom
    would be too. Fuck technology!

              JUWON
    You'll love Korea. And after your
    surgery, I'll show you everything
    in the world.

              KYLE
    Dad, it's not going to happen. I'm
    good here. I'll be ok. I got Sofie
    too.

Old man looks at his son. He can't wait to give him his gift, he tears up. For a moment, he forgets the gruesome incident that just occurred a minute ago.

              PLUSHIE
    No, please, don't kill me! No!
      (Korean)
    Please forgive me. Please. Please
    forgive me.

They both stop eating. Kyle looks back. Juwon is frozen. Then suddenly we see Kate's hand spring up and pulls Juwon's face with a plastic bag.

              BLACK OUT.

FIVE

"They've Got Something You Haven't. A Cock."

Exploring the Gendered Experience of Horror Filmmaking in Britain

Amy Harris

Despite the recent academic attention given to contemporary British horror cinema, the scholarship on women-authored horror has been slower to emerge, even though women have made interesting contributions to the genre.[1] Based on my survey for this work, of the sum 840 British horror films produced between 2000 and 2017, over 4 percent have been directed by women.[2] Although this percentage may seem small at first, it is a vast increase on the number of women-directed horror films produced pre-millennium in the UK. Furthermore, these figures have not included the other offscreen roles that women have played, for instance as screenwriters, editors, and producers. This is addressed by the "Calling the Shots: Women and Contemporary Film Culture in the UK, 2000–2015" project, headed by Shelley Cobb and co-led by Linda Ruth Williams, which produces annual reports on the numbers of women working in the UK film industry to evidence the gender imbalances across various creative offscreen roles. In their most recent survey of British films in production during 2015, they found that "women constituted just 20% of all directors, writers, producers, exec-producers, cinematographers and editors" (University of Southampton, 2016). Martha Lauzen, the creator of *Celluloid Ceiling*, a series of reports that have been compiled since 1998 to track employment statistics for women in Hollywood, calculates that the percentage of women working in these roles, specifically in the top 250 grossing films in America each year, has faced long periods of stasis (Center for the Student of Women in TV & Film 2020). She points out that if we suggest the numbers are getting better every year, we risk "creeping incrementalism"—a hope that women will gradually be involved in filmmaking until eventually the problem is solved and a 50/50 balance is achieved (Lauzen 2017). Of course, there is absolutely no evidence that this will be the case, and Lauzen implies that the numbers remain depressingly stagnant. Indeed, the slow progression seen in the industry gives no indication that reaching a balance will be imminent. In fact, for the most part, the evidence is still damning. Over the last 10 years, the top-grossing films made had a total of 1,069 male directors and only 45 female directors, demonstrating the transnational extent of the industry's gender imbalance (USC Annenberg School 2017).

Arguably, the gender imbalance seen in the film industry is caused and precipitated by a cycle of systemic issues. There are a low number of active women directors, which reinforces the male stereotype in positions of power, and fewer women are hired to direct because they are perceived as a riskier choice, particularly during times of economic uncertainty, which feeds back into the cycle of fewer women working as directors or in other primary roles. Melanie Hoyes, a researcher for the British Film Institute UK Filmography, points out that there has been a proven track record of the British industry favoring directors who are presumed a safer choice than lesser-known directors who are, so often, women (Hoyes 2019). The logic of nepotism within the film industry has been discussed at length by scholars and in their compelling article "Body of Proof" (2018, 8–9), written for *Sight and Sound*, Cobb and Williams collate precise statistics to argue that there is an unjustified assumption that women cannot successfully produce films with larger budgets. They state that "every few years a woman-led film does . . . do well at the box office or with critics, and the media hails it as the harbinger of change [but] the tendency is for the next year to return to the status quo, with celebrated cases as exceptions rather than rules." Despite the evidence that a significant number of women work in producing roles, Cobb and Williams point toward a kind of "postfeminist amnesia" in the media whereby women filmmakers are often hailed as the first of their kind and therefore celebrated in popular culture for breaking through in a male-dominated industry. In a sense, it can also be argued that whenever a woman director is given the chance to have her voice heard, she is often celebrated in popular culture simply for having the opportunity to have her film made. This is certainly reflected in the critical reception of some recent films, in part due to the language used to discuss and promote them. For example, Shelley Stamp's (2018) criticism of an article featured in *TIME* magazine on Greta Gerwig's coming-of-age drama *Lady Bird* (2017) identifies the patronizing discussion of Gerwig as a naive girl caught up in the glamor of Hollywood before being given the chance to have her film made. Stamp argues that the article wrongly portrays Gerwig's success as a rarity and thus disregards the pioneering work of women throughout cinema history and the extensive list of international work by women filmmakers that has gone unnoticed by the Academy.

With this context in mind, this chapter addresses how women have authored their experiences of filmmaking in Britain, particularly when faced with such unfavorable industrial conditions. Through reference to a selection of contemporary horror films, this chapter will demonstrate women's experiences of precarity within the British film industry and their own reflections upon and depictions of this, in order to understand what experiences they are authoring. Although this chapter will not provide a close reading of all of the films mentioned, it will provide a detailed analysis of Kate Shenton's *Egomaniac* (2017) toward the end of the chapter in order to illustrate how women have addressed these issues through their filmmaking. Aside from the fact that women-authored horror has been overlooked in academia, a point that this chapter will shortly return to, a specific focus on horror will demonstrate how women have reconfigured the tropes of a presumed masculine genre to encourage a counterhegemonic narrative that challenges structures of gender that uphold and maintain patriarchal structures (Williams 2012).

Since 2004, the number of British horror films that have been directed by self-identifying women has continued to slowly increase, with success stories such as *Prevenge* (Alice Lowe, 2017) drawing the attention of film critics toward British horror and women-authored horror, respectively. Nonetheless, aside from emerging scholarship on *Prevenge*, women-authored British horror seems to have been overlooked in film scholarship. Since the 1970s, feminist film theory has been occupied with reframing representations of women in horror, using a psychoanalytical framework to debunk the myth of the female victim archetype and replacing her with the monstrous-feminine archetype (see Barbara Creed), the powerful Final Girl, and the strong female lead (see Carol Clover), making the argument that women identify with horror narratives and their monstrous female characters in complex ways. There has also been a focus on the appeal of horror to female audiences (see Brigid Cherry, Isabel Pinedo, Linda Williams), which acknowledges that audiences are more complex than gender binaries, age, and taste distinctions can predict. Although this scholarship has been a useful starting point to think about women's relationship to horror, the much-needed shift toward thinking about women's offscreen roles as active filmmakers has been slower to emerge. There are several possible reasons for this. Firstly, existing British and non-British scholarship on women-authored horror tends to focus on productions from outside of the UK. Recent emerging work on women filmmakers explores international women-led film festivals that celebrate female authorship in horror (see Sonia Lupher); women-authored horror remakes and reboots (see Katarzyna Paszkiewicz); the emergence of *gynae-horror* (see Erin Harrington); and Alison Peirse's seminal edited collection *Women Make Horror*, as well as this edited collection, which promises to address the lacuna in existing scholarship. Despite these exciting developments, there seems to be a continued focus on overseas productions and so British horror is given less attention.

Secondly, scholarship on British horror has been preoccupied with Hammer Productions until recent interventions. Recognized for their Gothic films, which were produced in the mid-1950s until the late 1970s, Hammer Film Productions has become synonymous with British horror. Given this, Hammer tends to be the focal point of accompanying film scholarship on British-made horror, partly because it is the most financially successful horror film company in Britain, with the farthest international reach. At the end of Jonathan Rigby's *English Gothic*, published in 2000, he pessimistically states that "the chances of a uniquely British approach to horror being re-established remain slim" (2015). Other scholars have echoed Rigby's sentiments that if Gothic horror, primarily produced by Hammer, was dead, then so was British horror. Mike Simpson (2012, 12) points out that this assumption was made "by pretty much every fan, journalist and critic . . . that new British horror, if it ever appeared, would be the same as old British horror [drawing] from Britain's Gothic traditions. . . . Everybody was looking for the Next Big Thing. But they were looking backwards."

Scholarship on British horror cinema remained stagnant in a period in which women had no place as filmmakers. Indeed, Hammer productions tended to be male-created and male-controlled. Of the fifty-eight Hammer horror films made, none were directed by a woman. Finding scholarship about the offscreen roles of women working as filmmakers during this time is near impossible because, put simply, women were not employed in key roles by the dominant studio systems such as Hammer. Given this, women have been omitted from scholarship during this period of British horror cinema.

Interestingly, some of the scholarship on British horror cinema is also described in terms that evoke a specific image of British national cinema that reinforces gendered stereotypes. When documenting British cinema history, some scholars have described British production companies as "small production centres with an air of the family businesses . . . set on village greens" (Kuhn 2007). This description equates postwar British cinema as one of a "small-scale enterprise" with traditionally British themes which were understood as "celebrating the little man" (176–177). The construction of British cinema as the "little man" was further exemplified by Hammer Productions. Hammer's base between 1948 and 1950 consisted of large country houses, rather than studios, in order to capitalize on the notion that British productions were rooted in British traditions of family, domesticity and respectability (180–181). In 1951, Hammer Studios had finally settled in a large country house in Berkshire, where it remained until 1968, thus cementing its image as the wholesome, family-run studio. The gendered stereotyping of British production companies as patriarchal spaces, headed and run by paternal figures, reinforced the long-held belief that women simply were not making films, let alone horror, because they were not seen as playing any role within this space. Since contemporary film scholarship remained fixated on this period in British horror cinema's history, with Rigby and other scholars pining for a revival of "arrogant aristocrats, creepy castles, swirling fog . . . lobby cards, quad posters in the foyers," any work that women were doing went unnoticed (Simpson 2012, 12).

Unfortunately, the assumption that women were not making horror films in Britain from the mid-1950s onward is somewhat true. Jane Arden's experimental production *The Other Side of Underneath* (1972) was the only British feature film, of any genre, in the 1970s to be directed by a woman. Demonstrating the generic hybridity of art-film, Arden's horrific and violent film explores the troubled mind of a woman labeled a schizophrenic. The film remained invisible to mainstream audiences until a resurgence of public showings in 2009, and the BFI re-released a remastered version on Blu-Ray and DVD to pay tribute to Arden after her suicide.

A decade after Arden's film and following the eventual demise of Hammer in the early 1980s, women still struggled to find roles as directors for horror films. It was not until 1980 that British director Gabrielle Beaumont released her first feature film, *The Godsend*. In line with a cycle of possession films that proved popular at the time, *The Godsend* follows the story of a young family and their troubled adopted child—a storyline that imitates its better-known predecessor and American production *The Omen* (Richard Donner, 1976). Unlike its American counterpart, *The Godsend* was funded by a private production company, The Canon Group, who found success in producing low-budget English-language versions of Swedish soft porn films before facing financial struggles within the first decade of their inception. Comparatively, 20th Century Fox distributed *The Omen* and so it had a $2.8 million marketing campaign and became the fifth-highest-grossing film in the US in 1976, profiting over $60 million at the box office, earning two Academy Award nominations, and winning Best Original Score. As a result, like many British productions of the time, Beaumont's film was overshadowed by its American counterpart and quickly forgotten. The critical tendency to dismiss *The Godsend* from discussions of the possession horror cycle made popular during this period is interesting and warrants further research, particularly given the status of the film as directed by a woman.

Much later, in 1999, Antonia Bird directed her fourth feature film, and her first horror: *Ravenous*. Set in 1840, the film follows the story of a cannibalistic group fighting to survive in increasingly gruesome conditions. Film critic Roger Ebert (1999) praised the British director, writing that "she's a real filmmaker . . . wisely more interested in atmosphere than plot. . . . She does what is very hard to do: She makes the weather feel genuinely cold, damp and miserable. So much snow in the movies looks too pretty or too fake, but her locations . . . are chilly and ominous." Ebert's praise of Bird as "a real filmmaker" hints at a change in attitude toward the roles of women working in film in Britain since the days of Hammer, when they were previously not regarded as filmmakers. Nonetheless, the film's production conditions were notorious and resulted in the original director, Milcho Manchevski, choosing to abandon the project and leaving Bird to pick up the pieces. Much like other mid-budget British American coproduction studio projects made during this period, for instance horror films *Dust Devil* (Richard Stanley, 1992) and *Event Horizon* (Paul Anderson, 1997), *Ravenous* was deemed a box-office failure because it did not recoup anything close to its estimated $12 million budget. That women were unable to successfully produce and distribute films during this time suggests a gender imbalance within the British film industry. However, the failing success of British horror productions overall points toward the poor industrial conditions of filmmaking in the UK.

Aside from the fact that women did not seem to be making horror before the millennium, and thus were as a result omitted from the scholarship on British horror, the British film industry was in a state of crisis. Many filmmakers struggled to produce films that were deemed worthy of analysis. When contextualizing women's contributions to British horror, it is important to note the fluctuating industrial landscape of British cinema, which made it difficult for British horror to flourish. British cinema has a rich and diverse history, but behind the screen, the financial stability of the industry has been a source of trepidation. Compared to the dominance of US cinema, the British film industry is repeatedly described in terms of cultural specificity with limited transnational appeal, quite simply because Britain struggles to compete with the number of films financed and distributed overseas. By the 1980s, British cinema returned to the position in which it had found itself in the 1920s, when the government had first introduced a quota for British films (Street 2007, 185–187). Data from the BFI Filmography, which evidences the financial peaks and troughs of the British film industry, reveals that the decade with the fewest films released is the 1980s, where it witnessed "an all-time low of just 468 feature films," with only a minority of British films achieving a domestic gross of over £1 million (BFI 2019). Concerns about the decline in British production are discussed at length by Steve Chibnall (2001), who evidences that in 1971 only sixty-seven films of any genre were made in Britain and, in 1982, these figures dropped to forty-six films. New interventions such as funding by *British Screen* and tax incentives were quickly introduced in order to address the radical decline of British films. Chibnall goes on to locate the production of horror within this context to explore how the financial struggles across the British film industry impacted the production of horror.

Unsurprisingly, horror was likewise a victim of the drastically changing economic landscape, although it suffered less than other genres because horror films could be made cheaply. In his survey of British horror, Simpson (2012, 11) notes that cheap, high-quality equipment for production and postproduction was readily available for budding filmmakers, though he writes that skill and talent were still needed to make watchable films that would grab audiences, so "Sturgeon's Law applied."[3] Furthermore, in the mid-1980s, Hammer films, the last hope for British horror cinema, ceased production. This was partly because the rise of international video nasties continued to draw British audiences away from national productions. Moreover, mass hysteria over the corrupting effects of horror on Britain's youth, which was greatly encouraged by British educator and Conservative activist Mary Whitehouse, who targeted the genre as particularly obscene and threatening, contributed to the rapid decline in British horror productions and increase in bootlegged VHS imports. Given this, women were not the only group who faced challenges filming and distributing horror films. In fact, it seemed that most UK filmmakers failed to produce anything particularly noteworthy during this time and so the scholarship turned elsewhere for critical analysis. Ultimately, the absence of women-made horror films points to an absence of horror in general, demonstrating the trepidatious industrial climate of filmmaking in Britain pre-millennium. So if women were to find their feet in British horror, the British horror industry first needed a revival.

In their work on new British horror cinema, MJ Simpson (2020) and Johnny Walker (2016) suggest that there were signs of a horror revival in the early 2000s, explaining that long-held Gothic traditions were taking new forms by playing host to contemporary social and political allegories as Britain welcomed the turn of the millennium. The sudden shift toward a consideration of contemporary horror films suggested that women-authored horror might finally be included in discourse about British horror cinema, particularly as industrial changes meant funding opportunities were more widely available.

Simpson (2020) compiled a filmography charting the production of every British horror from the 1970s onward, through a combination of fan sites, dedicated horror publications such as *Fangoria*, IMDb Pro, film festivals, and word-of-mouth, which he recorded via an online blog and later published with Hemlock Books. His survey found a sudden spike in British horror productions, which, for the first time, included the work of women filmmakers such as Aimee Stephenson, Catherine Taylor, Susan Jacobson, and Tammi Sutton. Taken together, these films demonstrate the creative breadth of women's approach to the genre. Stephenson's supernatural horror, *Grave Matters* (2004), follows the story of a woman who "dreams of something better" because her husband is "a sexist, arrogant pig" whom she eventually batters to death (Simpson 2020). Taylor's lesbian vampire film, *Temptation* (2009), is a grueling tale of rape revenge, where sexually assaulted women empower each other through vampirism and devour male customers who attend their strip club. Sutton's *Isle of Dogs* (2011) is a gangster-horror hybrid where the submissive trophy wife of a mob boss remains on the periphery of the story until the final scene where she bludgeons her husband and flees with all of his money. The thread that ties these films together is a message of female rage against male oppressors, but the varied ways in which these themes are explored reflect the ways in which women are experimenting with tropes of the genre.

Walker (2016) also started to explore the accompanying industrial context, crediting three films for starting a revival of horror in the UK: *The Hole* (Nick Hamm, 2001), *Long Time Dead* (Marcus Adams, 2002), and *My Little Eye* (Marc Evans, 2002). He argues that the global popularity of horror, after the success of US slasher films *Scream* (Wes Craven, 1996), *Scream 2* (Wes Craven, 1997), and *I Know What You Did Last Summer* (Jim Gillespie, 1997), was enough to incentivize British producers to take a gamble on the genre. The introduction of tax relief in 1997 for British films with budgets of less than £15 million and the birth of the UK Film Council (hereafter UKFC) in 2000 was set to provide far more opportunity to filmmakers in Britain. Like Simpson, Walker notes that by 2004 there was a peak in British horror productions and, with this growing interest in horror, many UK filmmakers also secured funding through private investors.

Walker's work *Contemporary British Horror Cinema: Industry, Genre and Society*, celebrates this new age for British horror. He evidences how British horror allegorized national fears about an ostensible "broken Britain," a term later used repeatedly by Conservative party leader and Prime Minister David Cameron to encourage and feed off of "popular anxieties" (Gentleman 2010). The political tensions faced by the British population, particularly after the introduction of a New Labour Party government, encouraged horror filmmakers to respond to the changing political landscape in Britain. Films such as *28 Days Later* (Danny Boyle, 2002), *Shaun of the Dead* (Edgar Wright, 2004), and *Eden Lake* (James Watkins, 2008) address issues such as youth crime, antisocial behavior, welfare dependency, high unemployment rates, and isolation of the elderly, for example. British horror was back, albeit not under the control of women, who still remained on the periphery of Walker's discussion. Except for several titles that are given a brief mention in Walker's work, including *Jelly Dolly* (Susannah Gent, 2004), *Strigoi: The Undead* (Faye Jackson, 2009), and *Don't Let Him In* (Kelly Smith, 2011), most women-authored British horror films have, until now, been overlooked. It is unclear why women have been excluded from analysis of contemporary British horror, even though some scholarship admits that women are overlooked. It is not enough to argue that they are comparatively smaller-budget films because this exclusion also includes *Ravenous*, which, although a complicated text, was studio-led. If we consider scholarship on British cinema more broadly, the trend of excluding women from academic discourse continues. For example, Matt Glasby's (2019) recent publication on British cinema points out that the sense of British identity explored in early 2000s cinema is suggestive of male inclusivity, which does not extend to people of color or women. He briefly asserts that these marginalized groups remain underrepresented in the industry but dedicates only a few paragraphs of analysis to British Asian filmmaker Gurinder Chadha.[4] He does not address the number of women who produced exemplary films during his chosen period of study, such as Sally Potter and Carine Adler. My chapter intends to address these gaps and to make good on these inexplicable omissions. Inclusion of women-led films will feed into broader debates on the success of British horror cinema and will offer valuable contributions to the discussion of horror as a revived genre in Britain after the millennium.

Despite the enthusiasm concerning a new wave of British horror, women filmmakers continued to face the same financial challenges as before. The arrival of a supposed "new wave" of horror did not signal a conclusion to the problems faced by the wave that came before, as women and other marginalized groups continued to suffer from the previous economic crisis, despite the aforementioned funding initiatives put in place. Interestingly, Stella Hockenhull argues that the UKFC and its Leadership on Diversity in Film Group, led by Tim Bevan, brought about positive change for women directors. She suggests that the UKFC encouraged an increase in the numbers of women directors working across all genres. This was evidenced by data reporting that 15 percent of directors in 2011 were women, a significant rise from the first reported figure of just 6 percent in 2007 (Cobb 2020). Hockenhull argues that "the success of the UKFC cannot be underestimated for women directors" (Cobb 2020, 122). However, upon closer inspection of the data, the "Calling the Shots" team argued that

because women make up such a small number of directors of UK films, their fluctuating proportion year on year is more a product of the increase and decrease of the number of men than it is of their own ups and downs. Consequently, changes in the percentages of women directors can appear to indicate the improvement or the retrogression of women's presence in the industry when the actual numbers show stagnation. Although the numbers of women tripled after the UKFC carried out a study on women's represen-tation and, arguably, "a number of female film directors benefitted" from their diversity initiatives, those women were a small group, mostly making low-budget fiction film. (Cobb 2020, 122)

In line with this argument, Directors UK reported that over the ten-year period studied (2005–2014), the percentage of UK films directed by women increased by only 0.6 percent. This evidence suggests that while funding bodies such as UKFC and Film4 were somewhat willing to take a gamble on directors such as Danny Boyle, Edgar Wright, and Ben Wheat-ley, women were not afforded the same funding opportunities as their male counterparts.

Stacey Smith (2015) explains that this imbalance in funding opportuni-ties points toward civil rights issues because women "aren't being al-lowed to have the experience of the access." This is, in part, due to the un-conscious bias that women are unable to lead films with bigger budgets. The creation of this bias has historical roots, such as the aforementioned sustained belief that British production studios were small studios run by "the little man" and his family. Unfortunately, sustaining these biases has resulted in fewer films being directed by women, and so the existing gender inequality within the film industry creates and supports a vicious cycle. The unwavering lack of economic certainty within the industry leads to greater risk aversion and a greater reliance on the preconceived stereotype of the director as a man, thus women have less chance of re-ceiving funding (Directors UK 2016).

The assumption that women cannot handle big budgets has resulted in many women having to self-fund their projects. The second British horror film directed by a woman during the British horror revival, *Jelly Dolly*, was independently funded.[5] Gent wrote, directed, and produced *Jelly Dolly*, a surrealist horror set in Sheffield, about a woman whose inability to end a relationship causes her to mutate and hallucinate. Similar to other films of the time, Gent explored the crisis of identity, sexuality, and relationships in New Labour Britain. Despite its timely themes, *Jelly Dolly* is absent from scholarship, except for a brief mention in Walker's monograph.

In seeking to address why women-directed British horror has received minimal critical attention, with many titles omitted from scholarship al-together, it became obvious how difficult it is to acquire some of the films due to their narrow festival distribution and subsequent online release. *Jelly Dolly* was financed and distributed by Gent, who premiered the film in May 2004 at the Britspotting Festival in Berlin. Despite winning Best Feature Film, three months later, *BBC South Yorkshire News* (2004) wrote that "without a deal with a film distribution company, [*Jelly Dolly*] will not reach a large audience." In a follow-up article later that same month, Gent (2004) described her attempts to find a distributor, writing that she "had gone to Ireland to promote [*Jelly Dolly*] by showing trailers from the back of the van." In April 2010, six years after its production, the film was released on DVD. Disappointingly, many other women-directed British horror films have faced the same fate, and *Jelly Dolly* is not an anomaly.

Undoubtedly, British horror cinema has not been as diverse as one would hope. Despite the celebration of its revival, it seems preoccupied with the themes of lad culture and fragile masculinity in a New Labour government and plagued by memories of economic depression, evident in the perceptible militarization of British films after 9/11 such as *The Bunker* (George Schaefer, 2001), *Dog Soldiers* (Neil Marshall, 2002), and *Deathwatch* (Michael J. Bassett, 2002). Although these themes are not issues faced exclusively by men, it would seem that the dominant narrative on these themes are told from the same male perspectives, with a tendency toward male protagonists. The concern that the majority of stories are being told from a white, heterosexual male perspective has been explored in Amy Adrion's documentary *Half the Picture* (2018). The film opens with footage of an interview with actress Jessica Chastain (2018) at Cannes 2017 where she states that

> the one thing I took away from this experience [of being at Cannes] is how the world views women. From the female characters that I saw represented . . . it was quite disturbing. There are some exceptions [but] for the most part I was surprised with the representation and I do hope that when we include more female storytellers we will have more of the women that I recognize in my day to day life. Ones that are proactive, have their own agency, don't just react to the men around them, and have their own point of view.

Put simply, if the authorship is male, then arguably so are the perspectives within the story. Chastain points toward an ongoing problem of male authorship as dominant within the film industry. In this respect, it can be argued that British horror film would have a greater sense of recognition to the different identities within Britain if it included stories that reflect more hybrid and inclusive perspectives. Indeed, as noted by Shelley Cobb (2020), "The reality is that the goals of equality and diversity will require white, middle-class, male film-makers to be subject to a much lower chance of receiving funding and finding employment than has been the case in the past." The systemic, misogynistic belief that horror is inherently a male genre makes it even harder for women to receive adequate funding and recognition, and so the stories that are played out on-screen continue to be told from a male perspective. In order for the scholarship to respond to the more complex sense of identity that exists in modern Britain, it will have to take into account the films made by marginalized groups including, but not limited to, women.

A film that directly engages with gender inequality in the British film industry is Kate Shenton's directorial debut, *Egomaniac*, released in 2017 to Video-On-Demand platforms following its premiere at FrightFest in 2016. It is now hosted by Lawrie Brewster's independent production company Hex Media, which operates primarily on YouTube. Not only was *Egomaniac* directed by a woman, but it was also written and produced by one too. This demonstrates Shenton's full creative control over the project, thus avoiding quibbles around authorship and tenuous notions of the auteur. The plot of *Egomaniac* reflects Shenton's experience of filmmaking in Britain, serving to expose everyday examples of industry misogyny that lie behind the shocking data. In interviews, Shenton (Oughton 2016) has described how her own experiences of filmmaking, which inspired the film's plot, helped her growth as a filmmaker, stating, "It's a very surreal thing and it takes a lot of self-reflection, but it is also a very cathartic thing, and for me it was like closing that chapter of my life and then I could just move on." By describing the film as cathartic, Shenton draws attention to the emotional connection she had to the narrative. She continues to describe her inspiration behind the characters, stating:

> I think there is a real honesty to the brutal stereotypes of the characters. . . .
> Even though this film is not based on anyone real, the characters are an amal-
> gamation of different people that I've met. . . . I'm taking certain lines people
> have said and taking certain actions and combining into a character. It's a very
> fictionalized version of what has happened to me. We made sure in the script
> and in the performance that no one was an impersonation. . . . People who
> have watched a film have recognized characters in that they've experienced
> someone similar. They've had someone in their career that has done similar
> things and said similar things. It seems very close to the bone.

Shenton's feminist rage toward everyday instances of industry misogyny is played out through a series of horrifying and gruesome events within the film, when the female lead, filmmaker Catherine Sweeney (played by Nic Lamont), exacts revenge on all of the men who have wronged her. Set in the present day and directly mirroring Shenton's own journey of filmmaking, *Egomaniac* follows the story of filmmaker Catherine as she attempts to make a zombie horror-comedy. By placing a woman at the center of the narrative, *Egomaniac* addresses how women have fared historically as filmmakers in terms of industrial conditions. As this chapter has evidenced, the initiatives put in place by various funding bodies have failed to provide equal opportunities to British filmmakers. This is demonstrated in the film when Catherine is unable to get her project funded. Although Directors UK reported that the industry bias was not necessarily intentional, deeming unconscious bias responsible for funding decisions, in the film, Catherine is frequently humiliated by her male counterparts. She is told that in order to successfully fund her film, she has to include a talking dog in the plot. Seedy producers demand that she dress sexier to help market the film, forcing her to wear a leather bondage suit for a photoshoot that she protests is not needed and that makes her feel uncomfortable. She resorts to borrowing money from her long-suffering parents so that she is able to pay her rent because she spent all of her savings on self-producing the film, after being encouraged by her alcohol-dependent coproducer who, unknown to Catherine at the time, lives out of his car. Finally, she is advised to exchange sex for money so that she can ensure the film is presigned with a distributor because "that's how it works in this business, you know? You do me a little favor and I'll do you a little favor." When Catherine does the deed, she finds out shortly after that her script will be assigned to a different director who has "better" appeal (a vague description at best) and is advised that offering the distributor fellatio would have been a better option for her because it would have left him wanting more. The events in the film play out as a "satirical prod at the journey one goes through when making a film," although the dark comedy serves to expose the harsh reality of industry misogyny that Shenton has also come up against (Williams 2016).

Praise for *Egomaniac* can be given for its honest portrayal of the gendered experience of filmmaking faced by some women directors. In this way, the film serves to highlight the collective unhappiness experienced by women working within an industry that continues to ignore their valuable contributions to the horror genre. Like other women-authored British horror films, the self-reflexive plot of *Egomaniac* lends itself to broader analysis of women's precarity within the British film industry, marking it as an important film to study. Certainly, horror films that are authored by women can offer valuable commentaries on the misogyny of the industry.

When Catherine's film plays in an almost empty cinema, her name appears in every role from writer to producer, director and editor, to sound tech and so on, as the credits roll, indeed echoing the reality that many women filmmakers have to fulfill multiple roles in order to finish their films because there is limited funding available to them and that, unfortunately, their films do not reach a wide audience. In an interview, Shenton (cited in Fox 2017) explained that

[the film] is a celebration of independent filmmaking, just going out there and doing it against all the odds. It's one of the main messages of the film.

If you've got an idea, don't let anyone hold you back, just go out there and then make it. [However, the film] was made on £5,000 so naturally it was a bit crazy. . . . It was only a 10-day shoot and I don't think we could've made the budget stretch any further. I remember debating with myself about whether to get an extra memory card or a meat cleaver prop. We didn't have the luxury to afford both.

What is most poignant about *Egomaniac* is that it ends with Catherine presenting her completed film to an audience of one man whom she has gagged and bound, forcing him to engage with her work. This is reflective of women's concerns that their work will not reach its intended audience because of the limited distribution opportunities available for lower-budget or self-funded projects. As this chapter has demonstrated, women filmmakers are working against a variety of long-held gender prejudices in an industry that is largely male-controlled. This includes an assumption that when women are at the center of a narrative, the film will not profit at the box office, particularly if the film is directed by a woman (Cobb and Williams 2018, 8–9). Although *Egomaniac* headlined FrightFest, Shenton's work was not picked up by a film distributor and, similarly to Gent, she decided to showcase the film herself, via online platforms. Since the release of *Egomaniac*, the Female Filmmakers Initiative have declared that "there are differences in the types of companies that distribute male- and female-directed films. Movies with a female director were more likely than movies with a male to be distributed by independent companies with fewer financial resources and lower industry clout" (Smith 2015). The gagged and bound audience member also demonstrates women's frustrations that they have been ignored by the men who act as gatekeepers in the industry and who deny women funding without engaging with their work. Given this, Shenton's film is an excellent example of how women-authored horror can be used to address a plethora of wider issues within the film industry. When asked about how she wanted people to react to her film, Shenton (Oughton 2016) replied, "Maybe it'll start a discussion and maybe that discussion will make it slightly easier for someone who is just starting out."

This chapter forms part of an ongoing project that takes an industrial and critical approach to women-authored horror in the UK, to understand what experiences women are sharing through horror films. There is a diverse history of horror, and although the historical overview of women's horror from the 1970s through to present day in this chapter is by no means exhaustive, it demonstrates that there are many experiences shared among women directors that offer distinct responses to the stark diversity problems in the British film industry. The role of women within the film industry is a timely subject matter in academic discourse, particularly considering the Harvey Weinstein allegations that sparked the #MeToo movement on a global scale, resulting in Weinstein's subsequent convictions for sexual assault and rape. The accompanying media attention given to the long-standing problems and imbalances within the film industry resulted in a growth in scholarship pertaining to industry misogyny. This includes projects such as the Women Film Pioneers Project, which aims to rewrite cinema history to include women filmmakers, and Women and Hollywood, which educates, advocates, and agitates for gender diversity and inclusion in Hollywood and the global film industry. In line with this work, this chapter has initiated addressing the lacuna in the research by taking an industrial and critical approach to horror films authored by women and reflecting on the presumed masculine landscape of British-made horror in order to encourage a reassessment of the existing scholarship to include the creative work from women filmmakers. By highlighting women's hitherto undervalued work in contemporary British horror cinema through an exploration of the creative responses to an industry that privileges and is dominated by men, this chapter has contributed to the developing scholarship on women as active authors of horror cinema.

NOTES

1. Note that the term "author" is being employed as a gender-neutral term to describe the multifaceted primary, creative, and dynamic positions of filmmakers. It is not being used in association with auteurism, or potentially outmoded theories pertaining to that notion, because the director as the controlling mind behind a film poses the problem of romanticizing the individual and risks the erasure of others' contributions to the collaborative process of film production. That said, given the scope of this chapter, there has not been the opportunity to consider the other important roles that women have played in horror production. Therefore, in this chapter, the woman director as the "author" of the film somewhat represents a necessary gesture in the struggle for consideration on socially equal terms to their male counterparts.

2. Note that "British" has been defined using the *British Film Institute*'s cultural test, a points-based test where a film will need to achieve 18 of a possible 35 points in order to qualify as British.

3. Sturgeon's Law is an adage suggesting that, in general, the vast majority of the works that are produced in any given field are likely to be of low quality.

4. Note that this chapter has also failed to address intersections of gender and race. The number of BAME women working in key roles in the UK is reported by the BFI and Directors UK as significantly low. As mentioned, this chapter forms part of a broader project that will address the intersections of gender and race in more detail.

5. Note that Aimee Stephenson's *Grave Matters*, also released in 2004, is claimed as the first British horror directed by a woman according to Mike Simpson's aforementioned blog.

BIBLIOGRAPHY

British Film Institute. "New BFI Filmography Reveals Complete Story of UK Film 1911–2017." BFI Online, 2019. http://www.bfi.org.uk/news-opinion/news -bfi/announcements/bfi-filmography-complete-story-uk-film.

Center for the Student of Women in TV & Film. "Research." Accessed March 2020. https://www.womenintvfilm.sdsu.edu/research/.

Chibnall, Steve, and Julian Petley. *British Horror Cinema*. London: Routledge, 2001.

Cobb, Shelley. "What about the Men? Gender Inequality Data and the Rhetoric of Inclusion in the US and UK Film Industries." *Journal of British Cinema and Television* 17, no.1 (2020): 112–135

Cobb, Shelley, and Linda Ruth Williams. "Body of Proof." *Sight and Sound* 28, no. 3 (2018).

Directors UK. "Cut Out of the Picture: A Study of Gender Inequality among Directors within the UK Film Industry." Directors UK, 2016. http://www.directors .uk.com/news/cut-out-of-the-picture.

Ebert, Roger. "Ravenous." Roger Ebert Online, 1999. www.rogerebert.com/re views/ravenous-1999.

Fox, Zack. "Egomaniac: A Horror Film about the Horrors of the Film Industry." Gadgette, 2017. http://www.gadgette.com/2017/08/12/kate-shenton -egomaniac.

Gent, Susannah. "Jelly Dolly in Galway." BBC South Yorkshire Online, July 23, 2004. http://www.bbc.co.uk/southyorkshire/content/articles/2004/07/23 /film_jelly_dolly_2_feature.shtml.

Gentleman, Amelia. "Is Britain Broken?" The Guardian, March 31, 2010. www .theguardian.com/society/2010/mar/31/is-britain-broken.

Glasby, Matt, *Britpop Cinema: From Trainspotting to This Is England*. Bristol, UK: Intellect, 2019.

Hoyes, Melanie. Round table discussion, presented at De Montfort University Cinema and Television History Conference 2019: "Reclaiming the Screen— Overlooked Women in Film and Television." June 14, 2019.

Kuhn, Annette. "The British Film Industry." In *The Cinema Book*, third edition, ed. Pam Cook, 176–184. London: BFI Publishing, 2007.

Lauzen, Martha M. "It's a Man's (Celluloid) World: Portrayals of Female Characters in the Top 100 Films of 2016." *Center for the Study of Women in Television & Film*, 2017. http://womenintvfilm.sdsu.edu/wp-content/uploads/2017/02/2016 -Its-a-Mans-Celluloid-World-Report.pdf.

Oughton, Charlie. "Kate Shenton: Egomaniac." *Starburst*, August 30, 2016. https:// www.starburstmagazine.com/features/kate-shenton-egomaniac-interview.

Rigby, Johnathan. *English Gothic: Classic Horror Cinema 1897–2015*. Cambridge: Signum Books, 2015.

Salmon, Tom. "Jelly Dolly on the Move." BBC South Yorkshire Online, July 8, 2004. https://www.bbc.co.uk/southyorkshire/films/2004/07/jelly_dolly /jelly_dolly.shtml.

Simpson, Mike. *Urban Terrors New British Horror Cinema 1997–2008*. Bristol, UK: Hemlock Books, 2012.

Simpson, MJ. "Cult Films and the People Who Make Them." Blogspot, last updated October 3, 2020, accessed March 2018. www.mjsimpson-films.blogspot.com/.

Smith, Stacey. "Exploring the Careers of Female Directors Phase III." Female Filmmakers Initiative, April 21, 2015. https://time.com/wp-content/uploads/2015/05/phase-iii-research—-female-filmmakers-initiative.pdf.

Stamp, Shelley. "Women in Hollywood: Past, Present, Future." Presented at De Montfort University Cinema and Television History Conference 2018: "New Perspectives on Sci-fi, Horror, and the Monstrous On-screen." June 13, 2018.

Street, Sarah. "Contemporary British Cinema." In *The Cinema Book*, third edition, ed. Pam Cook, 185–187. London: BFI Publishing, 2007.

University of Southampton. "Calling the Shots: Women and Contemporary Film Culture in the UK 2000–2015." 2016. http://www.southampton.ac.uk/cswf/project/number_tracking.page.

USC Annenberg School. "It Doesn't Get Better: No Change for Female, Black, or Asian Film Directors in a Decade." 2017. http://www.annenberg.usc.edu/news/faculty-research/it-doesn%E2%80%99t-get-better-no-change-female-black-or-asian-film-directors-decade.

Walker, Johnny. *Contemporary British Horror Cinema: Industry, Genre and Society*. Edinburgh: Edinburgh University Press, 2016.

Williams, Jessy. "Egomaniac: Film Review." *Scream Horror Mag*, September 3, 2016. http://www.screamhorrormag.com/egomaniac-film-review/.

Williams, Linda. "Film Bodies: Gender, Genre and Excess." In *Film Genre Reader*, fifth edition, ed. Barry Keith Grant. Austin: University of Texas Press, 2012.

Six

At Our Table

Conceptualizing the Black Woman's Horror Film Aesthetic

Ashlee Blackwell

"The Future of Horror Is Black and Female" (Crucchiola 2019). It is a statement, an emerging movement, and a slogan I've stood by for years as a researcher on the topic. In this chapter, I examine how Black women filmmakers address harmful stereotypes of Black women by creating their own narratives, using history (and horror) to discover stories about Black women, and positioning Black women as the protagonists within their stories. In the *New York Magazine* article "The Future of Horror Is Black and Female" (2019), the editorial demonstrates a discovery of Black women working within the horror genre, *how* they incorporate their voices within a space that is overwhelmingly white, and *what* they are saying that adds texture to the genre that ensures they will never, from here on, go unnoticed. Nikyatu Jusu, the article's center, is an award-wining filmmaker who has managed to walk through some doors off her Black vampire springboard Sundance debut, *Suicide by Sunlight*. The story centers around Valentina (Natalie Paul), an oncology nurse and day-walking vampire in a tense custody battle for her two young daughters. She is feared as much as she is desired, and her supernatural identity is paired with her natural struggle for family. The audience accompanies her on a journey of exploring a future New York City where humans intermingle, navigate, and negotiate their relationships with Black vampires. The short blends Jusu's own Sierra Leonean heritage and broader "African diasporic" (Crucchiola 2019) mythos to tell a very universal story about socio-systemic oppression and family. *Suicide by Sunlight* is a testament to Jusu's own ambitious spirit for original storytelling. Arguably, it is everything horror needs in order to continue to reign as an exciting and progressive media genre.

Exploring the discourse around Black women horror filmmakers is new knowledge in its purest form. It is currently being developed and negotiated and is at the root of building a large body of work that is distinctive from what we've known horror to produce in content, characters, and themes consistently throughout its history. The Black woman's horror film ties itself to Black women's negative historical relationship with white supremacy, sexism, and classism but additionally works to dismantle and sever those bonds to produce work that centers the Black woman's current fears and collective anxieties. As artists, Black women horror filmmakers use visual storytelling to show how these intersections affect Black girls and women. In horror, they create an even bigger impact by jarring audiences into understanding how Black women are viewed and treated, using palatable symbols, formulas, trends, and traits of the genre.

In this chapter, I produce an overview of what a Black woman's horror film is by focusing on: various discourses surrounding the experiences Black women filmmakers use to create their work, historical depictions of Black women in horror and supernatural-themed genre films, the statistics that show the low numbers of Black women in certain positions in the film industry, and the work of Black women filmmakers who have embraced the supernatural in their work and laid foundational examples of the Black woman's horror film tradition. Black women horror filmmakers are looking to build their own opportunities in the business by working independently to showcase their own films, addressing the disproportionate, horrific circumstances and issues faced by Black people and Black women as well as developing and centering richly complex Black women characters in their work. As Black women working in the horror genre, they too are often an overlooked resource for exploring the fears and anxieties of Black women in ways rarely done, if ever, before in cinema. Here, Black women are free to be afraid, to be survivors, and to reclaim their humanity. These filmmakers ultimately have learned from their own experiences—as both audience members and artists studying the craft—in order to make the kind of horror films that more accurately depict the multiplicitous reality of Black women.

There is a reason why Patricia Hill Collins's flagship book *Black Feminist Thought: Knowledge, Consciousness, and the Politics of Empowerment* notes the critical implications of *experience* in her theory. When a "historically oppressed group" (Collins 2000, 9) such as Black women produce "social thought designed to oppose oppression . . . not only does the form assumed by this thought diverge from standard academic theory—it can take the form of poetry, music, essays, and the like," opposing racist and sexist practices imposed upon their livelihood in these ways. Simply put, "U.S. Black women participated [and continue to participate] in constructing and reconstructing these oppositional knowledges. Through the lived experiences gained within their extended families and communities, individual African American women fashioned their own ideas about the meaning of Black womanhood" (9). Experience is what drives this new, oppositional knowledge within the framework of Black women and horror. Black women filmmakers who enjoy and use horror to tell their stories are creating their own approach and style by using their personal experiences in their work in order to remove their perspectives from the margins. Black women are forming a new horror subgenre and dispelling myths that Black women filmmakers have no interest in having a creative, autonomous role in the horror film genre.

Screenwriter Tracy Oliver wrote an op-ed piece for *Cosmopolitan* online in 2018 where she addressed this pervasive lore:

> There's a bias against both women and people of color in the horror genre. When we were pitching *Survive the Night* [a novel written by Danielle Vega about a group of women that must endure the horrors of an underground rave outing gone awry], an exec plainly asked if black women like horror movies. He couldn't wrap his mind around women of color even *liking* the genre. . . . And yet, because that particular exec most likely neither knows many black women, nor had done any research, he made the assumption that the horror genre isn't for women like me. (Oliver 2018)

Oliver has been a fan of horror since her father showed her *The Exorcist* (1973) at a very young age and continues to enjoy the black communal experience of watching horror films in theaters. If these kinds of personal experiences give a Black woman creative like Oliver the excitement and confidence to pitch a horror story, it must be deflating for a potential collaborator to have no reference for her valid journey as a horror fan and writer. She continues:

> These faulty assumptions hurt the genre because they lead to the exclusion of so many talented storytellers of color who've got some unique, interesting movies in them. Somewhere out there, a woman of color has a horror movie that's as unique and fresh as *Get Out*, but she hasn't been able to get through the door because of biased thinking around who should get to write horror movies.

Despite these odds, Black women horror filmmakers continue to write and direct films that assert Black women's emotional range when faced with horrific scenarios that, I contend, should no longer be overlooked.

Historically, the focus on Black women characters as central players in the films created by Black women was the direct result of the persistent, negative stereotypes that infected the mainstream Hollywood canon. As we have moved forward as a system, a society, and a body of individuals who consume media with concern for the way in which images of Black women are presented, there's no precise way to affirm if those images have gotten better, worse, or a mixture of both. But there are moments in cinema's history concerning Black women that note a crucial need for the autonomy of Black women creators to produce images of Black women that are no longer homogeneous.

Horror films in the 1930s began to offer "more opportunities for 'real' Black actors" (Means Coleman 2011, 34), particularly Black women in cinema. However, Black women during this time were commonly written as sex-driven primitives or distrustful practitioners of Voodoo. Conclusively put by Dr. Robin R. Means Coleman in *Horror Noire: Blacks in American Horror Films from the 1890s to Present*, "It is Black women's sexuality—not Black romance or love—that captured the attention and imagination of image makers during the 1930s horror cycle" (38). These ideas of desirability, love, and acceptance would haunt Black women in horror in two glaring historical examples that demonstrate a consistent narrative of the undervalued, sinister Black woman.

The Voodoo (spiritual/supernatural) theme has been consistently tied to Black women in horror. In *The Love Wanga* (1936), a character named Klili (Fredi Washington) is anguished by her unrequited white male love interest, Adam (Philip Brandon). Her mixed race but passing appearance as a white woman[1] makes their potential relationship unattainable. He later falls for a white woman named Eve (Marie Paxton), which enrages Klili. Klili uses Voodoo spells and zombies to enact harm on Eve to halt her blossoming romance with Adam (Means Coleman 2011, 58). Because she is much more fair-skinned as a biracial woman, Klili is afforded a more reserved and dignified appearance on screen in regard to clothing and social position. However, her Blackness is coded as a stain on her identity, both in terms of her supernatural leanings on black magic and misfortune in her love of a white man. The movie implies that Black women are schemers attached to a horror trope that insists "Voodoo" is a practice predicated solely on evildoing.

A more contemporary example, *Ma* (2019), may not fall under Voodoo-themed horror fare, but it does investigate the pariah/stigmatized Black woman on screen in horror much like *The Love Wanga. Ma* presents a small-town veterinary assistant named Sue Ann (Octavia Spencer), who becomes friendly with a group of local high schoolers when she gives into their request to buy them alcohol. Upon her insistence, Sue Ann's basement/cellar quickly becomes the place for the teens to party. Her imposition on their social gatherings and odd behavior begin to raise suspicions. It is gradually revealed that she's targeting this specific group because of a nasty prank she endured when she herself was a teenager by a few of their parents.

It's clear that Sue Ann wants revenge, but what the deeper story never explored was the effects of bullying coupled with racism and the nuances of anti-Blackness represented in the film as a horror itself. What we see in flashbacks is Sue Ann as a bright and promising "nerdy" student with the typical desire to be liked, seen, and appreciated. But as a racial outlier, she's the target of discrimination. The shattering of that fragility is something Sue Ann carries as an adult. Her character continues to look for that acceptance by new (her boss, Dr. Brooks, played by Allison Janney) and older (the schoolboy crush who took part in the prank, Ben, played by Luke Evans) people in her life who continue to treat her poorly and who happen to all be white. In turn, her character is lonely and unstable; violence, aggression, and manipulation become her modus operandi when she doesn't get her way. An additional twist appears when the audience realizes she has a teenage daughter named Genie (Tanyell Waivers).

Genie is introduced to the audience at the beginning of the story in a wheelchair, alone in the high school halls where she's struggling for mobility. The protagonist and new-to-town peer Maggie (Diana Silvers) makes the effort to assist Genie as a kind gesture. But we don't see Genie again until she finds Maggie and friend Haley (McKaley Miller) snooping in Sue Ann's room for clues about her peculiar behavior. She tells the two that she is Sue Ann's daughter, and both seem genuinely surprised. Genie's role seems to simply be that of a secret Sue Ann chooses to hide in her home, convincing her she's too sick to go to school, keeping bars and locks around the upstairs hallway, and speaking to Genie in a tone of resentment, all in order to shield Genie (and possibly herself) from the trauma she has experienced. Her methods may be abhorrent and maniacal, but if we're taking into consideration the deep trauma of being emotionally stunted by a cruel prank, Sue Ann's actions in relation to her daughter are woefully sympathetic.

Ma can very legitimately be read as a film about inflicting generational trauma tied to the horrors of being a Black woman in everyday life, from adolescence to adulthood, yet white director/cowriter Tate Taylor just doesn't "see it that way" (Cea 2019). In an interview for GQ online, when asked by journalist Max Cea whether race is embedded in the film, Taylor responds defensively, suggesting he just wrote a film and wanted to give a talented friend (Spencer) a chance to break out of a type she's consistently cast as, even adding that Spencer herself has questioned why everyone thinks *Ma* is about race. Responses like Taylor's are irresponsible, Spencer's shortsighted. Yet other critics and writers viewed *Ma* as a painful reflection of how society treats and sees (or doesn't see) Black women and girls.

Kimberly Nichele Brown in her essay, "Decolonizing Mammy," which uses *Ma* as the crux of her argument, refuses to shy away from addressing the film's racial overtones. *Ma* offers "viewers a new archetype of black womanhood—the black female suburbanite" (2019), a character drowning in "the intersectional trauma black girls and women face in predominately white suburban settings that typically center around the politics of beauty, desirability, and popularity." *Ma*, as read by Brown, a Black woman whose personal experiences mirrored Sue Ann's, offers the film the layered reading it is unfortunately deprived of by its creators.

The common denominator of each of these examples is the fact that not one of them was written or directed by Black women. Black women characters in *The Love Wanga* and *Ma* were removed from the perspectives of actual Black women who could've informed and possibly produced much more whole and layered characters not riddled with one-note, harmful stereotypes. Given the model in mainstream Hollywood distribution, there seems to be a protocol to keep. Films marketed to the masses seem to reflect a social hierarchy dependent upon reproducing ideas of racial (white) and gender (male) superiority through the treatment and erasure of Black women. This is reflected in recent studies that examine who is behind the camera influencing what we see in front.

In the top 100 films of 2016, the presence of Black women characters was 14 percent (Lauzen 2017). What is more difficult to find are the numbers on how many of those characters had leading roles. If we were to imagine the landscape of top-grossing films, those that are virtually accessible and visible to the massive, general public in 2016, leading roles for Black women were likely fewer than the 14 percent reported. The most recent study on 407 directors who worked on films and television series during the 2014–2015 season reveals that only two were Black women (Strachan 2016; Smith et al. 2016). For Black women characters in the top 27 horror film box office performances in 2016, only 3.4 percent had supporting or minor roles (*The Numbers* 2016). No Black women characters occupied any of the year's leading performances.

A January 2019 report on the top 1,200 films between 2007 and 2018 showed that out of 1,335 directors, only 5 Black women occupied the director's chair. Out of the top 100 grossing films of 2018, there was only one Black woman director (Ava Duvernay) on that list. Over the ten-year study, only 5.1 percent of horror films were from Black directors; none of them were women (Smith et al. 2019). Sadly, there are no specific studies on the numbers of Black women actively working behind the camera specifically in horror or other speculative genres. Considering these abysmal figures, with particular attention to the horror genre, there are questions to ponder and discussions to be had with and about the Black women filmmakers who maintain an interest in creating films in the horror genre, how they address the real-life horrors Black women endure, and why centering Black women protagonists is so critical to the broader discussion about inclusion in media. What I seek to spotlight are Black women filmmakers who want to make horror movies. Discovering how their interests in real and personal subject matter are translated in their cinematic work reveals a template for a Black woman's horror film and the distinct way Black women are using the horror genre to tell their stories and expand the genre's transformative potential for all to embrace.

The involvement of Black women behind the film lens working outside of the Hollywood system dates to the 1920s (Dargis 2017). Likely the first and most notable Black woman filmmaker using supernatural themes we now tie to the genre was Eloyce Gist, who along with her husband James Gist traveled around Black churches (their core audience) with both of their silent films, *Hellbound Train* and *Verdict Not Guilty*, in the 1930s (Means Coleman 2011, 78). This was a time in Black filmmaking where Christian-based, morality tales of good vs. evil and the Devil's trickery were the primary inspiration for creators. *Hellbound Train* is the "horror" half of the Gist's short filmography, and Eloyce was crucial in writing and arranging several scenes. The film is a literal ride conducted by Satan where all manner of sin (bootlegging, drinking, dancing, lying, stealing, etc.) is on display as a message that those who partake have "no round-trip tickets, one way only [signed] Satan" (79). The Gists' filmmaking stint ended with the advent of sound, an expensive and ever-growing popular technique that made the demand for silent films obsolete (80). Eloyce Gist's work was the earliest indicator of the Black horror canon that would follow and certainly a foundation for a tradition of Black women exploring religious/spiritual themes in their speculative work. Future generations of Black women sought more varied, spiritual practices outside of the Christian good/evil dichotomy. Black women filmmakers told non-Christian supernatural stories on screen with nuance and care, removed from the old guard of the white filmmakers' imagination and cultural blind spots. Illuminating these themes more holistically, Black women filmmakers address and incorporate an intimate awareness of the bonds and tension Black women have and share with each other in their work.

Eve's Bayou (1997) was written and directed by a Black American filmmaker and screen performer named Kasi Lemmons. Its debut screening was at the Toronto Film Festival in 1997. Lemmons credits prolific film critic Roger Ebert for helping *Eve's Bayou* become "a hit indie film" (Althoff 2016). To this day, *Eve's Bayou* is beloved by many for its nonslavery, non–civil rights depiction of the Black experience in the American South and, most specifically, its multiple depictions of Black women of various ages, temperaments, and lifestyles. This film is certainly a universal tale about family strife, but also, *Eve's Bayou* is one of the strongest, most accessible models for the growing canon of the Black women's horror film. *Eve's Bayou* makes the supernatural a natural part of the lives of the women in the story.

The film opens with distorted black-and-white images accompanying a woman offscreen voicing a mild warning that "memories [are] a selection of images." The colorless moving parts are careful not to show fully what the close-up eye sees in its view. The voice continues with exposition about how old she (an adult Eve) was when she killed her father (with Voodoo). Further, she recounts the history of her known ancestors, John Paul Batiste and "an African slave woman called Eve," who, when he was close to death, saved him with a medicinal remedy. This circumstance brought the two together; he freed her and gave her land, and they went on to have sixteen children. The overlap of imagery is tall grass, swamp, and who we are to believe is Eve magically dissolving in the frame amid the dew-stricken plant life; never quite seeing her face, she points in a direction that the camera follows, transforming to color. The scene shows the land that now belongs to her descendants as the opening credits roll.

Eve is presented as a mythical yet very real woman. Her story is the context for what the Batistes are in the present day, their wealth and prestige dependent upon her fateful union. The voice also reveals that she was named after Eve. It is her story that begins when she was a young, spirited girl (Jurnee Smollett) who carries on the tradition of being an intuitive healer. Much like the "powerful medicine" her namesake conjured, Eve's "sight" doubles in meaning in the narrative. Young Eve witnesses the unpleasant sight of her father (Samuel L. Jackson) having a secret rendezvous with another woman that is not her mother, a sight far too sensitive for a girl her age. Her well-respected family crumbles under the weight of secrets like it. Eve's bond with her aunt Mozelle (Debbi Morgan) is fortified by sharing a similar spiritual gift. They both literally see memories of the past, spirits that are bound to the emotional anguish their passing invoked. Throughout the film, Black women characters utilize the supernatural to understand their lives, help others, and even at times arouse tension between each other. The young Eve, not yet disciplined enough to understand its power, uses magic for harm, to settle what appears not to be right. Lemmons brings forth a holistic balance in the presentation of Voodoo and other spiritual practices on screen. Lemmons's work has helped spark a tradition of demonstrating how Black women filmmakers can offer much more insightful and layered images of Black women on screen that can at times dismantle past and present stereotypes inflicted upon them.

In *Black Women's Films: Genesis of a Tradition*, Jacqueline Bobo asserts that "mainstream cultural forms are replete with devastating representations of Black women as victims, as pawns of systemic oppressive forces, lacking the will or agency to resist" (1998). Given this established structure, Black women filmmakers have approached filmmaking in terms of actively resisting Black women characters that are maligned both in presence and characterization. Black women filmmakers create autonomous and emotionally rich Black women characters by "utilizing aspects of Black women's cultural identity" (Gibson-Hudson 2009, 45), (the personal and political) that are intimately tied to "the politics of race, sex, and class" (44). Further, they want an audience to view Black women "as figures of resistance or empowerment" (43) that are authentic and active in their own stories and experiences. Black women filmmakers address harmful stereotypes of Black women by creating their own narratives, using history to discover stories about Black women, and positioning Black women as main, centered characters within their stories.

Black women's art is not simply "art for art's sake" as argued by Gloria J. Gibson-Hudson in *The Ties That Bind: Cinematic Representations by Black Women Filmmakers* (2009, 45). Rather, it is a critical factor in reversing the negative effects on Black women in our sociopolitical climate. Gibson-Hudson's premise is "that cinematic representations of Black women by Black women filmmakers are constructed by utilizing aspects of Black women's cultural identity situated within a specific socio-historic context." The story then, in many instances, begins with the creator herself and what it means to be a Black woman within the historical (past or present) frame she is a part of.

Black women filmmakers create characters that reflect themselves and the Black women they know, research, and feel will make their narrative a holistic depiction of the lives of Black women in an entertaining and introspective manner. Black women characters as subjects are the amalgam of a shared and distinct cultural identity, bonded by shared oppressive experiences in regard to race, sex, and class, and distinct by way of many factors including geography, cultural interests, and emotional temperament. Black women filmmakers create characters sometimes through the process of cultural memory, a term predicated on a fluid inclusion that provides "texture, complexity, and authenticity to the character and the narrative" (Gibson-Hudson 2009).

Daughters of the Dust (1991), written and directed by Black American filmmaker Julie Dash, includes inklings of the supernatural in its tale about a Gullah[2] family during the turn of the twentieth century embarking on a journey to leave their Georgia island for the US mainland (Gibson-Hudson 2009, 50). The film focuses on Black women that are connected by familial roots and cultural customs, but each character is contemplating their separate destinies of what this journey entails. Multiple generations of women (including the spiritual, not yet born) all exist simultaneously as complex representations of their lives on the land and of what's to come. One central character is Nana Peazant (Cora Lee Day), the matriarch of the family, who, "possessing traits and powers of conjurer, priestess, and/or practitioner of hoodoo," is a spiritual and material guide for the family, ensuring that the knowledge of their Black American folkloric traditions remain a source of both hope and empowerment (Gibson-Hudson 1009, 51). She is not a mirror of evil or pawn for ridicule such as in *The Love Wanga* or *Ma* but a depiction that visually relays how these traditions and practices historically aided in Black survival in the early twentieth century in the United States. These beliefs are the cultural memory and present in the cinematic lens of Black womanhood. As Lemmons's *Eve's Bayou* and Dash's *Daughters of the Dust* act as blueprints for the components of the Black woman's horror film, their contemporaries have more directly and actively embraced the use of the horror genre in order to tell these kinds of layered stories about Black women.

Filmmaker R. Shanea Williams's award-winning psychological horror short *Paralysis* (2015) explores the isolating nightmare of Jessica Sulloway (Nia Fairweather), a photographer suffering from sleep paralysis and possibly something supernatural. This film weaves Jessica's emotional weight and unnerving dread with dream-like visuals while addressing the concerning disdain the Black community has toward addressing issues of mental health. Additionally, *Paralysis* creates visibility for fully developed, central Black women characters in horror cinema. The short screenplay for *Paralysis* follows this chapter.

The film's story sheds light on the mental health issues faced by Black people that aren't depicted enough in the media and rarely in the genre. *Paralysis* is crafted as a quiet, dark piece to reflect Jessica's state of fragility due to her condition. When we meet her, she appears exclusively committed to basic, around-the-home routines but is severely distracted. She limits her contact with others and stays primarily confined to her apartment. Those she does encounter only fuel her distress, almost demanding she be proactive in leaving her apartment more, getting a good night's sleep, or feigning skepticism about what she's experiencing. The latter response, which comes about via an encounter with an even-toned white parapsychologist, Dr. Sylvia Woods (Antoinette LaVecchia), immediately suggests that the desperate Jessica has chosen the wrong doctor for treatment.

When she's alone, Jessica acts in ways that distort the perception of reality for both herself and viewers. Neither of us are certain whether the character's paranoid episodes are being ignited by a force that haunts her or if they're a physiological response to her lack of sound rest. By not revealing a "monster," we waver in our confidence as audience members to align with Jessica. But there's a balance brought to this uncertainty. To enhance our viewing experience, we learn just enough about Jessica to empathize with and take her seriously. Each of these carefully crafted moments points to her sleep paralysis as a crippling component of her quality of life and demonstrates how real disorders can influence (or enhance) our relationship with supernatural encounters. *Paralysis* stands apart as a ripened source of alternative discourse in horror criticism by way of its optics. The film takes the opportunity to address the complicated relationship to mental health in the Black community by focusing on a Black woman protagonist whose biggest hurdle may be the terror within her own mind.

The Health and Human Services Office of Minority Health report that "African Americans are 20% more likely to experience mental health problems than the general population" (Anxiety and Depression Association of America 2020). However, reluctance to seek treatment among African Americans has been an ongoing concern. The reasons for this often include a reliance on faith, lack of resources and access to professional mental health care providers, and cultural barriers that prevent Black patients from receiving a "safe space" treatment where they feel their stressful experiences with mental health issues such as the effects of racial discrimination won't be questioned (Anxiety and Depression Association of America 2020). These terms can make it difficult for many Black people to confidently pursue psychological or psychiatric care. Williams has taken to horror filmmaking to place a spotlight on these struggles:

> I always wanted to write about mental illness in the black community because it's a subject that is still taboo. I have struggled with depression and anxiety throughout my life and knew I wasn't alone in this struggle. I also love psychological horror—the idea of the mind itself being more monstrous than any creature or crazed slasher. I am also a fan of supernatural horror—this exploration of the unknown. . . . All my work is motivated by my desire to see African Americans, especially African American women, portrayed as intriguing, multi-layered characters. (Blackwell 2016, 34–37)

While addressing the issues surrounding mental health in the Black community is "largely absent from the public discourse," specifically in horror, Williams made it her intimate and artistic purpose to plant a film in the genre that is part of breaking that stony silence and shattering any resistance to a Black woman lead. *Paralysis* is only the genesis of the work we're seeing from Black women filmmakers who are interested in making films that fall under the horror category. Black women horror filmmakers have added what's missing in horror storytelling by focusing on issues they're passionate about. Commonly, those issues disproportionately affect Black women in society.

For example, missing persons reports on Black women and girls are a serious concern. This matter is fueled by outrage at the lack of care and urgency taken to solve these cases. In 2018, Black Americans made up 12.6 percent of the population (Index Mundi, n.d.), yet Black American minors alone are 36.7 percent of missing cases (S. Brown 2019). In 2014, it was reported that a disproportionate number of 64,000 Black women were missing, a high within the total number of cases reported (Mayes 2017). Despite these alarming rates, the variety of news-related television programs do not broadcast these cases as an imperative, attentive matter. While we know the names of JonBenet Ramsey, Natalie Holloway, or Elizabeth Smart, it is a challenge for most to name any Black women and girls who suffer similar fates. Black children, according to one report, only make up 20 percent of news coverage of missing child cases (King 2017). The dismissiveness, devaluation, and invisibility of Black women and girls when it comes to missing persons cases is heartbreaking. The horrors of missing cases alone, not knowing what happened to a loved one, are difficult enough. But having to contend with a systemic structure that doesn't bother to put maximum effort into discovering their whereabouts and bringing them home safely is extremely unsettling.

This lack of empathy for the humanity of Black women and girls specifically is explored by Chicago-based filmmaker Stephanie Jeter in her horror short, *Searching for Isabelle* (2017). Jeter, a Black woman, was deeply affected by her observation of how missing Black women and girls are essentially ignored by society and media. *Searching for Isabelle* is about a young Black college student named Isabelle (Charlee Marie Cotton) who becomes the target of a serial kidnapper. Once held captive, she discovers she has a supernatural ability to astral project. She rapidly learns how to control this gift in order to reach her friends Renee (Aida Delaz) and Tyler (Gage Wallace) to let them know that she is in trouble. While the white woman she's being held captive with, Lucy Grant (Stephanie Stockstill), has a $15,000 reward for her safe homecoming and is all over the news, there's virtually no mention of Isabelle. The detective working on her case was even pressured to focus more attention on Lucy's case. While using her ability, Isabelle can inform Renee and Tyler that her kidnapper is a regular patron of the restaurant she and Renee work for, and Renee and Tyler tail him to his home one night. Slightly panicked at the urgency of the matter, Tyler calls 9-1-1, leveraging the fact that Isabelle is being held captive with Lucy by telling the operator only that he "found Lucy Grant," assuming that the authorities will arrive more quickly based on the attention Lucy has received.

This beautifully shot, solemn horror film is a more psychological than visceral depiction of the terror humans can inflict on others while incorporating the intersections of race and gender into who is valued more in the cases of kidnappings and female victims. Lucy and Isabelle are equal in their terrible circumstances, yet the society they both live in uses Lucy's disappearance to draw attention to the same crime much more than Isabelle's. In order to receive any sort of visibility, Jeter uses the supernatural to give Isabelle a combative edge over her erasure in the world. Black women must be magical in order to be recognized by a society that insists they are not worth attention, respect, and care as human beings. This reality, drawn from statistics, experience, and the observations of Black women who must endure these harsh truths, is demonstrated with competence and talent by Jeter, who seeks to bring attention to this disparity through the horror genre.

With two recent demonstrations of a Black woman's horror film, both Williams and Jeter center Black women protagonists in a story that addresses real concerns in Black women's lives while telling a fictional tale in the horror genre that incorporates various elements of the supernatural. Throughout film and horror film history, Black women on- and offscreen have been maligned and sidelined with only a notable small handful of Black women filmmakers working to redirect, transform, and develop narratives that give Black women characters their just due as whole players with intriguing stories anyone could enjoy. Moving forward, it is my hope that work like this gains more exposure, coverage, and consideration. Cinematic horror stories as told by Black women are distinct, fresh, and vital if the genre is to progress in a direction that lessens any concern about the genre becoming complacent or going stale. While there's a slow ascendance of Black women leads in the genre, I'm always encouraged by work like Williams's, Jeter's, Jusu's, and other Black women like them who defy obstacles and biases and fully lean into their efforts toward building the future of horror cinema.

NOTES

1. The "tragic mulatto" is an early film stereotype attached to a female character "who tries to pass for white but finds disaster when her non-white heritage is revealed. . . . Filmmakers typically use the 'Tragic Mulatto' to critique racism by inspiring pity. But a pitiful character seldom becomes a fully formed protagonist" (Pak, n.d.).

2. "The Gullah and Geechee culture on the Sea Islands of Georgia has retained ethnic traditions from West Africa since the mid-1700s. Although the islands along the southeastern U.S. coast harbor the same collective of West Africans, the name *Gullah* has come to be the accepted name of the islanders in South Carolina, while *Geechee* refers to the islanders of Georgia. Modern-day researchers designate the region stretching from Sandy Island, South Carolina, to Amelia Island, Florida, as the Gullah Coast—the locale of the culture that built some of the richest plantations in the South. Many traditions of the Gullah and Geechee culture were passed from one generation to the next through language, agriculture, and spirituality. The culture has been linked to specific West African ethnic groups who were enslaved on island plantations to grow rice, indigo, and cotton starting in 1750, when antislavery laws ended in the Georgia colony" (Sumpter 2016).

BIBLIOGRAPHY

Althoff, Eric. "Lemmons Screens 'Eve's Bayou' Director's Cut at Ebertfest." *The Washington Times*, April 16, 2016. http://www.washingtontimes.com /news/2016/apr/16/kasi-lemmons-eves-bayou-director-applauds-more -wom/.

Anxiety and Depression Association of America. "Black Community." June 4, 2020. https://adaa.org/finding-help/blackcommunitymentalhealth.

Blackwell, Ashlee. "I've Met the Ghost of Horror Filmmakers Future, and She's Black." *Belladonna* 1, no. 3 (August 2016): 34–37.

Bobo, Jacqueline. *Black Women Film and Video Artists* (AFI Film Readers). New York: Routledge, 1998.

Brown, Kimberly Nichele. "Decolonizing Mammy." *black filmmaker magazine*, October 2, 2019. https://bfmmag.com/decolonizing-mammy/?fbclid=IwAR36ul ptEHoDh8xUxcvzD2euxks89PwzkvvtLOR40U5qHCD500JWsx2Eaoc.

Brown, Stacy M. "Our Black Women and Girls Have Gone Missing but Few Seem to Care." *New York Amsterdam News*, February 17, 2019. http://amster damnews.com/news/2019/feb/17/our-black-women-and-girls-have-gone -missing-few-se/.

Cea, Max. "The Director of Ma Will Not Let You Pee." *GQ*, May 30, 2019. https:// www.gq.com/story/ma-tate-taylor-interview.

Collins, Patricia Hill. *Black Feminist Thought: Knowledge, Consciousness, and the Politics of Empowerment*. New York: Routledge, 2000.

Crucchiola, Jordan. "The Future of Horror Is Black and Female—Ask Nikyatu Jusu." *Vulture*, February 13, 2019. https://www.vulture.com/2019/02/hor rors-future-is-black-and-female-just-ask-nikyatu-jusu.html.

Dargis, Manohla. "A Film Series Honors Black Women Directors." *The New York Times*, January 27, 2017. https://www.nytimes.com/2017/01/27/movies /black-women-directors-film-series.html.

Gibson-Hudson, Gloria J. "The Ties that Bind: Cinematic Representations by Black Women Filmmakers." *Quarterly Review of Film and Video* 15, no. 2 (1994): 25–44.

Index Mundi. "United States Ethnic Groups." Last updated September 18, 2021, accessed April 9, 2019. https://www.indexmundi.com/united_states/ethnic _groups.html.

King, Shaun. "Nearly 75,000 Black Girls & Women Are Missing Across the Country." *Black America Web*, March 23, 2017. https://blackamericaweb .com/2017/03/23/nearly-75000-black-girls-women-are-missing-across-the -country/.

Lauzen, Martha M. "It's a Man's (Celluloid) World: Portrayals of Female Characters in the Top 100 Films of 2016." Center for the Study of Women in Television & Film, 2017. http://womenintvfilm.sdsu.edu/wp-content /uploads/2017/02/2016-Its-a-Mans-Celluloid-World-Report.pdf.

Mayes, La'Tasha D. "Why the Crisis of Missing Black Girls Needs More Attention Than It's Getting." *Ebony*, March 24, 2017. https://www.ebony.com/news /missing-black-girls/.

Means Coleman, Robin R. *Horror Noire: Blacks in American Horror Films from the 1890s to Present*. New York: Routledge, 2011.

Oliver, Tracy. "Where Are All the POC in Horror Movies?" *Cosmopolitan*, October 29, 2018. https://www.cosmopolitan.com/entertainment/a24393125/tracy-oliver-survive-the-night-diversity-horror-movies/.

Pak, Geg. "'Mulattoes, Half-Breeds, and Hapas': Multiracial Representation in the Movies." PBS, n.d. http://www.pbs.org/mattersofrace/essays/essay4_mulattoes.html.

Smith, Stacy L., Marc Choueiti, and Katherine Pieper. "Inclusion or Invisibility? Comprehensive Annenberg Report on Diversity in Entertainment." USC Annenberg School for Communication and Journalism, February 22, 2016. http://annenberg.usc.edu/pages/~/media/MDSCI/CARDReport%20FINAL%2022216.ashx.

Smith, Stacy L., Marc Choueiti, Angel Choi, and Katherine Pieper. "Inclusion in the Director's Chair: Gender, Race, and Age of Directors Across 1,200 Top Films from 2007 to 2018." USC Annenberg School for Communication and Journalism, January 2019. http://assets.uscannenberg.org/docs/inclusion-in-the-directors-chair-2019.pdf.

Strachan, Maxwell. "What It's Like to Be a Black Woman in White Hollywood." *The Huffington Post*, February 26, 2016. http://www.huffingtonpost.com/entry/female-black-directors-hollywood_us_56cfbde9e4b0bf0dab31a4b9

Sumpter, Althea. "Geechee and Gullah Culture." *New Georgia Encyclopedia*, last modified October 19, 2016. http://www.georgiaencyclopedia.org/articles/arts-culture/geechee-and-gullah-culture.

The Numbers. "Box Office Performance for Horror Movies in 2016." *The Numbers: Where Data and the Movie Business Meet*, 2016. http://www.the-numbers.com/market/2016/genre/Horror.

PARALYSIS

Written by

R. SHANEA WILLIAMS

DRAFT 11

September 10, 2015

WGA REGISTERED 1782934
ROBIN SHANEA WILLIAMS

FADE IN:

1   INT. JESSICA'S APARTMENT - BEDROOM   1

CLOSE-UP SHOTS on a WOMAN'S LEGS TWITCHING. We never see her whole body, which is on the bed. Just the brown-skinned LEGS TWITCHING, RESTLESS... then the movement stops. Lifeless.

BLACK.

FADE IN:

2   INT. JESSICA'S APARTMENT - KITCHEN - EVENING   2

SOUND OF WATER BOILING.

A WOMAN'S BROWN-SKINNED HAND WITH BLACK-POLISHED NAILS opens a drawer and selects a KNIFE.

JESSICA SULLOWAY (33) is standing over a stove. One pot is boiling pasta noodles. The other is simmering tomato sauce.

Jessica dices cucumbers and tosses them in a bowl of lettuce. On her wrist there is an old SEVERE, JAGGED SCAR from a razor blade.

As she cuts, there's some fury in her eyes. She nicks her finger. She winces in pain, wringing her hand.

                     JESSICA
          Shit!

She puts her cut finger in her mouth. Then pulls it out and looks at it: it's still bleeding.

HER CELL PHONE VIBRATES. She picks it up off the counter. She sucks the blood from her finger as she answers.

                   JESSICA (CONT'D)
          Hi. This is Jessica Sulloway.... No
          I'm not taking any clients right
          now. I'm on a... um, a short
          vacation. I can recommend another
          photographer if you'd like. Ok, no
          problem. Buh-bye.

She ends the call and puts the phone down.

THE INTERCOM BUZZES.

3   INT. JESSICA'S APARTMENT - KITCHEN - LATER   3

Jessica stands by as her father ROMAN SULLOWAY fixes a plate
of spaghetti.

He looks around observantly.

                    JESSICA
          What?

                    ROMAN
          Nothing. Decent place. Nice.

                    JESSICA
          Yeah. It'll do.
               (beat)
          I'm still unpacking but it already
          feels like home.

                    ROMAN
          You doing okay?

                    JESSICA
          I'm fine.

                    ROMAN
          Are you?

                    JESSICA
          Dad, I'm fine. I promise.

Roman crosses over and sits down at the counter with his
plate. He forks a some salad onto his plate from a bowl.

                    ROMAN
          You know, I worry about you. Can't
          help it.

                    JESSICA
          Stop worrying. There's life after
          divorce. Jesus.

Jessica forks spaghetti onto her own plate.

                    ROMAN
          Are you having trouble sleeping?

                    JESSICA
          No.

                    ROMAN
          Good. But if you do, promise me
          you'll take your medicine.

                         JESSICA
          I will.

Roman's attention is on the scar on Jessica's wrist. She
notices. She rubs the scar.

                         JESSICA (CONT'D)
          This was a million years ago.

4   INT. JESSICA'S APARTMENT - BEDROOM - NIGHT   4

On her bureau is a small altar of seven blue candles. Jessica
lights the candles one by one.

Roman appears at the entrance of the bedroom, wearing his
coat.

                         ROMAN
          What are you doing?

                         JESSICA
          These are divine protection
          candles. Supposed to ward off evil.
          Put the mind at peace. The blue
          represents tranquility.

There is a nervousness in Jessica that she cannot quite mask.

                         ROMAN
          You don't look so good, sweetie.
          Maybe I should stay. I could sleep
          on the sofa.

                         JESSICA
          Dad, I'll make it through the
          night. And the next night and the
          next.

5   INT. JESSICA'S APARTMENT - BEDROOM - LATER/NIGHT   5

A small NIGHT-LIGHT glows dimly. (Note: she always has a
night-light on in the dark)

Jessica sits on her bed. Tears are painted on her cheeks. She
sniffles them back.

She picks up her PILL DISPENSER on the night stand. She
stares at it a moment, then puts it down.

6 INT. JESSICA'S APARTMENT - KITCHEN - NIGHT 6

Jessica is at the counter, pouring herself a cup of coffee.

She HEARS A CAMERA CLICKING SOUND. She turns around, curiously. Then it stops.

7 INT. JESSICA'S APARTMENT - BEDROOM - LATER/NIGHT 7

Jessica lies wide-awake in her bed. Staring at the ceiling.

We see THREE COFFEE CUPS on the night-stand.

It's oh-so-quiet until we hear

THE SOUND OF RUNNING WATER.

She sits up, the SOUND OF RUNNING WATER CONTINUES.

She cautiously walks into the

8 INT. JESSICA'S APARTMENT - KITCHEN - CONTINUOUS 8

She turns on the light. The sink is running water. She turns it off but she stands there, completely bewildered.

9 INT. JESSICA'S APARTMENT - BEDROOM - EARLY MORNING 9

GLOWING RED NIGHT-LIGHT illuminates the room.

Jessica is lying in bed, asleep, on her back. One blanket twists around her body. Dead silence.

Suddenly we hear THE ANGUISHED SOUND OF A WOMAN WHIMPERING. It's a dreadful, hair-raising sound.

THE WHIMPERING SOUNDS GROW LOUDER.

Then... INCESSANT SCRAPING NOISES ON THE WALLS.

Jessica's eyes are open. Her body is FROZEN in place. She can't move. She attempts, FIDGETS SLIGHTLY. Her feet TWITCH. Then her hands TWITCH. Then nothing. No movement.

Suddenly she jolts up, sweating profusely and gasping. (The Strange Noises Stop)

She takes deep breaths trying to calm herself. She's completely drenched in sweat.

10   INT. JESSICA'S APARTMENT - LIVING ROOM - DAY   10

Jessica is methodically going through a few boxes unpacking
her photography equipment: her cameras, lenses, filters, etc.

INCESSANT FLICKERING LIGHT.

Jessica looks to the bathroom where the flicker apparently
originated. The bathroom door is open. It's dark.

11   INT. JESSICA'S APARTMENT - BATHROOM - CONTINUOUS   11

She enters and turns on the light. She hears that CLICKING
SOUND again.

Suddenly she can't breath. It's like the air is leaving her
body. She gasps. She drops to the floor and struggles to
crawl out of the bathroom. When she gets out of the bathroom,
her breath returns. She exhales. Relieved. But scared.

Abruptly, she starts coughing. Blood spatters from her mouth
into her hand.

12   INT. JESSICA'S APARTMENT - BEDROOM - NIGHT   12

Jessica jolts up from her sleep. Terrified. *Was that a dream?
Was it real?* She looks around.

She sees splatters of BLOOD on her pillow. Her eyes overwhelm
with horror. She picks up the pillow squeezes it to her
chest, closing her eyes.

                         JESSICA
                       (muttering)
          This is a dream. This is a dream.
          This is a dream.

13   INT. JESSICA'S APARTMENT - KITCHEN - MORNING   13

Jessica sits at the table, eating a bowl of cereal. Her
tired, reddened eyes are filled with dark despair. She stares
blankly as she spoons the cereal.

This is the desolate look of a woman who hasn't slept a full
night in days.

HER CELL PHONE VIBRATES LOUDLY. It startles the shit out of
her.

She picks it up off the table and sees DADDY CALLING. She
answers.

>   JESSICA
>   (into phone; groggy)
>   Hey Daddy. Yes, I'm.. I'm great. I
>   was um, headed to the park. Getting
>   some fresh air. Okay. I will. Bye.

She ends the call and places the phone back on the table. She
puts her hand out and it trembles uncontrollably.

14   INT. JESSICA'S APARTMENT - BEDROOM - DAY   14

Jessica is lying across the bed, taking a nap. The sunlight
floods in through the blinds, washing over her.

CLICKING SOUND IS INCESSANT. She awakens. Jolts up. DEAD
SILENCE.

THEN...KNOCKING ON THE FRONT DOOR. It takes her a moment to
process what is "real".

15   INT. JESSICA'S APARTMENT -LIVING ROOM - DAY   15

Jessica lethargically approaches the door. She looks in the
peephole.

>   JESSICA
>   Who is it?

>   VICTORIA (O.S.)
>   It's your neighbor.

Jessica cautiously opens the door.

VICTORIA, a black woman, stands at the entrance, wearing
excessive make-up making it impossible to guess her age.
Dressed eccentrically. Everything about her is "over doing
it". She's a little too strange for comfort.

She holds a wine bottle.

>   JESSICA
>   Hi.

>   VICTORIA
>   Hi there. I live down the hall. I'm
>   Victoria.

>   JESSICA
>   Oh hi. I'm Jessica.

She hands Jessica the wine bottle.

                    VICTORIA
        I hope you're not an alcoholic.

                    JESSICA
        I'm not. Thanks for your concern.
            (beat)
        Come in.

Victoria enters, with an air of caution. Jessica closes the
door behind her.

Victoria stands close to the door.

                    JESSICA (CONT'D)
        You can have a seat?

                    VICTORIA
        No. No. I'm fine.
            (beat)
        You doing okay in here?

                    JESSICA
        Yeah. Why would you ask that?

                    VICTORIA
        Just making sure. The last girl
        that lived here wasn't so lucky.

                    JESSICA
        What do you mean, "wasn't so
        lucky?"

                    VICTORIA
        Probably shouldn't tell you this.

                    JESSICA
        Tell me what?

                    VICTORIA
        Last girl... She was real sweet.
        But then she went nuts. Just
        completely crazy. Outta nowhere.

Jessica is stunned.

                    JESSICA
        Crazy?

                    VICTORIA
        Yeah. She had some kind of
        breakdown. She was dragged outta
        here kicking and screaming. It was
        awful.
            (MORE)

                    VICTORIA (CONT'D)
          I mean, I can still hear those
          screams. They were loud enough to
          wake the dead.

Jessica is unsettled by this.

Victoria studies Jessica's disposition; the dark circles
around her tired eyes.

                    VICTORIA (CONT'D)
          It's really none of my business but
          when's the last time you had a good
          night's sleep?

16   INT. JESSICA'S APARTMENT - BEDROOM - NIGHT   16

Jessica sits on the edge of the bed. She opens her PILL
DISPENSER and begrudgingly takes a pill.

17   INT. JESSICA'S APARTMENT - BEDROOM - MORNING   17

Jessica opens her eyes and sees that she is gripping a KNIFE.
She jumps up, gasps; hysterical.

She looks at her arm where her scar is and her arm is BRUISED
severely. She winces in pain, holding her arm close.

18   EXT. APARTMENT BUILDING - DAY   18

Jessica exits the building and starts walking down the steps
of the apartment building.

19   INT. DR. WOODS'S OFFICE - DAY   19

DR. SYLVIA WOODS (40ish, White woman) and Jessica sit in her
cramped office. Very cluttered. Dr. Woods is a
parapsychologist. (Note: We see INTER-CUTS OF BIZARRE DREAM-
LIKE IMAGES throughout this conversation)

                    JESSICA
          I was diagnosed with a sleep
          disorder when I was 10 after my
          mother died. I had sleep terrors.
          But the worst was the sleep
          paralysis. I was terrified to go to
          sleep. It got so bad, I even tried
          to kill myself when I was 16. But
          since then it's mostly been
          manageable. Some bad nights but
          manageable. Until now...

                    DR. WOODS
          It's all come back?

                    JESSICA
          Yes. And..and I hear this clicking
          sound. Click. Click. Click. I--I
          don't know what that is.

                    DR. WOODS
          Jessica, how did you find me?

                    JESSICA
          Online.

                    DR. WOODS
          I'm a parapsychologist. Do you know
          what parapsychology is?

                    JESSICA
          It's the study of supernatural
          phenomena, right?

                    DR. WOODS
          Yes. I ask because what you're
          telling me sounds psychiatric in
          nature. I don't think I can help
          you.

                    JESSICA
          I stayed for 3 years just so I
          wouldn't have to sleep alone.

                    DR. WOODS
          I just don't know how I can help
          you.

Jessica rolls up her sleeve. Her arm is still bruised.

                    JESSICA
          I didn't do this to myself. I wanna
          know who or *what* did this to me?
          Wouldn't this qualify as
          unexplained phenomena?

                    DR. WOODS
          It would. I just--

                    JESSICA
          When I go to sleep at night, I feel
          someone, *something* hovering over
          me. I hear strange noises. Is that
          crazy?

                    DR. WOODS
          No it's not crazy. But from what I
          know of sleep paralysis, people who
          suffer with this often feel a
          presence.

                    JESSICA
          This is different! Are you even
          listening to me? I never felt this
          before. I had a knife in my bed.
          How did it get there?
                    (calming herself down)
          I mean when I was a child, the
          monsters were in my dreams. But
          now...I don't know what's dream and
          what's real. That's why I'm here. I
          need to make sense of this.

                    DR. WOODS
          Well, in ancient folklore and still
          prevalent in some cultures, sleep
          paralysis was characterized as a
          demon or a monster sitting on one's
          chest or hovering over one's body.
          Perhaps the monsters aren't just in
          your dreams anymore--

                    JESSICA
          Wait, monsters? You think monsters
          are real?

                    DR. WOODS
          Well, there are all kinds of
          monsters.

Jessica is struck by those words.

                    JESSICA
          What am I supposed to do?

                    DR. WOODS
          Okay, how about this? Can you take
          some pictures for me of all the
          rooms in your apartment?

                    JESSICA
          Yeah. How will that help?

                    DR. WOODS
          Often cameras can capture what the
          eyes cannot.

20   INT. JESSICA'S APARTMENT - LIVING ROOM - DAY   2

Jessica prepares and sets up her camera as if she's prepping for a photo shoot.

21   INT. JESSICA'S APARTMENT - LIVING ROOM - LATER   21

Jessica sits at the table. Images upload on her laptop.

VARIOUS IMAGES of the bedroom, living room and bathroom appear on the screen. Nothing out of the ordinary.

Jessica seems both relieved and disappointed by this.

22   INT. JESSICA'S APARTMENT - BEDROOM - NIGHT   22

Jessica is lying in her bed, on her side, awake. It's very quiet, then...

CLICKING. CLICKING. FLASHES. CLICKING. FLASHES.

Jessica remains in her bed, trembling in fear.

> JESSICA
> God help me.

Tears stream from her eyes.

23   INT. JESSICA'S APARTMENT - BATHROOM - MORNING   23

Jessica enters the bathroom turning on the light. She stares in the mirror. The bruises on her arm are gone.

> JESSICA
> Am I dreaming?
> (beat; staring in mirror)
> Wake up. Come on. Wake up. Wake up.

She looks at her arm oddly and vigorously scratches her scarred wrist. Blood gushes from her wrist onto the floor.

The lights go out completely. TOTAL DARKNESS.

CUT TO:

24   JESSICA'S LEGS TWITCHING (FROM OPENING SCENE)   24

> JESSICA (O.S.)
> (desperately; terrified)
> Wake up. Wake up. Wake up.

EXTREME CLOSE-UP: JESSICA'S HORRIFIED EYES

25   INT. JESSICA'S APARTMENT - KITCHEN - MORNING   25

Unnerving quiet.

The laptop is sitting opened on the counter.

On the laptop, we zoom into an EERIE IMAGE we didn't see
before. It's a PHOTO of Jessica lying in bed asleep. Who took
that picture?!

FREEZE ON THE PHOTO.

                    JESSICA (O.S.)
              You think monsters are real?

                    DR. WOODS (O.S.)
              Well, there are all kinds of
              monsters.

· FADE OUT.

THE END.

CREDITS ROLL.

SEVEN

Women in Horror Film Festivals

*Representation, Dark Storytelling, and an
International Community of Filmmakers*

Kate R. Robertson

The subject of women horror filmmakers has become increasingly visible over the past few years, fueled in part by the international success of directors like Ana Lily Amirpour, Julia Ducournau, Coralie Fargeat, Jennifer Kent, Issa López, and Lynne Ramsay. But this is not a new trend: women have been making horror throughout cinema history; the cultural gatekeepers just have trouble finding (and funding) them. The creation—and success—of film festivals dedicated to women in horror reflects a push for representation, showcasing the diverse work being made and encouraging its continued momentum. They offer practical opportunities, such as education and networking. Encouraging collaboration and support, women in horror festivals have facilitated the growth of a global community. One of the first was Viscera Film Festival (2007–2013), a touring festival based in California, followed by other US examples like Etheria Film Night (2012), Ax Wound Film Festival (2015), and Women in Horror Film Festival (2017). In the UK, there is Jennifer's Bodies (2011), in Australia Stranger With My Face International Film Festival (2012), in Japan Scream Queen Filmfest Tokyo (2013), in Canada Bloody Mary Film Festival (2016), and in Germany the Final Girls Berlin Film Festival (2017).

In exclusive interviews with women at the forefront of women in horror festivals, this chapter provides unique insight into how these events and programs promote new voices and fresh perspectives, while supporting emerging women filmmakers by facilitating networking, cultivating an international community, and offering opportunities for collaboration, education, and support. In this chapter, insights are drawn from a series of never-before-published interviews with women in horror festival founders to reveal a shared goal of building a community of filmmakers, programmers, and also viewers through their events and programs, while emphasizing the importance of, and continued need for, festivals for women filmmakers. In keeping with the ethos behind women in horror festivals (community and collective engagement), I hope that by exploring the history of these festivals, and the approaches taken by their founders, other aspiring filmmakers can read this chapter and gain an awareness of the resources that exist for them, thus furthering the overall goal of the project. This chapter also delves into what it means to be a woman film-maker working in horror, revealing how their festivals reflect and shape a collaborative and supportive international community.

The growth of women in horror film festivals is not a response to a new trend as much as a continuation and celebration of a long history of women working in the genre. Alice Guy-Blaché was making horror films at the start of cinema; Ida Lupino directed the noir *The Hitch-Hiker* (1953); and Roberta Findlay, Stephanie Rothman, and Doris Wishman made exploitation films in the 1960s through the 1980s. Women helmed low-budget offerings like *Blood Bath* (1966), which Stephanie Rothman almost entirely reshot, and *Humanoids from the Deep* (1980), which Barbara Peeters condemned for gratuitous scenes added without her input. Jackie Kong's *Blood Diner* (1987) is a riotous sequel to Herschell Gordon Lewis's *Blood Feast*. *The Slumber Party Massacre* (1982) is Amy Holden Jones's take on a meta-slasher. Women also made studio films, like Mary Lambert's *Pet Sematary* (1989) and Mary Harron's *American Psycho* (2000). Since their original releases, Kathryn Bigelow's *Near Dark* (1987) and Antonia Bird's *Ravenous* (1999) have found strong followings. It also bears mentioning that women screenwriters are responsible for some of the best-known horror films. For example, Daria Nicolodi cowrote *Suspiria* (1977), Debra Hill *Halloween* (1978), and Karen Walton *Ginger Snaps* (2000). Women have also been instrumental in organizing significant horror film festivals. For example, Adele Hartley established Dead by Dawn in Edinburgh (1993–current); Kier-La Janisse created CineMuerte in Vancouver (1999–2005); and Rachel Belofsky cofounded ScreamFest in Los Angeles (2001–current), the longest-running horror film festival in the US. Their work helped lay a foundation for expanding women's roles in the genre as well as the development of women in horror festivals.

Viscera Film Festival was one of the first festivals dedicated solely to women in horror. Founded by actor, filmmaker, and entrepreneur Shannon Lark in the Bay Area in 2006, it launched as a grassroots initiative the following year. "There weren't many opportunities at the time for women who make fantastic films to be noticed and supported, especially early on in their careers," says Lark (2020). "I had been running festivals for a couple years in Oakland and decided to do something different with Viscera." Two key decisions were to not charge submission fees and to give every filmmaker feedback from the judges. Most importantly, Viscera was designed as a touring festival, rather than a single event, that local organizers from around the world could incorporate into their programming; its films traveled across the United States and Canada to the United Kingdom, South Africa, Australia, Sweden, and Italy. "Viscera became the place that programmers and event directors would come to when they needed great content by women," Lark (2020) explains. Its digital catalog of hundreds of genre films by women was the starting point for several women in horror festivals.[1] Despite continued growth—2012 involved thirty-five events—it closed at the end of 2013, primarily because of funding, something Lark recalls as "one of the hardest things I have ever done in my life" (2020).

Viscera's director of programming was Heidi Honeycutt, a journalist, programmer, and filmmaker who had been involved in the horror community for many years. In 2004, she established Pretty/Scary, a website dedicated to women in horror, along with filmmakers Amy Lynn Best and Jennifer Whilden. This space for networking and promoting films and writing by women led to Honeycutt's first experience organizing a film festival. In November 2005, they decided to host the Pretty/Scary Film Festival as part of Genghis Con in Pittsburgh, a convention organized by Best and her husband, Mike Watt. In the callout for submissions, Pretty/Scary solicited indie horror films where a woman played a prominent role behind the camera, as a producer, director, writer, or cinematographer. Honeycutt (2019) remembers screening their selections on a television in a meeting room at the hotel where the convention was held. "We had no idea what we were doing; we just knew we really wanted it to be about women . . . about camaraderie and [a] celebration of the feminine in horror, which was not something that was widely written about or talked about at the time." She adds, "It was really a unique thing at the time—there weren't a lot of places that women felt welcome in, in terms of film festivals."

By 2012, Viscera was receiving a lot of submissions, some of which were not quite horror but which Honeycutt really wanted to screen. So she created Etheria Film Night, expanding the scope to include fantasy and science fiction, which was first held in Somerville that September. Honeycutt also established Full Throttle, for action films, describing both as Viscera sub-brands. When Viscera shut down the following year, she decided to continue Etheria, working with former colleagues Stacy Pippi Hammon and Kayley Viteo. In July 2014, Etheria partnered with American Cinematheque to copresent its first annual showcase at the Egyptian Theatre in Hollywood and also launched a world tour. Honeycutt's continued aim with Etheria is to expand the concept of what it means to be a woman director making genre films and to encourage more to do so. She mentions feeling a pressure to make the selections really strong because of the inherent bias against women filmmakers but also notes this has become easier as the number of submissions has skyrocketed; she finds herself rejecting great films that have screened at large festivals.

One of the most important turning points in the growth of women in horror festivals was Women in Horror Month (WiHM), established by Hannah (Neurotica) Forman in February 2010. Forman was already a familiar name in the burgeoning community of women in horror as the creator of the zine *Ax Wound*. Started in 2004, this handmade labor of love explored the relationship between gender and horror. After sharing the message "FEBRUARY AS WOMEN IN HORROR RECOGNITION MONTH" across social media in 2009, Forman expanded with a manifesto, explaining:

> I posted it originally as just that—a proposal. That is no longer the case. Instead I am fucking claiming it. As a woman I have spent most of my life afraid to claim space for myself in the world. . . . So, in the spirit of punk rock, DIY (Do-It-Yourself), and a little sprinkle of blood-saturated glitter . . . I officially claim February 2010 the first annual WOMEN IN HORROR RECOGNITION MONTH.

Encouraging people to hold their own events, this grassroots initiative took hold in a way Forman never imagined. Across the Atlantic, in February 2010, Nia Edwards-Behi organized Ghouls on Film in Birmingham, UK. Furthermore, back in the US (Athens, Georgia), the Women in Horror Film Festival was directed by Andrew Shearer, who the following year brought the Viscera World Tour to the city. Honeycutt was also involved in WiHM from its first year, collaborating with Dione and Andrew Rose on the Pretty Scary Blood Bath Film Festival in Addison, Texas. In the same year, Brenda and Elisabeth Fies held a special edition of BleedFest Film Festival (2010–2011), which they were running monthly in Sherman Oaks. WiHM was also the impetus for the Stiletto Film Festival (2011–2012) in Clinton, directed by Megan Sacco. It also inspired Jovana Dimitrijevic to host the week-long Girls Can Do Horror (2013) in Belgrade.

After several years of planning, Forman held the inaugural Ax Wound Film Festival in Brattleboro in October 2015. The program included thirty-six short films written and directed by women and two filmmaker panels. Forman looks for stories that fit into a fluid definition of horror. She insists that while some festivals prioritize recognizable names, which obviously helps their marketing efforts, she strictly considers films on their own merit. Ax Wound also specifically tries to support emerging filmmakers, creating a place to screen films—something Forman realizes is incredibly hard—as well as hosting workshops on topics like crowdfunding, distribution, and special effects. Discussing stand-out moments at the festival, Forman (2020) mentions a group of local high-school girls leaving a screening "talking animatedly about these badass women making horror movies and how they should make one together." The festival has facilitated professional relationships, with many women who met there progressing to working together. This collaboration is "one of the things that makes me the happiest," Forman (2020) insists.

When Jennifer Cooper organized the first Jennifer's Bodies Film Festival in Glasgow in 2011, it was a fairly spontaneous decision. On hearing that there would not be a second edition of Ghouls on Film, which she had helped Edwards-Behi promote the previous year, Cooper suggested on Facebook she might host something. She recalls immediately receiving encouragement and support from the WiHM network, including Honeycutt, Forman, and Jen and Sylvia Soska. For the Jennifer's Bodies Festival, not only do submissions not require fees but some of the screenings have also been donation-based, with proceeds given to charity. Jennifer's Bodies has shown the work of many of the same filmmakers as other festivals, like Gigi Saul Guerrero, Jill Sixx Gevargizian, and Karen Lam, and also of other organizers, like Lori Bowen and Lark, Forman, and Nakanashi. When choosing films to screen, Cooper (2020) looks for a strong female presence, both in front of and behind the camera, as "while women have always been an essential part of horror, they have always generally been either weak or strong, virgin or whore, smart or dumb; they have been what men have wanted them to be." She feels that horror can be both a form of escapism and a way to reflect on the world. "Horror is something that looks into the darkness of the human mind," she says. "To define horror, is to define ourselves." She credits the genre as inspiring her interest in animal rights from a young age, pointing out, "Look at how the human race treats animals the world over; it is beyond barbaric, but most don't think about it as it happens behind closed doors and away from the public eye, at least here in the West." But Cooper also points out, "Of course there is the fun side of horror, I mean, who doesn't love blood, guts, and gore, right?"

Similarly focused on female perspectives in horror, Stranger With My Face International Film Festival was founded in Hobart, Australia, in 2012 by filmmakers Briony Kidd and Rebecca Thomson. Named for a novel by Lois Duncan, it focuses on women's dark storytelling, a broad description that reflects a fluid and evolving genre. Kidd and Thomson conceived of the festival as a contribution to WiHM. Starting with a collection of Viscera shorts, including Lam's *Doll Parts* (2011), Honeycutt and Leslie Delano's *Wretched* (2007), and Kidd's *The Room at the Top of the Stairs* (2010), they added local shorts and the Soskas' first feature, *Dead Hooker in a Trunk* (2009). They also developed an education program geared to nurturing new talent, including seminars, roundtables, and the first Short Script Challenge. Sixty people signed up to write a ten-page horror script in ten days, with Honeycutt and Lam as two of the judges. Kidd continued to prioritize industry-driven initiatives when she took on the role of festival director in 2013. In 2021, Stranger With My Face launched the "Tasploitation Challenge," a forty-eight-hour team film-making event, as well as the Mary Shelley Symposium, a series of talks with academics, critics, and filmmakers. Before that, in 2016, it added the Attic Lab, with nine invited participants attending group and one-on-one sessions on development and pitching, concluding with presenting to an industry audience. Stephanie Trepanier (director of development, Snow-fort Pictures), who established Frontières Market at Fantasia, was the key mentor, along with Honeycutt and Nakanashi, who joined remotely, and horror filmmaker Sean Byrne. One of the participants, Natalie James, worked on her first feature, *Relic*, which was then cofunded by Screen Australia and Film Victoria and premiered at Sundance 2020. Stranger With My Face demonstrates how mentorship directly benefits emerging filmmakers, reflecting Kidd's aim to aid career progression. She also acknowledges her own advisors, mentioning Honeycutt, who "never tires of generously promoting women's work," and Kier-La Janisse, "a real force for genre cinema" (Kidd 2020). Kidd decided that films in competition must be woman-directed, but she welcomes international participation, believing Stranger With My Face needs "to be part of a bigger conversation, even while being very specifically rooted in its location in Tasmania." It is clear here that film festivals dedicated to women in horror point to a push for increased visibility and representation. They offer practical opportunities, such as networking and collaborations, facilitating the growth of a global community.

In 2013, Mai Nakanishi founded Scream Queen Filmfest Tokyo, "the only female-centric genre film festival in Asia." Nakanishi balances a career in distribution with her work as a filmmaker, including *Hana* (2018), the first short she wrote, produced, and directed. While studying at the Vancouver Film School in 2012, she attended a Viscera screening hosted by Lam. She recalls the powerful impression this made, with so many examples of strong female characters, unlike the stereotypes typical to the genre. The following year, Nakanishi submitted her first short, *No Place Like Home* (2012), which she wrote and coproduced, to Viscera, where it was accepted. At the festival, she met Lark and Bowen, a filmmaker and tour coordinator at Viscera, who supported her decision to create Scream Queen. Drawing from the Viscera catalog, she launched her festival just three months later in October 2013. Scream Queen accepts a broad range of genre films, including noir, fantasy, thriller, science fiction, and grindhouse, though features must be directed or codirected by a woman and shorts must have a woman in at least three creative roles. Nakanishi

(2019) says, "I always try to program films by filmmakers that Scream Queen hasn't showcased before. It's important to showcase outstanding works by veteran or prominent filmmakers, but I feel that it is equally important to give opportunities to aspiring filmmakers." She is also aware she is appealing to a Japanese audience. "We hand out surveys at every screening at the Tokyo event and I read every single comment and feedback from the audience for better programming." Scream Queen has also traveled to Osaka, Nagoya, and, in 2016, Singapore. For Nakanashi (2020), "genre cinema reflects dark sides of humanity, human instincts and desires in imaginative ways. Women are equally smart and creative to make great genre films, from intelligent horror films to blood-soaked slashers."

Founded in 2016, Bloody Mary Film Festival in Toronto is named for the legendary mirror ghost. One notable point of difference for this festival is that codirectors Laura Di Girolamo and Krista Dzialoszynski decided to only program films directed or codirected by Canadian women, wanting to screen work by local emerging filmmakers to a local audience. The film school graduates shared a frustration with the lack of women's perspectives in genre films, both in mainstream theaters and festivals; Girolamo names *The Babadook* and Ducournau's *Raw* as turning points in the impetus to create Bloody Mary. These filmmakers look for women creators and predominately women's stories from "the hard end of the genre spectrum—gory horror, sci-fi in space, magical fantasy—to dramas or comedies with a genre slant," Girolamo (2020) explains. What she wants to see is horror that comments on cultural fears, offering interesting perspectives on international politics, race, and gender issues—"I think horror films are among the smartest films being made out there and exactly what I want in my life right now." Bloody Mary has offered an Audience Choice Award since 2017, with the winner receiving $5,000 toward camera rentals for their next project. The following year, the festival also launched the Creators Coven Genre Film Generator, giving filmmakers with a feature project a year of script development and mentorship. Such talent initiatives provide a platform for underrepresented creative voices in the industry, as they work to unite a strong network of collaborators, promote talent, raise ambitions, and produce more encouraging conditions for women filmmakers.

The Final Girls Berlin Film Festival was first held in 2017 by Lara Mandelbrot, Elinor Lewy, and Sara Neidorf, with the latter two serving as codirectors since 2018. Knowing that February was Women in Horror Month and aware of festivals like Etheria and Ax Wound, Lewy (2019) says, "As avid feminist horror fans, we wanted to be get involved here in Berlin." Final Girls Berlin has grown into one of the longest festivals, with four days of screenings, workshops, and talks. It welcomes submissions directed, written, or produced by women and nonbinary

filmmakers. Lewy explains they look for films with a clear point of view
and that do not reflect tired, retrograde, and sexist ideas. "What I love
about horror is that it tackles very human fears, the things we repress;
blurring the boundaries between what is real and what is not, what
can be shown and what can't," she says. Final Girls Berlin (FGB) also
works to connect women working in the genre. At the 2020 edition, for
example, Lewy (2020) points to connections made between experts like
Honeycutt, Amanda Reyes, and Andrea Subissati: "You could feel like
there was something in the air. People want to connect, collaborate, and
support each other!" Final Girls Berlin has also toured around the world,
including to Stockholm, Innsbruck, Tel Aviv, Glasgow, London, Oslo,
New York, Philadelphia, and Seattle. Lewy mentions organizing a "Best
Of" in Chile in 2019, which inspired the hosts to start Final Girls Chile.
Discussing regional differences in horror cinema, Lewy (2019) points out
that FGB is the only women in horror festival in Germany, which "unlike
France or Italy, for example, doesn't have a big modern horror film scene.
. . . One of my theories is that the real-life horror that occurred here in the
30s and 40s made fictional horror far less palatable to the population."

In the same year FGB was launched (2017), across the Atlantic, the
Women in Horror Film Festival was launched in Atlanta. Cofounders
Vanessa Ionta Wright, the current director, and Samantha Kolesnik are
filmmakers who had worked together on two shorts before starting
Women in Horror. Unlike the other festivals, it does not exclusively
screen films directed by women, accepting submissions where women
hold three or more creative roles as: director, writer, producer, cinematographer, composer, SFX artist, editor, production designer, and/or lead
talent. "We created a criteria that promotes balance rather than exclusion," says Wright (2020). "We wanted to be able to shine a light on the
creative contributions outside of the director's chair." When choosing
films for the program, Wright assesses craft, originality, and also passion.
"We love to see filmmakers and screenwriters who think outside the box,
giving us fresh perspectives and that make those hairs on the backs of
our necks stand up," she explains. Women in Horror also has competition
categories, with winners awarded a one-of-a-kind "Lizzie" trophy, with
an arm holding an ax wedged into a film reel.

Founded by women filmmakers, these women in horror festivals are
guided by insights into what works for the program, participants, and
audience. "What does it mean to be a programmer and a filmmaker? It
means I eat, sleep, and breath film," Wright (2020) enthuses. Nakanishi
(2019) feels "being a filmmaker gives me a better understanding of the
hardship and also joys of filmmaking, so naturally it gives me the motivation to create a platform to support fellow genre female filmmakers
and showcase their labor of love!" The other organizers similarly mention

how knowing firsthand what goes into making a film creates an appreciation for the submissions they receive. Lark believes watching hundreds of
films by women each year, and sharing these with an audience, made her
both a better filmmaker and programmer. The organizers also recognize
the lack of opportunities to screen genre films, especially for emerging
filmmakers. Kidd (2020) found Stranger With My Face empowering as,
"rather than waiting for people to approve of my work or give me opportunities, I was able to make things happen." She emphasizes how vital it
is that audiences are able to watch films in a public space that allows for
discussion "so film culture remains more than just the solitary consumption of 'product.'" Forman also specifically imagines how submissions
will be experienced in a cinema with an enthusiastic and genre-loving
audience, even when watching alone on a small screen. "Being genre fans
and film fans really means that we know what we as an audience would
want to see," Dzialoszynski (2020) adds.

Discussing what they look for when programming, these women all
agree that originality is vital. For Nakanishi (2019), this is at the very heart
of the genre, which "reflects dark sides of humanity, human instincts, and
desires in imaginative ways." Wright (2020) affirms, "If a film is filled
with the same tropes and stereotypes we have seen for decades, we won't
be impressed." Pointing out that budget and quality don't necessarily go
hand in hand, Forman prioritizes unique stories over style (though she
points out submissions have to be watchable). Kidd (2020) shares a similar
approach: "I'm interested in promise and originality of voice, more than
I'm interested in perfection," she maintains. "If you only go for the most
polished and the most irreproachable films in the world, you're going to
end up with a program that may be impressive but also feels a bit soul-
less . . . then what's the point? These events should be about discovery."

The founders also share the goal of building a community of filmmakers, programmers, and also viewers through their festivals. "Fans often
become filmmakers and filmmakers remain fans, so there's a lot of camaraderie," Honeycutt (2019) enthuses. Technology has changed this ability
to connect with people across the world; before digital media became so
ubiquitous, before social media or podcasts, finding this community was
much harder. Forman (2020) started her zine in part because connecting
with other female horror fans was so difficult: "Being feminist and a horror fan could be a very lonely feeling!" She insists that WiHM "is only
successful because of the ever-evolving network people who continue
to carve out spaces and opportunities for each other." Cooper (2020)
points out that, being from a small town in Scotland, her festival would
not have been possible without online relationships created through this
network: "What Hannah did when she started Women in Horror Month
was change the status quo; she started a revolution where women were

sick and tired of not being heard or appreciated and thought fuck it, let's do something about this!"

Honeycutt (2019) describes the women in horror community as "a sisterhood of sorts of women looking out for other women. . . . We all collectively make this movement stronger." This network extends to the organizers, who frequently collaborate. Many have screened their own films at each other's festivals, such as Honeycutt's *Wretched*, Kidd's *Watch Me*, and Nakanishi's *No Place Like Home*. Honeycutt and Nakanishi were mentors at Stranger With My Face in 2012 and have attended FGB, in 2020 and 2019 respectively. Dzialoszynski (2020) finds women programmers across festivals are eager to help one another. "We all want the same things . . . to make sure these films get seen and hope that that can be a great help to filmmakers in the early stages of their careers." The network of women in horror is also demonstrated more formally in the Women's Alliance of Fantastic Film Festivals (WAFFF), founded in 2015 by Forman, Honeycutt, Kidd, and Nakanashi. Though currently inactive, its aim was to help women genre filmmakers reach a wider audience and strengthen programming, with members agreeing to event support and cross-promotion.

The network of women in horror festivals has directly helped filmmakers progress. For example, after Heidi Lee Douglas won the inaugural Short Script Challenge at Stranger With My Face in 2012 for *Little Lamb*, she made the film, which premiered at the 2014 festival. Later that year, it had its international premiere at Fantastic Fest, became a 2014 Etheria Tour selection (later appearing in the anthology *7 From Etheria*), and screened at festivals including Ax Wound, Scream Queen Filmfest Tokyo, and Women in Horror Film Festival. Another script challenge success is *Blood Sisters*, written by Hannah White in 2014. When the finished film premiered at the 2017 festival, director Caitlin Koller met filmmaker Elizabeth Schuch; her recommendation landed Koller her first feature *30 Miles from Nowhere* (2018). Honeycutt (2019) and Lark (2020) mention several filmmakers whose work they screened who progressed from shorts to features, including Lam, Jovanka Vuckovic, and Jenn Wexler. Both also note the success of Guerrero, who was most recently appointed director on *10-31*, produced by Eli Roth. Honeycutt adds that Chelsea Stardust's first short, *Where Are You?* (2015), was selected for the 2016 Etheria tour— in 2019, she released her first feature, *Satanic Panic*, as well as *All That We Destroy* in Hulu's *Into The Dark* series. Gevargizian's short *The Stylist* (2016) screened at most women in horror festivals; she is turning this into her first feature in 2020.

The importance of, and continued need for, these festivals for women filmmakers is demonstrated in Jason Blum's offhand and poorly considered comment in 2018: "There are not a lot of female directors period, and even less who are inclined to do horror" (Patches 2018). He would only have needed to turn to anthologies like *XX* (2017) or *The Field Guide to Evil* (2018) or look at a program from any horror film festival to have a ready-made list. His huge horror-driven production company Blumhouse has since hired Guerrero, Stardust, Hannah Macpherson, and Sophia Takal to direct films for *Into the Dark* and Takal the feature *Black Christmas* (2019). Blum's sentiment, however, is unfortunately not unusual. It reflects a broader problem of visibility and opportunities for women filmmakers, who are not nonexistent but underrepresented in all above-the-line roles. In 2018, of the top 250 top-grossing movies in the US, women made up 26 percent of producers, 16 percent of writers, 8 percent of directors, and 4 percent of cinematographers. Of the top 100, 108 directors were men and 4 women, a ratio of 27:1. While this discrepancy is clear, these numbers actually show an improvement: across the top 1,200 films from 2007 to 2018, just 4 percent of directors were women. Women are, however, better represented in behind-the-scenes roles that are considered feminine. For example, in the top 265 films from 2016 to 2018, women outnumber men as department heads of costume, hair, and makeup. However, in the same time period, men almost exclusively filled most crew positions, such as key grip (272 men, 4 women), best boy electric (292 men, 1 woman), and gaffer (281 men, 0 women) (Lauzen 2019; Smith et al., 2019). It bears mentioning that all these statistics are even lower for women of color. Women are also underrepresented at festivals. For instance, of the 1,727 films selected in the official competition at Cannes from 1946 to 2018, just 82 are directed by women. This is not just an issue from the past; in 2010 and 2012, there were no women-directed films in competition. For more than forty years, women-focused film festivals have been actively attempting to right this imbalance by making space for women filmmakers, like International Film Festival Assen (1980), Feminale in Germany (1984), the Barcelona International Women's Film Festival (1993), and Seoul International Women's Film Festival (1997). Women in horror film festivals continue this work within a genre from which women have been excluded, both as filmmakers and audiences.

The programming at these festivals repositions the complicated relationship between women and horror, a genre overwhelmingly assigned to men as creators and as the target audience. These female founders love horror, with almost all having done so from a young age. "I guess you could say horror made me," Cooper (2020) offers. Kidd (2020) delves into how:

> The scarcity of opportunities for women to direct gave rise to this very widely accepted idea of men being the "masters of horror." Once that became ingrained, the type of horror being made by men began to be consid-

ered "horror" and whatever women were making was considered something else. A sort of near miss.

She identifies how this leads to a double standard: when women directors push the boundaries of the form, they are often dismissed from the genre, in a way that men who do this are not. This is why many women horror filmmakers have been underappreciated or, in some cases, had their legacies deliberately obscured, she points out. So at Stranger With My Face, Kidd also programs retrospective screenings to draw attention to under-recognized women directors, like Anne Turner and Gaylene Preston. Similarly, Nakanishi's goal with Scream Queen is not just to promote women genre filmmakers, who are rare in Asia, but to work toward eliminating bias against them. Lark (2020) firmly believes there is a stigma around being a woman filmmaker: "It's systemic, pervasive, and destructive, and it segregates genders into stereotypical roles. It's a vicious cycle that feeds itself if we buy into it." It follows that one of her most memorable moments at Viscera was when filmmakers said it "helped them to believe they can and should continue to make films. That they were on the right path. Damn right they are."

These women share an aim to combat preconceptions about horror films, showing they can be more than thin stories dominated by gore and nudity. Lewy (2019) looks for characters who thwart the history of women "flattened into passive victim roles and other uninspired, cliché stereotypes." She adds that viewers are accustomed to cinema reflecting the white male gaze, which is positioned as normal and neutral. Women-made horror, however, draws from anxieties and fears experienced in everyday life. Lewy (2020) describes how it takes "the threat of harassment, the complexity of motherhood, the socialization we received that we often want to fight against, and displays it on screen in all of its ambivalent, messy glory." Forman (2020) finds she increasingly has no time for the "celluloid cycle of white male rage." Adeptly dismantling the status quo of men creating stories about, and presumably for, the same audience, she proposes, "We need new filmmakers to tell their stories, fresh perspectives of fear. The voices of women, and any underrepresented group, live with fears and anxieties that others do not, and their stories are ripe for the genre. Horror can breed empathy." The programmers all see the need for increasing diversification of voices. For Kidd (2020), "striving towards a more intersectional approach became increasingly important as the festival evolved. . . . I'm absolutely sure I didn't always succeed in this with Stranger With My Face, but it's at least a conversation that needs to be had, and had often." Cooper (2020) looks toward a future where, hopefully, the industry hires "more women from all walks of life, irrespective of where they came from or the color of their skin, or sexual orientation."

The impact of these festivals both aligns with and has encouraged changes across the industry. There is certainly an increasing awareness of the underrepresentation of women in roles both in front of and behind the camera and a call for more diverse voices. But progress is slow and women filmmakers face issues at multiple levels, including financing, distribution, and marketing. Dzialoszynski (2020) suggests that the rise in festivals that strictly program films made by women puts more pressure on larger festivals to address the underrepresentation of women in their programming. "I love this platform that we've created and the community we're building here but ultimately, I would love there to not be a need to have a festival that only screens films made by female-identifying filmmakers," she says. Girolamo (2020) echoes that "I definitely think that the film industry is collectively becoming aware of how big a draw horror films are and how passionate its fans are, and how much audiences want diverse voices. There's been a bit of change in this direction, but not as much as there should be."

A point these women repeatedly raise is the disconnect between the films people want and those that get made. "The industry is still very male and very white because it's still seen as a risk for major studios to back minority filmmakers even if audiences want it," Girolamo (2020) explains. Forman (2020) points out that it is the financiers who keep recycling remakes by the same male filmmakers who then complain about the lack of originality. Cooper also laments this claim, believing "it is not because the work isn't out there, it is; most are just never given the opportunity or the creative control to bring about their vision." But there is an undeniable correlation between diversity and quality, Kidd (2020) finds, believing the wider you cast the net, the greater the rewards: "It's not about compromise; it's the opposite of that." Lewy also points out that, though women make up half the student body at most film schools, when they enter the industry, they don't get as many opportunities, as "being a female filmmaker is still seen as something out-of-the-ordinary." For Cooper (2020), women in horror festivals showcase the possibilities of the genre and the talent available. "We have obviously come a long way over the past ten years, and I absolutely believe that Women in Horror Month has played a valuable part in that," she says. "But it has been a long and arduous struggle, and there is still so far to go."

The growth of film festivals dedicated to women in horror does not point to a new trend as much as a recognition and celebration of a long tradition. These festivals show that it is not that there are not women doing the work, or wanting to do the work, which draws attention to a lack of visibility and opportunities. Their creation of space is also a response to the often-hostile treatment of women at genre events—something Honeycutt describes at length—which are typically dominated by white men. The founders of these festivals wanted to—and did—enact change. Through supporting emerging filmmakers, their festivals encouraged and celebrated new voices and stories. By facilitating networking, they culti-vated an international community, offering collaboration, education, and support. The programmers themselves share resources and sometimes at-tend or even show their work at each other's festivals. But the festivals are also about audiences. While horror is a genre that appeals to a wide de-mographic, encompassing a broad range of films, these festival founders reveal that their attendees seek unique and diverse perspectives. Often these are from filmmakers who might not gain the attention of a main-stream audience but are recognized in independent cinema or, more spe-cifically, the horror community. For example, Etheria Film Night secured the world premieres of Gevargizian's *The Stylist* in 2016 and Guerrero's *Into the Dark* segment *Culture Shock* in 2019, before it became available on Hulu. In 2016, Stranger With My Face held the Australian premieres of festival favorites *Evolution* (2015) and *The Love Witch* (2016). The success of these women in horror festivals demonstrates that they have tapped into an audience who view horror through a broad lens, looking not for "women's stories" but for new voices and approaches to craft. They also allow opportunities for viewers and filmmakers to experience and discuss cinema together in a supportive communal setting. "Connection and reflection through storytelling are vital," Kidd (2020) insists. Looking forward, the founders hope that increasing opportunities for women film-makers will lead to new stories from a diversity of perspectives, helping horror evolve into a more inclusive and richer genre.

Figure 7.1.   Viscera Film Festival Poster 2011.

Figure 7.2.　Etheria Film Night Poster 2014.

Figure 7.3. Bloody Mary Film Festival 2017.

Figure 7.4.   Ax Wound Film Festival Print Flyer 2019.

Figure 7.5. Etheria Film Night Poster 2019.

Figure 7.6.   Final Girls Berlin Film Festival Flyer 2020.

NOTE

1. For example, Viscera films were presented at the Women of Horror Film Festival in Chicago, directed by Mitchell Wells, held in April 2009 and May 2010. In October 2012, they showed at Day of Herror, organized by four Lund University students in Sweden—Jeanette Höljefors, Afsaneh Larsson, Isabel Rescala Larsson, and Frida Wallin. Viscera also featured at the inaugural Stranger With My Face and Scream Queen festivals. In 2010, Viscera held its first annual red carpet ceremony in Los Angeles and also became the not-for-profit Viscera Organization.

BIBLIOGRAPHY

Cooper, Jennifer. Interview by Kate Robertson. January 30, 2020. E-mail.

Di Girolamo, Laura, and Dzialoszynski, Krista. Interview by Kate Robertson. January 5, 2020. E-mail.

Forman, Hannah. Interview by Kate Robertson. February 16, 2020. Telephone.

Honeycutt, Heidi. Interview by Kate Robertson. November 15, 2019. Telephone.

Kidd, Briony. Interview by Kate Robertson. February 22, 2020. E-mail.

Lark, Shannon. Interview by Kate Robertson. January 15, 2020. E-mail.

Lauzen, Martha M. "The Celluloid Ceiling: Behind-the-Scenes Employment of Women on the Top 100, 250, and 500 Films of 2018." Center for the Study of Women in Television & Film, 2019. https://womenintvfilm.sdsu.edu/wp-content/uploads/2019/01/2018_Celluloid_Ceiling_Report.pdf.

Lewy, Elinor. Interview by Kate Robertson. November 22, 2019. E-mail.

———. 2020. Interview by Kate Robertson. March 14, 2020. E-mail.

Nakanishi, Mai. Interview by Kate Robertson. November 30, 2019. E-mail.

Patches, Matt. "Blumhouse Has Never Produced a Theatrically Released Horror Movie Directed by a Woman—but Hopes To." *Polygon*, October 17, 2018. https://www.indiewire.com/2018/10/jason-blum-female-horror-directors-blumhouse-trying-1202012834/.

Smith, Stacy L., Marc Choueiti, Angel Choi, and Katherine Pieper. "Inclusion in the Director's Chair: Gender, Race, and Age of Directors Across 1,200 Top Films from 2007 to 2018*." Annenberg Inclusion Initiative USC, 2019. http://assets.uscannenberg.org/docs/inclusion-in-the-directors-chair-2019.pdf.

Wright, Vanessa Ionta. Interview by Kate Robertson. January 8, 2020. E-mail.

EIGHT

"But Are You Really Into Horror?"

The Importance of Female-Centric Horror Film Festivals, Horror Curators, and Industry Champions

Anna Bogutskaya

There has been much written about the so-called new wave of "feminist horror." I use scare quotes here because it is a reductive term layered with assumptions but one that's catchier and fits better with the pop culture feminism that permeates the mainstream. It is catchy because it is, on the surface, an oxymoron. For many, horror cannot be feminist: the implication being that horror is inherently misogynistic, not a genre that is inviting for women, neither as filmmakers nor audiences. So to call a subgenre of horror feminist is quite a statement. The truth is that horror is a highly flexible and inherently generative format (Paszkiewicz 2017, 96) that women enjoy watching and making, despite the prevalent misconception that it's fixed and restrictive (a patriarchal, antifeminist product that limits artistic vision). Following on from Robertson's superb overview of the growing global trend for women-led festivals in chapter 7, here I document the motivations, challenges, and successes that go into, and come out of, working outside the conventions of mainstream horror fandom in a case study of seven women-centric horror events and curatorships founded between 2013 and 2016. This chapter offers a rare auto-ethnographical view of the DIY methodology that informs much of the work around female horror filmmaking, hinting at universal obstacles and regional differences in grassroots film programming.

Since 2014, two phenomena have intersected: horror films becoming slowly but surely embraced by the mainstream "filters of quality" of the film industry (namely, prestigious film festivals, the critical community, and film awards bodies) and a series of female-made feature-length horror films drawing the attention of critics, programmers, and industry gatekeepers from outside the horror scene. I use 2014 as the benchmark year because *The Babadook* (Jennifer Kent) and *A Girl Walks Home Alone at Night* (Ana Lily Amirpour) were both released that year to great critical acclaim and enjoyed successful festival runs. While these two feature film debuts became festival darlings and catapulted the careers of their directors (both of them already having a body of work in short films), it should be noted that the same year saw the premieres of *Honeymoon* (Leigh Janiak) and *Goodnight Mommy* (Veronika Franz, Severin Fiala).

This is not to say that there were no horror films directed by women before 2014, nor that there weren't critically acclaimed horror films (directed by women or otherwise) before then either. The fact that both *The Babadook* and *A Girl Walks Home Alone at Night* were stylish reinventions of familiar horror tropes (the central monsters in both films are heavily influenced by German Expressionism), had female writer-directors at the helm, were critically acclaimed, and very distinctly centered the female experience made them easy to fit into the narrative of a "new wave," as if it were a trendy new subgenre of horror cinema, like slashers or torture porn had been before.

This trend, combined with the blending of arthouse and horror, resulted in horror films being elevated into the realm of acceptability. The coincidence of both these simultaneous trends, as well as the appearance on the scene of more female-directed genre films over the next few years, would reinforce an idea that there was a "new wave of female horror." In 2015, there was *Evolution* (Lucile Hadžihalilović) and *The Invitation* (Karyn Kusama). The following year, we got *Always Shine* (Sofia Takal), *Prevenge* (Alice Lowe), *Raw* (Julia Ducornau), *The Love Witch* (Anna Biller), *Dearest Sister* (Mattie Do), and *The Bad Batch* (Ana Lily Amirpour). In 2017, international film festivals were awash with new takes on familiar horror tropes, all directed by women, like *M.F.A.* (Natalia Leite), *XX* (Roxanne Benjamin, Sofia Carrillo, Karyn Kusama, Jovanka Vuckovic, and St. Vincent), *Revenge* (Coralie Fargeat), *Tigers Are Not Afraid* (Issa López), *Good Manners* (Julian Rojas, Marco Dutra), *Most Beautiful Island* (Ana Asensio), and *Berlin Syndrome* (Cate Shortland). A trend had begun. Journalists, critics, programmers, producers, and development executives had taken notice.

2019 was a bumper year for women making genre films. To quote Alexandra Heller-Nicholas's report on the Toronto International Film Festival's program for the Alliance of Women Film Journalists, "This year's iteration of the festival—running from 5–15 September—presents even further proof that women filmmakers are a creative, original force to be reckoned with when it comes to things that go bump in the night" (Heller-Nicholas 2019). Some of the notable films that made the festival rounds were: *Saint Maud* (Rose Glass), *The Wind* (Emma Tammi), *Promising Young Woman* (Emerald Fennell), *Ever After* (Carolina Hellsgård), *The*

Devil's Doorway (Aislínn Clarke), *The Long Walk* (Mattie Do), and *The Other Lamb* (Malgorzata Szumowska).

There have been plenty of think pieces, listicles, features, reviews, and hot takes trying to determine why this sudden wave of filmmakers were using genre to tell stories, or more deliberately wanted to make horror films exclusively. These articles seemed to suggest that there was no real interest by women filmmakers to make horror films before this. There's always an element of incredulity in these pieces: Why *horror*? Why *now*? Why *you*? The implication being, of course, that horror as a genre has a "right" creator/audience and a "wrong" creator/audience—the latter being the female creator/audience. This is in part why women have been historically excluded from horror cinema, both industrially and through film criticism (Paszkiewicz 2017, 9). Despite this, or perhaps because of it, women-centric horror events and curatorships are emerging across the globe. It is thus vital to consider the birth of these projects, their connections to each other, and especially their role in propping up new female talent through funds, prizes, publicity, distribution projects, and serving as a quality filter for the horror film industry. This chapter seeks to raise some questions about what is at stake when women directors make horror films and when woman (like me) spotlight them.

FRUSTRATED FEMALE FANS AND THE BIRTH OF THE FINAL GIRLS COLLECTIVE

My own curatorial project, The Final Girls, was born out of a desire to challenge both of these notions—that women enjoy neither watching nor making horror films. Cofounded by Olivia Howe and myself in 2016, it was initially defined as a film collective dedicated to exploring the intersections of horror film and feminism. At that point, we were both working in the same office and had bonded over a shared and secret love of horror films. What started as a shared fandom became a sharing space for similar frustrations that we've both since heard a myriad of female horror fans tell us: we didn't talk about liking horror because it was "weird" and it always surprised people because "we didn't look like horror fans." Because, you know, some genres are seemingly more "suitable" for women audiences (and filmmakers).

In a story we've told many times over in talks, presentations, and Q&As, the initial idea behind The Final Girls came together very naturally and very quickly. Through a series of early morning WhatsApp conversations, the name, ethos, and first film choice were decided. We wanted to do a screening series; we wanted to screen the weird and the horrific; we wanted to give the screenings care and attention; we wanted to call it

The Final Girls. The joke being, of course, that there's only supposed to be one "final girl" (Clover 1992)—but we wanted there to be many of us (however, this wouldn't prevent men trying to explain to us that the name of the collective made no sense because there can only be one final girl at the end of the film). We were careful about not using the term "film club" in order to give more weight to our ambitions. Even though we were, essentially, a film club, we wanted to use the same language we'd seen applied in arthouse cinema to horror, hefty terminology like "curation" as opposed to "films we like." A "film collective" implied community as opposed to exclusivity; it implied that the audience was just as important as we were in bringing the screenings to life. We also wanted to, eventually, grow the collective beyond just ourselves. Both having come from the world of festivals, we didn't have any intention of putting on a festival because that would have meant losing out on programming repertory screenings (we would be expected to prioritize first-run films every time, as opposed to showing classic or notable older films) and would put us in the endless race against time to put on a large-scale annual event. Instead, we wanted to experiment with repertory programming, unearthing lost horror treasures, experiential events, and contextualized screenings.

The policing of women's tastes, particularly when it relates to horror, has always been fascinating—and hasn't been as explored. Female cinephilia and fandom studies (how women interact with cinema that is both supposedly "meant" for them and that isn't) are only now starting to take form, with proper critical appraisals of how female audiences engage with culture beyond the derogatory or simplified. It's the old "What's a girl like you doing in a place like this?" approach but tacked onto a whole cinema genre. I've always been interested about the why behind this assumption, that horror (both in literary and visual form) has been instinctively associated with male audiences. Why is it so controversial for female audiences to enjoy the macabre? Bela Lugosi, the Hungarian actor most known for portraying the first onscreen Dracula in Tod Browning's 1931 adaptation (Lennig 2003, 61), is supposed to have said: "It is women who love horror. Gloat over it. Feed on it. Are nourished by it. Shudder and cling and cry out—and come back for more." Horror literature has always been equally penned by women and men but somehow became narrowly viewed as a masculine genre. Let's remind ourselves that arguably one of the most influential horror novels ever written, Mary Shelley's *Frankenstein* (1818), was penned by a teenage girl. Women are also major on-screen presences in horror films.

A recent study compiled by Google (2020) and the Geena Davis Institute on Gender in Media used computer analysis to recognize patterns in gender, screen time, and on-screen speaking time in major films. In horror films, women held 53 percent of the on-screen time and 47 percent of the speaking time. This is where film marketing comes in. While romantic comedies are actively marketed to female audiences, horror films tend to prioritize male audiences in the way they are marketed (from poster design, talent appearances, press champions, and media partnerships). So while horror is actually the film genre where women have more lines and more visibility on-screen, as a genre it has been historically marketed to male audiences. Yes, we all know that horror was considered the nemesis of early feminist criticism, given its association with fairly horrifying stereotypes, not to mention the smorgasbord of violence against women, yet it has been acknowledged, for a good deal of time now, as a productive site of ideological disruption and reimagining (Paszkiewicz 2017, 19).

Many female-identifying horror fans have had the experience of feeling uneasy in horror film festivals, or at horror events, because we have to "prove" that we really like horror movies. Being there is not enough—there is always a test of some sort, a test of knowledge that is really a camouflaged test of belonging ("Have you even seen enough horror films to be here?"). This extends to a lot of culture in general, especially anything that's been mostly considered a male-dominated scene, but it does become particularly jarring when applied to the horror community. In a community of people who band together with a shared status as outsiders or weirdos, feeling like you still have to prove your right to be there is extremely draining. Being a fan is both an individual and a communal experience.

In her book on female music fans, *Fangirls*, Hannah Ewens (2019) writes: "To be a fan is to scream alone together." Film fandom manifests itself not just by the act of watching but by sharing the experience with others. With horror film fandom in particular, it's the comfort of knowing that enjoying horror might make you weird to the mainstream, but here's a whole group of other weirdos who you can enjoy horror with. It's finding a tribe. But if that tribe questions your right to be there—to just *enjoy* horror films—as if there was a test one needed to pass before purchasing a ticket, it invalidates the communal aspect of fandom. Going to horror film screenings and local genre festivals as a young woman, I was often chatted up by men who asked whether I was waiting for a boyfriend or if someone had dragged me there. The one time I did go to a horror festival with a boyfriend, I'd actually dragged him there.

Like author and horror film producer Mallory O'Meara writes in her book *The Lady from The Black Lagoon* (2019):

> Growing up a horror fan is harder when you're a girl. You have very few role models and they generally all look the same. They're white, they're beautiful, they're thin, they're straight, they're able-bodied, and they only fight the monster because they have to, because everyone else has been killed off.

They don't direct the monster, they don't make the monster, they don't go off in search of monster adventures.

Being a horror fan that doesn't fit into the popular mold that's been presented to us through the very genre we love (namely, a straight, white, cis man) means that this misogyny is internalized by female horror fans as well. You learn to either brush aside the issues or wear the "I'm-not-like-the-other-girls" badge with pride. A lot of what's discussed in this chapter has been informed personally by my experiences as a horror fan and professionally by my work as a curator. How a film festival experience is designed is extremely important and part of the work of a programmer. Everything from the price of the ticket, the name of the event, the film choices, the copy, the venue, the holding slide, the way audiences are addressed, who does the introduction and hosts the Q&A's—all of these are small decisions that together form the experience. Each of these decisions is deliberate and designed.

AN OVERVIEW OF WOMEN-CENTRIC HORROR EVENTS AND CURATORSHIPS FROM THE INSIDE

The Final Girls collective was, unknowingly to us at the time, a part of something larger that was brewing on the international horror scene. Between 2013 and 2016, seven film festivals were founded that were dedicated to female filmmakers working in the genre space. It is difficult and perhaps reductive to batch these festivals together. But it is no coincidence that they emerged at the same time as this "new wave" of mainstream female horror filmmakers (such as Kimberley Peirce, Karyn Kusama, and Sophia Takal) gathered momentum and attracted the attention of industry gatekeepers. The shared lines of their curatorial strategies address female horror fandom and the dismissal of the existence of female filmmakers interested in genre. Festivals traditionally act as filters of quality, of critical validation by programmers and experts. From that, film industry gatekeepers such as development executives, distributors, producers, talent spotters, agents, commissioners, programmers, publicists, and more have a handy way of finding new talent. A hit film at a festival gets people talking, impacts on deals, and offers a glimpse at the audience potential of a film. Of course, this is not a science and not all festival darlings or award winners become commercial success stories or have lengthy careers, but in an industry where every film is a prototype, it's the closest we have to an indication of interest and appetite.

Stranger With My Face Festival was the first of them, founded in 2012 and based in Tasmania, Australia. Founded by filmmakers Briony Kidd and Penny Vozniak, the event took place over four days in March, coinciding with International Women's Day. Scream Queens Filmfest Tokyo came in 2013, with a mission to showcase and promote emerging and established female genre filmmakers. They have existed since then as a film festival and a touring program (a showcase of their selections touring across Japan throughout the year, outside of festival dates). Etheria Film Night, of which McCollum (coeditor) is a Finalist Judge, was founded in 2014, based in Los Angeles, and is very directly designed to be an address to the industry. The event positions itself as such: Etheria puts the women directors who want to make genre films and TV in front of the people who want to hire them. Since 2018, they have also awarded the Stephanie Rothman Fellowship to female film students who make, or want to make, horror, science fiction, action, fantasy, and thriller films. In 2016 came Sick Chick Flicks Film Festival (Chapel Hill, North Carolina), Bloody Mary Film Festival (Toronto, Canada), and Women in Horror Film Festival (Marietta, Georgia). The following year saw the creation of the Final Girls Film Festival in Berlin, Germany. This festival is the first that defines more curatorial ambitions than industry-facing ones and is the first that explicitly includes nonbinary and trans filmmakers in their language.

Notably, most of these festivals have one or all of the following: (a) a festival program primarily focused on short film; (b) a competitive element, either a short and/or screenplay competition or a competitive program; (c) an engagement with the industry in order to engage the filmmakers directly with gatekeepers. It's not a coincidence, I think, that most of these festivals are founded or cofounded by filmmakers, women who are likely just as frustrated with being told that there is no room for them to make the sort of work they want because there is "no audience." A film festival is a perfect platform to both disprove that and to offer networking opportunities for both fans of the genre and future horror storytellers.

The driving inspiration behind setting up my own The Final Girls (UK) was to create a space that was both highly curated and that invited smart conversations about the genre, platforming female voices (both filmmakers and critics) and reappraising films that, for one reason or another, had been deemed "antifeminist" or "inappropriate" for women to like. We wanted to avoid badging anything as "feminist" but rather open up room for discussion. Audiences should be able to disagree with us on whether a film we had chosen had anything to say about the female experience or whether it contained feminist ideas. The Final Girls wanted to create a space that was welcoming for seasoned horror fans, arthouse audiences, and people (particularly women) who had not felt comfortable going to traditional, mainstream horror events.

Our first screening was in May 2016 (on Friday the 13th) at the Prince Charles Cinema, an independent two-screen cinema in Leicester Square. The film was Claire Denis's 2001 cannibal love story, *Trouble Every Day*. By sheer good fortune, we were able to locate a pristine 35mm print of the film. We cold-e-mailed the cinema with our pitch and were offered an early evening slot. This was a show of faith by the cinema, which we have continued to work with very happily over the years across different projects and which has always embraced new programming ideas. Our pitch was clear: a horror crowd, a female audience, and we had sorted out the print already. At that point, *Trouble Every Day* had not screened in London for close to a decade. I had been fascinated with the film (and with the enigmatic French actress Béatrice Dalle) since I first saw it on library VHS at Central Saint Martin's.

Since then, we have worked with distributors on theatrical campaigns, special events, and panel discussions, all connecting female audiences with horror audiences. For the first two years of the collective, the screenings were mostly repertory screenings: *Office Killer*, *Single White Female*, *Carrie*, *Slumber Party Massacre*, and *Slumber Party Massacre II*. Our key aspiration was that every screening was an event: all of them were introduced by us, there was a zine produced for each event and given out to attendees, and, in some cases, the screenings were followed by panel discussions. We also experimented with special events, like an all-nighter dedicated to horror icon Jamie Lee Curtis (we screened six horrors from her body of work at an all-nighter event in the Genesis Cinema) and a "bloody prom party" after a screening of *Carrie* (which included a bucket of blood made from red rope, a prom photo set, and a specially designed fortieth anniversary poster by Spanish artist Tasio).

In an event that was part of the Film4 Summer Screen Series, we organized a screening of short films focused on the figure of the final girl, followed by a panel with critic Anton Bitel, lecturer Dr. Charlie Allbright, and filmmaker Todd Strauss-Schulson (*The Final Girls*). These panel discussions invited a combination of journalists and academics, always designed to explore specific female tropes in horror, female themes explored in films deemed problematic, or the legacy and context of female-made films. For each screening, we created bespoke zines, with original writing, references, artwork, and collages inspired by the film(s) we were screening. The idea of the cinephile artifact—film magazines, posters, fanart—was always appealing to me partly because of my fascination with punk culture and, in particular, riot grrrl culture (the punk subgenre originated in the 1990s that had a vibrant zine culture centered on women's writing and creative expression). On a programmatic level, it allowed us to give audiences something to take with them, to remember a screening by. On a marketing level, it was highly Instagrammable content.

Alongside our repertory screenings, The Final Girls worked with distributors to reach female audiences for horror releases *The Love Witch* (Anna Biller, 2016) and the all-female horror anthology *XX* (Jovanka Vuckovic, Sofía Carrillo, Karyn Kusama, Annie Clark, Roxanne Benjamin). With the former, we organized a UK-wide tour of previews, each accompanied by a Q&A with the director Anna Biller or, if she was unavailable, an eventized approach to a screening. At Sheffield Showroom, we organized a postscreening tea party, taking visual inspiration from the aesthetic of the film. With *XX*, which was not going to have a theatrical release at all, we experimented with the one-night-only model, putting the film into independent cinemas around the country on the evening of May 3, 2017. These screenings were the only theatrical showings of the film in the UK outside of a festival context.

WE ARE THE WEIRDOS: CURATING SPECIAL SHOWCASES WITHIN A FEMINIST HORROR FILM COLLECTIVE

Inspired by these experiences, in 2017 we started an independent distribution project titled We Are the Weirdos: a curated program of horror shorts directed by women that The Final Girls distributed in independent cinemas across the UK. When I say "distributed," I mean everything from curating the program, producing the DCPs, creating marketing materials (poster, graphics, social media assets, postcards, merch, etc.), contacting cinemas for bookings, negotiating a box office split, keeping track of sales, marketing the events, and processing the box office receipts after the events.

The project garnered substantial press attention, giving a platform to filmmakers who had not yet directed their first feature. Without the insight of a savvy publicist, or even a proper press release, the project got coverage in, among others, *The Telegraph, Little White Lies*, and, through a media partnership, *Broadly*. This project gathered attention because of the noteworthy weirdness of this formula (women + horror = huh?). In her feature covering the project, journalist Rebecca Hawkes (2017) opens with:

> Horror movies and feminism, at first glance, don't seem like natural bedfellows. On-screen women are regularly terrorised, chased, drenched in blood, mutilated and murdered in the name of cinematic scares. Unpleasant things happen to male victims too, but traditionally it's been the girls who get the really nasty deal.

We Are the Weirdos was designed as a mission statement from the very start—that's evident in the title. It comes from a moment in the 1996 cult film *The Craft*: the four teenage witches get off the bus in the middle of nowhere (they're going there to perform a series of rituals) and are warned by the good-natured bus driver to be careful because "there's a lot of weirdos out there." Without missing a beat, Nancy Downs (played by Fairuza Balk), the de facto leader of the group, retorts: "We are the weirdos, mister." The quote is instantly recognizable to fans of the film, and it deliberately owns the disparaging term "weirdo," imbuing it with a sense of community. We are the weirdos together.

The horror shorts were selected through a combination of scouting and open submissions. Accessibility was a key element, so the submissions were kept free and managed through the submission platform FilmFreeway. More than 1,300 submissions were received from all over the world and viewed by us. The criteria was specific: submissions were open to shorts up to twenty-five minutes in length; films must have been directed by a woman or female-identifying director; films must have been completed in the past two years; and we accepted fantasy, thriller, and horror films from all countries, production techniques, forms, and budgets. Most of the films, as we expected, did not fit this criteria. But through a combination of scouring these open submissions and the shorts selections of film festivals from previous years, we put together a program of ten short films: *The Puppet Man* (Jacqueline Castel), *Undress Me* (Amelia Moses), *Pulse* (Becki Pantling), *I Should Have Run* (Gabriela Staniszewska), *Sorry, We're Closed* (Alexis Makepeace), *A Mother of Monsters* (Julia Zanin de Paula), *Dead. Tissue. Love.* (Natasha Austin-Green), *Don't Think of a Pink Elephant* (Suraya Raja), *Shortcut* (Prano Bailey-Bond), and *I Want You Inside Me* (Alice Shindelar). The selection premiered at the fiftieth Sitges International Film Festival and screened at eleven cinema venues across the UK (not including free events or private screenings). The selected films were presented under the Weirdos banner, the first edition in October 2017 (coinciding with Halloween activity). Some of the non-UK-based filmmakers (including Castel and Moses) were present for some of the London screenings to take part in Q&As about the films. The cinemas we approached were welcoming and open to the project. Short films rarely get a place to screen in the regular program of a cinema outside of the context of a short film festival—We Are the Weirdos provided an alternative. Additionally, contrary to film distributors, who rarely achieve an identity strong enough to be recognizable by audiences, a curatorial collective has a personal touch, and we could speak directly to our audience—as fans, as curators, and now as distributors. The promotional approach for We Are the Weirdos was not based around sales but around a shared interest with our horror audience.

The second edition of Weirdos was presented in February 2019 (to capitalize on Women in Horror month). This time around, we engaged the services of a genre-specialized publicist to help promote the project and increased the amount of coverage for the program, which included *The Skinny*, *The A.V. Club*, *Bustle*, and many genre-specialized outlets. The decision to move the project was partly an experiment: with October dominated by horror-themed activity, it's easy to get lost in the shuffle; in February, it was much more likely to get press coverage due to the hook of Women in Horror Month. This edition included ten shorts: *Catcalls* (Kate Dolan), *The Lady from 406* (Lee Kyoung), *Inseyed* (Jessica Hudak), *Hair Wolf* (Mariama Diallo), *Puppet Master* (Hanna Bergholm), *#EAT-PRETTY* (Rebecca Culversome), *Cerulia* (Sofía Carrillo), *Goodnight* (Diane Michelle), and *Blood Runs Down* (Zandashé Brown). As with the first edition, we made efforts to find a widely different variety of films: different visual styles (including the always-interesting horror animation), tones, and subject matters. We are currently prepping for the third edition, due to happen in late 2020 in an updated format in response to the ongoing COVID-19 situation. The underlying mission of We Are the Weirdos is to challenge the idea that female filmmakers can only make one type of horror film. It's all about the multiplicity of voices, themes, and approaches that female filmmakers can have to genre.

CONCLUSION

Since that first screening of *Trouble Every Day* in 2016, The Final Girls collective has been redefined as a film collective focused on exploring feminist themes in horror cinema and highlighting the representation and work of women in horror, both in front of and behind the camera. Continuing that thinking, in November 2019, we launched a podcast. Initially designed to be an accompaniment to the season, *Here Be Witches* the podcast was a series of conversations with female contributors (critics, horror fans, and filmmakers) about a selection of witch films. The films ranged from the horrific (*Black Sunday*, *The Autopsy of Jane Doe*, *The Craft*) to romcoms (*Practical Magic*, *I Married a Witch*, *Bell Book and Candle*) and television series (*Buffy the Vampire Slayer*, *Chilling Adventures of Sabrina*). It was important with the podcast to center female voices, so all the guests are womxn (an intersectional term that signals the inclusion of those who have traditionally been excluded from white feminist discourse). In every episode, myself and a guest would discuss a witch film in depth.

As part of the evolution of the collective (which thus far had been, ironically, just Olivia and myself), we wanted to create a platform that would center female voices and thoughtful, bold writing on horror in a way that was longer term than screenings and panel discussions. So, in May 2020, to coincide with our fourth anniversary, we launched *Bloody Women*, a horror film journal committed to platforming viewpoints on horror cinema, TV, and culture by women and nonbinary writers. We hired a commissioning editor to work with emerging writers on essays and also invited filmmakers, fans, and writers to contribute a personal essay on how their viewing habits evolved during lockdown.

Programming events is, essentially, an ephemeral experience. The value of the shared experience is in the cinema and cannot really be captured later on. While The Final Girls never intended to be a media platform, our increased prioritization of new talent evolved into wanting to support and grow the multiplicity of voices in writing and podcasting. The key thinking behind this is also the ability to reach wider audiences outside of a single event or a single season. We do not record the conversations, panel discussions, or introductions we do as part of the events, but with the podcast and *Bloody Women*, we are able to have these discussions live online and be accessible to audiences without the usual barriers of price, geography, and access.

Hollywood history is littered with the lost and wasted talents of female creatives. Partly this has to do with proper crediting (Who gets credit for work? Where are these names listed? How are they preserved?). Sometimes this is omission or incompetence. In her documentary dedicated to the film pioneer Alice Guy-Blaché (explored in chapter 1 of this volume), director Pamela B. Green discovered that a few simple misattributions of Guy-Blaché's work to her then-husband meant these films are not attributed to her, sometimes due to malice. O'Meara, in her book on the creature designer Milicent Patrick, uncovers ill will and scheming against her by the then-head of the makeup department, Bud Westmore. In terms of who is talking about the work, the role that critics and curators play is extraordinarily important because they provide a record of what is being made, who is making the work, and how it's being received and discussed at a particular point in time. The way people talked about *Carrie* in 1976 is not the way we talk about *Carrie* in 2020; we are all, of course, victims of our own inherent biases. It's the job of the curator to look *wider* and *harder*. And in the case of horror curatorship and criticism, it's our job to let our voices (quite literally) be heard.

What these festivals and The Final Girls are doing is trying to address the idea that there are "not enough" women working in genre—filmmakers, critics, writers—from an early point in their careers. These festivals and curatorial initiatives are intent on not letting that happen to new generations of filmmakers. They will never be a substitute for A-list festivals or major showcases that pride themselves on prioritizing "quality" over any sort of gender quota or inclusivity policy (that's a subject for a whole other book), but that's hardly their intention. Through networking opportunities, press attention, and other modes of platforming new talent, these initiatives perform the most necessary task of any film festival or curatorship: they filter. A film festival is a filter of quality. A curatorial project like The Final Girls is a filter. The quality of the films and the talent that goes through a festival is the best possible qualifier of a festival's taste. If a festival supports the work of a new or up-and-coming filmmaker, it's a vote of confidence in them and the beginning of a relationship that might last for the duration of that filmmaker's career. Hence, curation is never (or should never be) taken lightly by film festival programmers. It is, after all, our main tool—the ability to spot a diamond and find a way of connecting it with the right audience.

These initiatives respond to the complaint that "there is not enough talent" or "no audience" for female-led horror projects with a resounding cry of "Bullshit!" There *are* enough female-identifying filmmakers out there who want to make horror films; there *are* enough films to showcase; and there *are* enough audiences that want to support them.

BIBLIOGRAPHY

Clover, Carol. *Men, Women, and Chain Saws: Gender in the Modern Horror Film.* Princeton, NJ: Princeton University Press, 1992.

Ewens, Hannah. *Fangirls: Scenes from a Modern Music Culture.* London: Quadrille, 2019.

Google. "The Women Missing from the Silver Screen and the Technology Used to Find Them." *Google Study,* 2020. https://about.google/main/gender-equality-films/.

Hawkes, Rebecca. "We Are the Weirdos: Meet the Women Changing the Face of Horror." *The Telegraph,* October 26, 2017. https://www.telegraph.co.uk/films/0/weirdos-meet-women-changing-face-horror/.

Heller-Nicholas, Alexandra. "Women Horror Filmmakers at TIFF 2019." Alliance of Women Film Journalists, September 4, 2019. https://awfj.org/blog/2019/09/04/women-horror-filmmakers-at-tiff-2019-report-by-alexandra-heller-nicholas/.

Lennig, Arthur. *The Immortal Count: The Life and Films of Bela Lugosi.* Lexington: University Press of Kentucky, 2003.

O'Meara, Mallory. *The Lady from the Black Lagoon: Hollywood Monsters and the Lost Legacy of Milicent Patrick.* London: Simon and Schuster, 2019.

Paszkiewicz, Katarzyna. *Genre, Authorship and Contemporary Women Filmmakers.* Edinburgh: Edinburgh University Press, 2017.

NINE

Short Sharp Shocks

An Interview with
Women Who Make Horror Shorts

Brian Hauser

This chapter is constructed around semistructured interviews with several women filmmakers who work primarily in short-form horror filmmaking, about their insights and experiences as short-form horror filmmakers. I have made minor edits in spelling and punctuation for clarity and stylistic consistency while also attempting to preserve individual voices. The four filmmakers interviewed (over e-mail) for this chapter include: Jennifer Trudrung, an actor, writer, and producer known for *Unbearing* (2017), *Indolence* (2019), and *Here There Be Tygers* (2019); Izzy Lee, a writer, director, actor, and producer known for *Innsmouth* (2015), *Rites of Vengeance* (2017), *My Monster* (2018), and *The Obliteration of the Chickens* (2019); Aislínn Clarke, a writer and director known for *Short Sharp Shocks* (2015), *Childer* (2016), and *The Devil's Doorway* (2018); and Vanessa Ionta Wright, the filmmaker behind shorts such as *I Baked Him a Cake* (2016) and *Rainy Season* (2017), as well as cofounder of the annual Women in Horror Film Festival.

Following the interviews with horror directors Trudrung, Lee, Clarke, and Wright, I provide a narrative analysis of the filmmakers' individual stories highlighting important aspects of their insight, particularly as it pertains to the benefits of short-form horror filmmaking from an aesthetic, economic, and practical perspective. The interviews analyzed in this chapter reveal a broad range of opinions and perspectives regarding the extent to which these filmmakers choose to situate their work along the lines of gender identity. Some see their gender identity as integral and inescapable to their work, while others prefer to be received simply as horror filmmakers. As such, gender is discussed both as inspiration and hurdle. At the same time, the interviews illuminate the potential for the horror genre to assist in the achievement of broader gender parity in the motion picture industry.

Q: Was your decision to make horror shorts primarily pragmatic, economic, or aesthetic?

Trudrung: My decision to make short films is that I'm just a true horror geek. I absolutely love horror. I have been reading horror books and watching horror films since I was an angst-riddled kid. I'm a scaredy-cat and not much of a risk taker, so horror is my way to get that healthy adrenaline rush in a safe manner. My imagination is also ripe with scary ideas. I tend to try not to think too hard on what lurks in the corner, but I'm also riddled with fears. So making short horror films came quite naturally. I have children, and honestly a lot of my films deal with a parental fear or a childish nightmare. I delve quite a lot into the what-ifs of a normal family household.

Lee: I went on this journey because I wanted to try telling stories in a new medium that had the potential to reach a large amount of people. That and because I had no choice. If you're in filmmaking for real, it chooses you. There are so many easier and less heart- and wallet-breaking careers out there with sane hours. That said, directing is the most fulfilling thing I've ever done.

Clarke: My first films were by necessity short anyway—experiments, attempts at testing the limits of what I could do. When I studied film at university, there was only one camera available for students to borrow—there wasn't the easy access to equipment there is now. My early films were made on 8mm film cameras, so they had to be short. I would treat the films with food coloring, dyes, whatever I could to create unexpected effects. The pragmatic and aesthetic were always combined. I was never working to fulfill an ambition but to make art. However, making art requires a pragmatic mind. When I came to make my first dramatic shorts, the aesthetic and pragmatic combined too. I had always loved horror films, so I was always going to make them—that aesthetic, an interest in the dark in human nature, was my primary concern. However, the nature of horror is such that it can be distilled into single moments, into gestures, actions, and turns—for a short film, horror is a pragmatic choice, the format is so well-suited to it. That pragmatism—working within the limits of your resources—necessitates bold aesthetic choices. The system of film development in Europe and the UK encourages the short format, as a testing ground. Thus, when I received a small amount from NI Screen to produce a short in 2015, I produced *Short Sharp Shocks*—three microshorts, a minute each, all filmed in the same house on the same day. This was a pragmatic choice, using the limited funding to produce the most work, distilling each film down to a single horror beat, allowing me to funnel the resources into the production design and focusing the story on that moment. It was through these three shorts that I got my UK agent.

Wright: My reason for starting with a horror short was both economic and aesthetic. I hadn't directed or produced a film professionally, and I really wanted to get my feet wet with a short. I decided to adapt and direct a Stephen King short story through his Dollar Baby program. Horror, or suspense thriller in this case, seemed a natural fit, as I grew up watching these types of films and have a deep appreciation of the genre. This was a phenomenal learning experience and has really helped shape how I approach future projects.

Q: Even if your professional or artistic goals focus on a career in features or streaming series, do you find that short films offer any particular opportunities in horror that longer forms do not?

Trudrung: I feel that making short films in any genre is very important and especially helpful in the horror genre. Horror film festivals have been where I have made close friends in the industry and also important networking connections. Making a short film is a more affordable and realistic way to get your unique voice out into the world. It's a less daunting format also and an easier way to get your work on a social platform. It's also important to write your first script even if you don't know the proper format yet. It's just important to try. The horror community is especially supportive and welcoming. We all just want to be scared or creeped out or challenged in a new way. It's a community ripe for new ideas or even fresh ideas on old tropes. Short films are a great way to get your foot in the door with this amazing community.

Lee: Yes. You can create stories that make a great impact in little amounts of time. And if you can't afford film school, then shorts are a fantastic way to learn actual filmmaking. Being on set is so much more important than being in a class anyway. Shorts also provide an excellent way to easily digest what your peers are doing, in the sense that there can be themes hanging around in the zeitgeist that some of us—across the world—are working in.

Clarke: Different ideas demand different forms. You can drill down into some ideas and find depth and character; others offer up everything almost straight away. Some ideas demand concentration and focus; other ideas are ruminations. The short film is concentrated, only a moment in time. And because it is only a moment in time, it isn't constrained by cause-and-effect or logic in the way that a feature or a series is. The thing that happens is the thing that happens and that has no consequence for the storytelling. There is no expectation that you will follow it with anything. Rather, like a joke or an anecdote, the short film exists primarily to get its honest reaction—a laugh, a scream, a single earned tear. Anything after or beyond that is a bonus. This makes it a form equally useful to the formalist and the experimentalist—as long as you hit that moment of re-action, you've succeeded. The viewer is waiting for that moment, and you either hit them between the eyes or surprise them with a blow to the back of the head. Probably before I ever saw a horror film, I sat down with my family to watch *Tales of the Unexpected* on a Sunday night. This might have been my first experience of filmed horror, short twenty-minute bites with a nasty twist in the tail. And while horror fans grow to love the feature films and the franchises, the returning monsters, I think this is how most of us come to love horror—*The Twilight Zone*, *Goosebumps*, classic short stories—waiting in anticipation for *the* moment, whether it's a jump scare, a twist ending, or the feeling of release when the blade finally meets the blood. The short film offers that moment without any filler, and many horror films are a series of short films stitched together.

Wright: Generally, short films can be more cost effective and faster to produce. There are many factors that affect cost and production timelines, so this is speaking in very generic terms. If you are a first-time filmmaker and you do not have the funds or resources to make a feature film, making a short film can allow you to showcase your skills as a filmmaker in a more economical way. If you have a contained story that can be shot in one to two days and access to cast/crew who are willing to lend their time to your project, you can make a film and then use that as your calling card for more ambitious projects. This goes for all genres, not just horror.

Q: Does it seem like these films have substantive defining qualities or characteristics beyond the basic descriptive facts of "women-led horror"? If so, what are they?

Trudrung: I think that women-led horror is immersed in the idea of "smart horror." It's also very character driven and can be quite emotional and profound horror. I think women who make horror normally make personal horror. In terms of the type of horror scripts and films I have made, I would say I fit into this idea of "women-led horror." I tend to write about my personal fears and experiences, and most of my short films involve my children, who are both actors. So I can take a very personal fear from a parent's perspective and bring it to life. That can be both disturbing and hard for me, but also it's like lifting a weight off my chest. And it's truly rewarding to work with my daughters. My youngest is a budding FX makeup artist who has done a lot of her own makeup on my sets, and both girls are creative with rich imaginations. Neither one of them are lovers of horror though (not yet . . .).

Lee: What films? Does that mean "women-directed horror"? Horror films directed by women subvert the male gaze, which is the subjective view of male filmmakers and stories in a male-dominated industry. Not only are female characters in these films not viewed as sexual objects, but these characters have agency and motivations of their own. They're not simply pawns or devices to get male characters from point A to B.

Clarke: There are different voices at different festivals, and, ideally, every film has its own voice. I'm not sure that filmmakers should be singing in unison anyway. Certainly, we see recurrent themes that represent the elements of the female experience that are shared, if not universal: motherhood, sex from the female point of view, caring roles, the victim's experience of sexualized male violence, the female body, etc. That said, the themes of sex, violence, dominance, and responsibility are foundational themes of horror anyway. We shouldn't be surprised that women bring their experience to these themes. That the female perspective on these topics represents a fresh take is somewhat sad and certainly not something that I would want to be seen as a defining quality or characteristic of my work or of anyone else's work. The range and quality of films that women produce and that appear at "women-led" horror festivals is varied. There are derivative, by-the-numbers slasher flicks made out of love; there are experimental films and political screeds. In all, they amount to the breadth and variety of horror cinema. It seems to me that much less work has been put into identifying substantive defining qualities in "man-led" film than in films made by women and with just as much success. Certainly, the ways in which female socialization and industry sexism might differentiate female filmmakers from male filmmakers (for example, how they conduct themselves on set, how they are managed by producers and funders, etc.) are not necessarily evident on screen.

Wright: They should [have additional defining qualities]. It depends on the subject matter of the film and how the story is told. It's important to create visibility, but one thing women, and other disparaged groups, do not want is to be pandered. We do not want to exist in a vacuum. The defining qualities of any horror film, short or feature, should be irrelevant to the gender of the filmmaker.

Q: Do you think that the gendered experiences of women lead to unique work?

Trudrung: Yes. Absolutely yes. I was raised in the South. I was raised to be polite and respectful to the cost of my own confidence and independence. I feel that becoming a mother to two daughters forced me to learn to speak up and stand up not only for myself and my daughters but also for others who have experienced repression and sexism. I can remember so many times questioning myself because a man told me I was wrong, being flirted with or touched inappropriately by a superior, and demurring to avoid conflict because of lack of confidence. I think women carry our history within our hearts and minds, and there is also a current of anger at our current social and historical injustices. Women have unique, strong, and fierce voices, and horror is such an excellent way for us to express ourselves.

Lee: Our lives *are* horror, whether it's oppression, harassment, gendered violence, or just fill-in-the-blank. We're the perfect conduits to bring fictional horror to life. Besides, it's nice to see a different perspective on screen. Film is a vehicle for empathy.

Clarke: All human beings are different—but taking women as a class, there are experiences that are shared and that are not reflected in the dominant male experience and, therefore, on screen. However, if female filmmakers focus on female experiences, they are reaching for universals, not singularities. Unique work comes from an individual artist's aesthetic originality, their control of the language of film. For example, Anna Biller's work is unique and it's hyperfeminine, but that is not a condition of her being a female filmmaker. If female filmmakers focus on work that explores their female experience, the result will be works that share themes, motifs, and insights. Among those, there will be unique works by individual artists—their work informed by their female experience but not contingent on it.

Wright: This is a tricky question; I think it can. However, beyond gender, we all have our own unique experiences that lead to a certain perspective for the way we tell stories. For example, my own experiences aren't necessarily unique because I'm a woman, rather, because of so many other variables that contribute to the experience at hand. You could take something that is uniquely female, like giving birth; however, there are many women who have not given birth that would not be able to tell a story through that lens simply because they haven't experienced it. Thus, specifically female experiences aren't necessarily shared across gender. I've heard many say, "Oh, I'd love to see a woman direct this film; it would be great to see it from the female perspective." What does that even mean? I've seen work by women that is so misogynistic that one could assume it was created by a man, and I've found the opposite to be true as well. I am strongly in favor of fresh perspectives in storytelling, and I would really like to see more inclusion across the board. It's easy to fall into the rut of "this works; don't change it," and we get an influx of regurgitated stories. It's exciting to see creatives think outside of those boxes and color outside the lines a bit.

Q: What does the phrase or concept "women-led horror shorts" mean to you? In what ways does the phrase or concept "women-led horror shorts" make sense to you? In what ways does it fall short, if any?

Trudrung: This is a really good question. It's multifaceted of course. I love embracing "women in horror" because it is a genre that women are underrepresented in and are fighting to make our voices heard. We bring a fresh perspective to the horror genre, and it's important that the uniqueness of women-led horror shorts find their following and voice. The goal would be that we wouldn't need a label of any sort. That men, women, LGBTQIA would all not need a label in the horror world. We would all just be horror filmmakers or writers.

Lee: It's a spotlight, but it's also a form of ghettoization until we've reached gender parity and we're simply looked at as "filmmakers."

Clarke: To me, it means what it says: horror shorts led by women. "Led by" means directed by, for, although film is a collaborative art form with many departments and contributors, the film itself is mediated from start to finish by the director (excepting interfering funders and executive producers). The director is the film's custodian until its release. When we talk of "women-led" films, we should talk only of those films actually led by women—directed by them—where the film is led wherever the woman, as an artist, wants to take it. A "woman-led horror short" is not led by female subject matter; it is not led by our feminist goals; it is led by the woman who makes it, however she makes it. The meaning should be small but significant. Perhaps film does a disservice by focusing on the director, making invisible the contributions of female screenwriters, editors, producers, etc. Although hidden, the impact of women such as Alma Hitchcock and Thelma Schoonmaker—in the roles of script and film editors—is undeniable. But we want to see films led by women, not because women are already invaluable in cinematic storytelling, but because we want them to be visible and credited. Credit and visibility go to those at the helm.

Wright: I interpret "women-led horror shorts" to generally mean one of two things: that the story is heavily focused on the journey or experiences of female characters or that the story itself was perhaps written and directed by a woman. Where this term could fall short is that the focus of the film now becomes all about the gender of the characters or filmmaker and less about the story. If the story is about a group of women who get trapped in a cave and discover a terrifying species that targets them one by one and kills them, are we, the audience, thinking about this terrifying experience, who or what these creatures are, or are we sitting in the theater thinking, "Hmmm, this cast is all women; there are no men—*groundbreaking!*"? I think it's important to think about how you want to label or market yourself and your films. Also, whether or not you want the focus on you or your work. Do you want to be known as a female filmmaker or simply a filmmaker? Is your film about a woman's journey or simply your character's journey? The other side of this is that the industry is hungry for new and emerging talent, and if being a filmmaker who is female helps you stand out from the crowd and gets eyes on your project, the better for your project and all involved. Many film festivals are actively seeking more diverse and inclusive programming, so if there is something unique about you, your crew, or your cast, add that information to your marketing strategy.

Q: In your experience, is there a community of women horror film-makers? If so, how does that community interact with, overlap with, or resist the wider horror filmmaking community?

Trudrung: There is absolutely a community of women horror film-makers. I have attended several women in horror film festivals and have formed quite a network of friends and acquaintances in the industry. It's a very supportive community. There are numerous women filmmakers that are seriously kicking butt in the horror industry, and they are an inspiration. Quite honestly though there are an incredible amount of men and nonbinary people in the horror community that are huge supporters of the women-led horror community. I love it. I feel that horror as a whole brings creative people together because fear and being scared is such a universal and fun experience. It brings back a kind of childlike innocence. Reminds of us our first roller coaster ride in some ways. So I would say overall the horror filmmaker/writer pool is super supportive.

Lee: There is a community of women horror filmmakers. I started call-ing us #coven online, and it's caught on with many of us. We see each other at the same film festivals; we're part of the same online groups and directors' organizations. We don't see ourselves as any different from male horror filmmakers, except that we have more obstacles in our path. That's changing a little, but institutional bias means that many of us will be much farther away down the career ladder or away from our goals than men in our peer group.

Clarke: I think there are several communities that exist in much the same space. There is a community of women filmmakers who make films, many of them making horror films. This is a mostly supportive and encouraging group, conscious of the challenges and obstacles that women face in this industry. However, as with all human communities, it is not always coherent or harmonious. Why would it be? How could it be? The group exists not through the will of the members but because filmmakers who are female exist. There is a concurrent community comprised of people with an interest in the former group as a coherent entity. Many in this community are, understandably, female horror film-makers, but they are also academics and film-lovers, many of them men. For them, the female horror filmmaker is an observable phenomenon, in which they take a positive interest, concerned with the group as much as any individual. There is also, of course, the inverse of this: a community that takes exception to the female filmmaker as a category of special interest. There are probably other variations. In my experience of the horror community—on the surface anyway—their main consideration is the horror itself. But it is difficult to talk of one's experience in the community of women horror filmmakers because you are invariably part of a discourse over which you don't have control. It is a community but also, sometimes, a ghetto. Sometimes it feels like a demerit, while we are also being told that it is a selling point.

Wright: There is a huge community of female horror filmmakers who are integrated nicely into the wider horror community. We may still be in the minority, but I have not seen any resistance to letting us in. This is speaking in reference to indie filmmaking, as this is where I exist. I couldn't answer this in reference to the larger, studio part of the industry, as I don't have firsthand experience in that arena. As a consumer of films, I would like to see more progress being made beyond the indie level. We still have a long road ahead, but great strides are being made and progress is actively happening.

Q: Can you talk about the experience at film festivals for women-led horror shorts? Do you experience festivals as community-building events?

Trudrung: Yes, women-in-horror-centric film festivals are the absolute *best*. And yes, talk about female power and strength in numbers: these festivals are truly a love fest and huge support system for women creatives. I've been so impressed with the quality of work I have seen at these women-centric horror film festivals. Don't get me wrong: I also love horror film festivals that aren't women centric, but there is something truly special about these film festivals that choose to celebrate female filmmakers, writers, and actresses. There is a level of comfort and support that isn't always at other festivals.

Lee: Yeah, we become more friendly at film festivals. We're away from home, and we end up bonding, hanging out, going to each other's films. Sometimes we become collaborators and make some pretty cool things together.

Clarke: I was lucky in that my first experience of a women-led horror festival was the inaugural Women in Horror Film Festival in Atlanta in 2017. In terms of open, welcoming events, it was exceptional. There was a definite sense of community there and a will to make the festival—and its attendees—succeed. I made friends and supporters at that festival who have and will remain great friends and whose support has been a great help in my career. My short film *Childer* played at WIHFF, as well as many other international festivals, taking prizes at festivals with a female focus and those without. However, it was clear that, in the first instance, festivals with a female focus related to and recognized the power and horror in its theme: the pressures of motherhood and bodily autonomy. The film's appeal was not limited to a female audience, but positive reception at these festivals gave it credibility moving on, overcoming some barriers that a female-helmed short might face. It is now available through the Alter short film platform, where it has 1.5 million views. Not all festivals—whether women-led or not—have quite the same friendly atmosphere as that first WIHFF. Most film fests are still competitions, so they have a competitive air. However, horror festivals in general are community-building, even the bigger ones. As they get bigger, the community grows more diffuse, and one finds filmmakers and audience separated further and further. However, the biggest horror festivals retain some element of purpose and passion for horror, which distinguishes them from the cool, detached mainstream and industry festivals.

Wright: I definitely feel that festivals can be community-building events, depending on the atmosphere of the fest, that is. Programmers and fest directors that take the time to put the filmmakers and screenwriters first generally create a great sense of community. It boils down to the people. If you're putting energy into an event that creates a sense of welcome, that you are honoring someone else's art to the best of your abilities, this is where magic happens. Whatever you put out is exactly what you are going to attract. If you are building an event to create inclusion, to create visibility, to create balance, to create relationships and connect artists to other artists . . . that's an event I want to be a part of.

Q: How does social media (as another potential source of community/ networking/marketing) intersect with/overlap with/resist the in-person dynamic of film festivals?

Trudrung: I think if you can attend a film festival, that is a much better way to truly connect with fellow creatives. There isn't much better than meeting someone and sitting with them in a theater and experiencing great horror with them. And you take that connection, and it lasts through the disconnection that social media can sometimes bring. Face-to-face is always better. But it does cost money to attend if the festivals aren't local to where you live, so you do have to pick and choose. I have made many connections through attending film festivals that have led to community networking with people I haven't met in person also though.

Lee: It's simply a continuation of friendship and networking. It helps us keep in touch. It's nice to fill in the gaps between festivals because that can be a long time for some of us.

Clarke: If used in a natural manner, I think that social media can be more "in-person" than a film festival. On social media, you are communicating as yourself, contributing to conversations as yourself, rather than being a part of a panel or a screening block. There is still the sense of a community, but it is a community as a living thing, existing in real time, rather than a group that materializes in various locations throughout the year.

Wright: Social media can be a very valuable tool for both filmmakers and festivals. It's used by employers and schools as a way to check out prospects. It matters how you behave on social media. It can be a dangerous tool if not used properly, but I'll stick to some of the more positive aspects. Everyone uses social media in one way or another, so finding the right type of social media and using it properly can really help spread the word about your event or your work as an artist. For my festival, we have utilized social media to promote the artists and supporters involved with us. We even set up a closed, private group on Facebook that allows selected artists to connect before the event in order to make attending more relaxed. By the time our event rolls around, you already know many of the people there and a bit about their work, and it creates a very supportive and friendly environment. As a filmmaker myself, I have attended festivals before where I don't know a single person, and it can be daunting to meet a room full of strangers. By using social media in this way, attendees at WIHFF have an opportunity to meet and get to know each other before the event.

Q: What has your experience been with regard to seeking and/or securing work in commercial filmmaking? Have you been instantly disadvantaged (as a woman or otherwise) by Hollywood's power structures?

Trudrung: I'm not going to have the best answer for this, as I'm relatively new to the commercial world of filmmaking and screenwriting. I've been making small low-budget short films for about five years and definitely had it on my radar that one of my short films could be "discovered" or go viral and my career could gain momentum that way, and that hasn't happened. And I don't think that has anything to do with my gender. I think it's hard for any indie filmmaker and writer to "make it" commercially. I think within the horror community you hear more about male upcoming filmmakers because it's still a male-dominated genre. I again feel this is changing, and I'm excited to be part of the change. I will add that my experience with *The Bewailing*, a feature screenplay I wrote that is currently a feature film in postproduction and due to have its theatrical release this fall, was interesting in regard to this question, though. I was approached by a local production company and asked if I had any feature screenplays that would fit an ultra-low budget SAG (Screen Actors Guild) feature film model. I know they had requested screenplays from numerous other writers, and the two previous films they had produced were both by male screenwriters. I feel that the producer not only liked my screenplay enough to make it but was also motivated to work with a female screenwriter in order to bring a different feel/story to the films his company wants to make. I think that female, minority, and LGBTQ+ filmmakers bring a uniqueness to the table in the horror commercial film-making world because the male-centric gaze has been leveled there for so long. We are a fresh, strong, and powerful voice in the horror genre, and I feel that it's our time to take the reins.

Lee: I've been actively trying to "do it right" and access funds to make a feature for the last four years out of nearly eight that I've been making short films. Men tell me again and again (when do they not tell women anything?) that it's a good time to be a woman filmmaker because now they can't get meetings and we're the "hot commodity" that production companies look for—a new voice from an oppressed segment of society. It's laughable because while I've been able to have a few general meetings, for the most part, it doesn't seem that these studios and production companies really mean it, that they're being shamed into hiring a woman. So be it. Hire us, you cowards. It's way past time for any of us to be hired. I understand that being a filmmaker is an extraordinarily hard path; I do. I don't begrudge my male peers their success, no matter how well-earned . . . or not, in many cases. I don't know if I've ever actually been taken seriously, and I'm tired as hell of this. Whether they realize it or not, men have been erasing our voices and our names from history. It's time that it's stopped.

Clarke: I find myself attached to lots of projects to write and direct. Some of those projects are with producers who specifically want to work with female filmmakers and others who have no particular interest in that at all. Given the way in which a lot of development is funded in Europe, there are plenty of funding programs now focused on female representation. This is a positive and a negative—it presents opportunities in which your being female is an advantage, rather than a disadvantage, but there is the feeling sometimes that you could be any female director and that the project comes from the opportunity to access the money more than to work with you as an artist. They like your work, otherwise they wouldn't have asked you, but the primary reason they've approached you is because you're a woman and this or that opportunity is for women. In America, where there is no public funding, the process is different. There are certainly producers who want to work with female directors, for whatever reason: personal integrity, optics, or an eye on the market. They dream of the perfect female-led vehicle. However, it's hard for them to get their dream. When it comes to it and they have to put trust and money down, they don't. As we see time and time again, the more perceived risk there is—i.e., the higher the budget is—the more likely it is that producers and studios will go with a male director. When I was studying film, I was told by someone in the industry that I didn't have the "right personality to be a director," which meant commanding, domineering, single-minded, loud, stubborn, obsessive: masculine. The archetypal Director with a baseball cap, loudspeaker, and a bad attitude. I was making good work and getting top grades, but many of the traits that serve me very well as a filmmaker—kindness, thoughtfulness, a cool head under pressure—were read as negatives because they didn't fit the mold. Human beings respond to archetypes, even while we think we are above that. We've all seen it happen that a male peer in the industry is given trust automatically, whereas females in the industry must work to earn that trust. Men are often assumed to be competent unless they prove otherwise. There are so many examples of men being given the keys to studio franchises and big-budget movies after just making perhaps a couple of shorts—I don't know that this has ever happened to a woman. There are plenty of people who hold the ideal of working with a female director, but, when it comes to it, mostly subconsciously, a female doesn't meet their ideal of a director. A lot of work has to be done to dismantle this subconscious bias around what a director "is." I also find myself frequently offered scripts, written by male writers, about pregnant female characters or female characters that become pregnant magically or female characters that were pregnant, had babies, and must protect them or had babies but lost them and must overcome the grief. Or stories about women who are the victims of male violence—some of whom seek revenge! Those stories are important and sometimes they even are written by female writers, but when they fall in the lap of production companies, the producers know they have to play it safe: if this script isn't directed by a female filmmaker, the production will come under criticism. Film history is already littered with films that display a male director's cack-handed understanding of a female's experience. The result of this is the continued ghettoization of female filmmakers—their share of scripts and job offers is heavily filtered through this political negotiation. Some of this comes from personal experience; some is anecdotal from conversations with other female filmmakers. I don't know that it amounts to being instantly disadvantaged, but you certainly recognize patterns of difficulties that female filmmakers have to get around. Sometimes these obstacles are purely on an individual level; sometimes they are informed by the current political conversation. However, the same is true of the benefits of being a filmmaker—sometimes it helps on a personal level; sometimes it just feeds into the discourse.

Wright: This is a tough one to answer from personal experience, as I haven't been actively seeking to secure any commercial work yet. I am very new, as far as writing and directing are concerned, and I'm still trying to build a body of work. I haven't directed a feature film yet, and it's next to impossible to land a commercial feature directing gig without a proven body of work or some professional connections. I think it's tough for all indie filmmakers to break out into commercial/studio work, regardless of gender. However, if you look at the percentage of male directors making the leap from indie to commercial, you'll notice a huge disparity in the percentage of women making that same leap. The end goal is balance and equality. Women should be able to both fail and succeed at the same rate as their male counterparts. We just aren't there yet, but I'm hopeful.

ANALYSIS

As we can see from these interviews, there are various perspectives regarding the category "women-led horror shorts," and indeed there are various points of view on whether this is a question of sex, gender, both, or neither. Some acknowledge that such films exist but that the category is not meaningfully different from any other person-led horror shorts. Perhaps more to the point, there is general agreement that there shouldn't be any considerable difference, and insisting upon it goes some way toward reifying the sorts of gaps we might otherwise wish to eliminate. We often read that a primary goal is simply to be received as a horror filmmaker and not a variously gendered or otherwise identified filmmaker. However, there are some who embrace the concept "women-led horror shorts" as valuable and meaningful. For them, their identity and how that identity exists within various wider power relations is an integral part of the way that they see and produce their art. For instance, both Lee and Trudrung mention the ways that living as a woman inside the wider power structure is itself to partake of horror. From this point of view, we might go so far as to suggest that women horror filmmakers could have a more intimate understanding of horror as an emotional and aesthetic experience than their male peers.

One of the things that struck me most forcefully about these answers is the line drawn both implicitly and explicitly between independent and studio-driven filmmaking. On the independent side of the line, there is often (if not always) a welcoming and supportive community of filmmakers that is seemingly eager to broaden representation among artists. All of the interviewees talk about the sorts of connections and benefits that they have found as part of both local filmmaking communities as well as broader independent film and horror film communities through festivals and social media. Trudrung and Wright in particular speak in very positive terms about the shared sense of purpose and mutual reinforcement of effort among the indie horror filmmakers with whom they work. And yet there is also a clear sense from both Clarke and Lee that, while the independent community may well be more supportive and collaborative than Hollywood, there are still significant hurdles facing a woman who wants to move into commercial filmmaking (Lauzen 2019; 2020). Clarke points out that European funding models encourage a certain level of better hiring behavior in this regard, but that specific pots of money for hiring women directors does not translate into equal professional respect. Lee is even more direct in calling out the more or less hollow claims that it is a good time to be a woman filmmaker in Hollywood right now. If it is such a good time, as these claims insist, then why are there still such massive inequities in the employment of men and women in film (both independent and studio-driven)? Where are the opportunities for talented and capable women?

It may still be the case that the road to greater gender equality in horror film production may be paved with the efforts of independent women horror filmmakers. Due to their relatively low cost and short turnaround time on production, short horror films are one of the most accessible opportunities for women directors finding their way into commercial filmmaking. The short screenplay for Aislínn Clarke's *Childer* follows this chapter. As the filmmakers interviewed here have highlighted in different ways, the restrictions on resources, duration, and intended effect often serve to motivate bold aesthetic choices. In a short that successfully delivers on the intended horror effect, bold aesthetic choices also help the filmmaker stand out from the crowd. In addition to making short horror films, direct efforts to promote more women in the filmmaking community can have real effects. The Women in Horror Film Festival, founded in 2016 by Vanessa Ionta Wright and Samantha Kolesnik, is just one example of a platform offering a bright spotlight for up-and-coming horror auteurs. Trudrung discusses how her feature screenplay for *The Bewailing* was picked up by a local production company, which prior to that time had worked primarily with male writers. And while Clarke does acknowledge the double-edged sword of women-centered funding opportunities, the fact does remain that funding models do fund real work that allows women film professionals to showcase their talent and hard work.

Horror films have long been a genre that blurs the lines between studio and independent fare, allowing some filmmakers to achieve big-budget commercial success without necessarily requiring front-end studio involvement. Horror films, and specifically horror short films, may offer a singular opportunity on the border between these categories. Relative to studio tentpoles, especially in an era lacking studio-backed mid-sized films, feature horror films are most often lower-budget entries into the market, making it easier for them to achieve commercial success by having a lower bar (in real dollars) in terms of profitability within the context of a genre that is still popular with audiences. While this success is never guaranteed, horror and similar genre films have long been considered among the better bets when it comes to low-budget financing. In particular, horror films can often find success without name actors, which is generally a tougher sell in other genres. These factors make it more likely that early-career filmmakers in the independent horror field could produce low-budget films that either garner enough success to be profitable on their own (in the case of features) or attract the attention of producers in search of new talented filmmakers who can helm profitable features or series (in the case of shorts or features). If this path can actually be an effective way for women filmmakers to find more opportunities at higher budget levels, then their visions and voices can take their rightful places in an increasingly global motion picture culture.

It is important to remember that filmmaking remains a tremendously difficult and expensive enterprise, despite the digital revolution putting powerful tools into the hands of almost anyone with an interest in the craft. Economic, social, and political barriers still exist for many filmmakers, and gender forms only one axis of potential difficulty, even while it also exists as a profound source of inspiration. However, the insights and lessons learned by one group of people will hopefully be of use not only to others in similar positions but also to people grappling with different trials and tribulations. This is especially true if those challenges arise from a wider power structure that places the artist at an instant disadvantage. Still, while positive changes in the proportions of gender representation in both the independent and Hollywood film worlds are frustratingly gradual, the grit, talent, vision, and spirit of collaboration displayed by these four horror filmmakers and their peers are encouraging signs that these improvements will nevertheless persist.

BIBLIOGRAPHY

Clarke, Aislínn. 2020. Interview by Brian Hauser. May 12, 2020. Google Doc.
Lauzen, Martha M. "The Celluloid Ceiling: Behind-the-Scenes Employment of Women on the Top 100, 250, and 500 Films of 2019." Center for the Study of Women in Television & Film, 2000. https://womenintvfilm.sdsu.edu/wp-content/uploads/2020/01/2019_Celluloid_Ceiling_Report.pdf.
———. "Indie Women: Behind-the-Scenes Employment of Women in Independent Film, 2018–19." Center for the Study of Women in Television & Film, 2019. https://womenintvfilm.sdsu.edu/wp-content/uploads/2019/06/2018-19_Indie_Women_Report.pdf.
Lee, Izzy. Interview by Brian Hauser. May 12, 2020. Google Doc.
Trudrung, Jennifer. Interview by Brian Hauser. May 2, 2020. Google Doc.
Wright, Vanessa Ionta. Interview by Brian Hauser. May 13, 2020. Google Doc.

CHILDER

Written by

Aislinn Clarke

AUDIO ON BLACK -

The tinkling of a child's musical nightlight. The soft voices
of a bedtime tuck in. Mark is 7 years old.

                    MARK
          Where do childer come from?

                    MARY
          Children come from a cabbage
          patch at the bottom of the garden.

EXT. FOREST AT FOOT OF THE GARDEN - DAY

Cabbage patch. A garden spike reads CABBAGES. A green forest
presses against the edge of the garden.

So much green. Living green. Leaves blow gently in a slight
breeze. Behind them the forest is darker and darker and then
darker again. Something SCUFFLES amongst the darker thickets
towards the back. A SCURRYING sound and then a SINISTER
GIGGLE.

A leaf lands at a woman's polished shoe as she stands on her
very neat lawn, a lawn that's surrounded by thick forest.

She picks the leaf up and SCRUNCHES it to death.

Mary is 36. Very neatly presented. Her clothes are ironed and
starched impeccably. Her shoes shine. She marches over to the
bin and puts the dead leaf in it. She casts a look at the
forest beyond her garden and we see one boy, then another,
then a snot-nosed girl peering between branches.

She turns on her heel and goes into the house.

INT. HALLWAY - DAY

Mary brushes non-existent mud off her shoes in the hall. Mark
bounds out of the living room holding an empty jam jar in one
hand and bouncing a GREEN BOUNCY BALL in the other.

                    MARK
          Can I go outside to play?

                    MARY
          No.

                    MARK
          But I have to collect mini beasts
          for school tomorrow and you said I
          can't have them in the house.

                    MARY
          Ok, but stay beside the house and
          don't go near those children.

Mark peers out the window.

                    MARK
          Childer? Where.

                    MARY
          There are strange children in the
          forest. Don't go near them. They
          are dirty.

DING DONG. The doorbell rings. Mary JUMPS. Mary slowly opens
the door. Mark peers at the door from behind the staircase
banisters.

It is the postman, Mr Cooper. He is kind-faced and gentle-
looking. He holds out a package in brown paper.

                    MR COOPER
          A wee delivery here for you.

Printed on it are the words "Mystery Book of the Month Club".
Mary takes the package.

He hands her a pad and pen.

                    MR COOPER (CONT'D)
          Sign here please.

She signs.

                    MR COOPER (CONT'D)
          It's a good one this month. You
          know, we have a little book group
          that meets in the library, third
          Tuesday each month, and we discuss
          that month's book. We have wine and
          biscuits...

Mary hands him back the pad and pen.

                    MARY
          I don't drink wine.

                    MR COOPER
          Or coffee if you'd prefer...we call
          it 'Bodies in the Library' ha ha!

                    MARY
          Caffeine gives me migraines.

There is a slight awkward pause. Mary starts to close the
door.

>   MARY (CONT'D)
>   Thank you. I have to go.

Mr Cooper NODS. He then notices Mark behind the banisters and
salutes at him.

>   MR COOPER
>   Alright Chief.

Mark waves back as Mary SHUTS the door.

INT. KITCHEN - DAY

Mary stands chopping red cabbage by the sink. She CHOPS
neatly with an expression of focus. She scoops the chopped
cabbage into a bowl and cleans the worktop. She washes the
cabbage. Some reddish cabbage water splashes on the floor.
She gets down on her hands and knees and cleans it. She then
washes her hands. She washes them again. She dries them.
Again she turns on the tap but stops herself.

She puts her hand to her face, weary.

>   MARK
>   I'm hungry.

Mary JUMPS at his voice.

>   MARY
>   Ok I'll get you something now. Wash
>   your hands.

INT. KITCHEN - DAY

Mark is eating a boiled egg and soldiers. His GREEN BOUNCY
BALL sits on the table beside him. He DUNKS buttery
'soldiers' into the runny egg. Mary watches this process
closely with a faraway look on her face.

>   MARK
>   Mrs Grey says there is a baby in
>   her tummy. So we are going to have
>   to get a new teacher.

Mary is knocked out of her daydream by his voice. Mark chews
on the egg and soldier.

>   MARY
>   Don't make a mess...

                    MARK
          But how did the baby get into her
          tummy?

Mary watches him dunk another soldier and raise it, dripping
with egg.

                    MARY
          Be careful. That's messy.

Mark chews and looks at the chopped heads of cabbage on the
worktop.

                    MARK
          Does the mummy...eat them?

Mary SIGHS.

                    MARY
          Don't be silly.

Mark dips a soldier in the runny egg. His voice gets far away
as Mary stares at the action of him dunking and then chewing
eggy soldiers. He babbles about needing to bring a jar to
school for frogspawn tomorrow because they have to grow frog
babies.

Mark drips a spot of yellow yolk on the table as he speaks.
This snaps Mary back to the present moment and Mark's speech
becomes clear again. Mary stares at the drip.

                    MARK
          Was I in your tummy one time? Eww
          Would it not be all blood and guts
          in there?

                    MARY
          I told you to be careful! That's
          disgusting. Don't be disgusting!

Mark recoils as Mary scrubs at the drip with a cloth.

                    MARK
          I'm sorry mummy, I'm sorry...

She looks at his trembling face and sighs. Her face softens.

                    MARY
          It's not your fault. I'm sorry.

EXT. GARDEN - DAY

Mary hangs clean white sheets on the line. Mark is playing
with a tennis racquet that has a ball attached to it by a
string.

The Childer lurk in the forest beyond the garden.

A SINISTER SNIGGER attracts Mary's attention to the trees.
The sheets FLAP in the gentle breeze.

A RED BALL flies out of the forest and lands at her feet. It
lands in the mud and SPLASHES one of the clean white sheets.
Mary turns to face the forest.

                    MARY
          Get away from here!

No one can be seen. A muddy rock hits another sheet with a
WET SPLAT.

The Childer GIGGLE. Mary marches towards the forest, furious.

INT. FOREST - DAY

Mary peers through the trees. It is darker in the forest
because the canopy of trees blocks out so much light. A
GIGGLE behind her makes her spin around. We see a child
disappear behind a tree.

Another GIGGLE makes her spin the other way.

                    MARY
          Stay away from us.

She says this to no one we can see. There is a responding
GIGGLE.

She CLENCHES HER FISTS. A BUZZING FLY lands on her cheek. She
SLAPS it off.

                    MARY (CONT'D)
          Just stay away.

There is no one to be seen. She turns and leaves the forest.

INT. GARDEN - DAY

She walks back towards the house. Mark is no longer at the
tennis ball pole. The front door is wide open.

Mary quickens her step towards the house.

A GIGGLE comes from inside. She stops and then runs.

There is a spot of blood on the front step.

INT. HALLWAY - DAY

There are DRIPS of blood all along the hall leading to the kitchen.

Another GIGGLE.

Mary rushes to the kitchen.

INT. KITCHEN - DAY

Mark GIGGLES as Mr Cooper speaks quietly to him. Mark is sitting on the worktop. His mouth is bleeding. Mary stands aghast in the doorway.

>   MARK
>   Look! I lost a tooth!

Mr Cooper holds a small baby tooth in his hand.

>   MR COOPER
>   I'm afraid young Mark here got into
>   the wars with that tennis ball.

He smiles. Mary stares at him.

>   MR COOPER (CONT'D)
>   I'm sorry for coming in...he was
>   crying.

Pause.

>   MARY
>   There is blood all over the
>   floor...

>   MR COOPER
>   But he's ok now, aren't you son?

Mary stares at the blood on the floor.

>   MARK
>   Mr Cooper my teacher is having a
>   baby so you could be our teacher!
>   It's better than being a postman
>   because you can do painting
>   everyday.

Mr Cooper smiles at Mark then at Mary. She does not smile back.

>   MR COOPER
>   I'm sorry...I just...

Mary stands to one side to make space for Mr Cooper to walk through the door.

Mr Cooper looks at the door and nods. He lifts his post bag.

>   MR COOPER (CONT'D)
>   Your letters are on the table.
>   (to mark)
>   Bye now son.

He nods at Mary as he passes.

>   MR COOPER (CONT'D)
>   Bye now.

She turns her head away as he leaves.

INT. BATHROOM - NIGHT

Mary is in the bath. We can hear a kid's TV programme from the other room.

Mary looks absent-mindedly at her red fingernails as her hand floats just under the blue/green surface of the water. The taps DRIPS into the bath.

We are close on Mary's face. She looks down into the water and raises a hand. There is blood on her fingertips.

Mary gets out of the bath quickly, as though panicked.

Mary stands in the bathroom shivering in a towel as though she has just had a quick escape.

In the bath tendrils of blood float on the blue/green surface. Mary PULLS the plug. The water GARGLES down the drain.

INT. KITCHEN - DAY

A calendar reads October 30th. Mark sits at the table eating breakfast.

Mary stands by the sink staring out the window. The Childer are playing in the trees in the forest at the bottom of the garden. The trees are leafy and green.

               MARY
It's nearly November. Why aren't
they dead yet?

Mark is humming to himself as he eats.

               MARY (CONT'D)
I'm sick of picking up leaves.

Mark pipes up.

               MARK
Can I dress up for Halloween?

               MARY
No. Halloween is dangerous.

Mark SIGHS.

               MARK
But all the other Childer...
     (quickly corrects himself)
...children are!

Mary looks at him. Suspicious.

               MARY
What children?

               MARK
At school. We are having a dress-up
day.

Mary thinks.

               MARY
I can make you a ghost? We have
lots of white sheets.

               MARK
I don't want to be a ghost. I want
to be a fireman or a superhero or a
knight or a soldier or at least a
dinosaur. Ghosts are for girls.

Mary looks at him bemused.

               MARY
Ghosts are not for girls. Ghosts
are for everyone.

Mark rolls his eyes. He's resigned to it.

> MARK
> Ok, fine. I'll be a ghost.

Mary raises her eyebrows at him.

> MARY
> Did I hear a thank you?

> MARK
> Thanks Mar...mammy.

There is a KNOCK at the door.

INT. HALLWAY - DAY

Mary answers the door. Five scruffy CHILDER stand there.
Their noses are snotty, faces dirty, and clothes covered in
mud and what might be baked beans smeared on jumpers. There
is a moment of hesitation and then a RIBBIT.

A little girl holds out her hand. There is a frog on it.

> GIRL
> If you kiss him, he will be a
> prince.

Mary looks at her incredulously. A boy pipes up.

> BOY
> Our big sister kissed a frog once
> but she's dead now.

One of the Childer touches the doorframe and leaves a SMEAR
of something on the clean paint. Mary SHUDDERS.

> MARY
> Get away from here this instant.

They SNIGGER and run away, leaving the frog on the step.

RIBBIT.

INT. BATHROOM - EVENING

Mary is cleaning the bath. A young green-leafed tendril
appears to be growing out of the plug hole. She stares at it
in disbelief before plucking it out and pouring bleach down
the drain.

INT. BEDROOM - NIGHT

Mary is sleeping. The window is open. One of her legs is outside of the sheets. A thin tendril of green with a little leaf at the end wraps around her painted toe. The tendril travels up her foot, ankle, and leg gently. She STIRS in her sleep. The tendril travels up across her knee and then to her inner thigh. She SIGHS in her sleep and then WAKES UP. She SCREAMS as branches hold her arms down on the bed and further tendrils shoot up under the sheet. Mary SCREAMS.

We pan out to reveal that her bed is in the middle of the forest.

Mary WAKES UP in her own room. She is drenched in sweat and panting. She pulls back the white sheets and of course there is nothing there.

EXT. GARDEN. - DAWN

It's very early in the morning. Mary is outside using a hand held DustBuster to hoover up any forest debris from the perimeter of her garden.

INT. KITCHEN - DAY

The calendar reads OCTOBER 31st. Mary is putting Mark into his ghost sheet.

He wriggles.

                    MARK
          I don't like it.

Mary TUTS.

                    MARY
          Don't be rude. I went to a lot of
          trouble to make that for you.

The costume is on. It's quite cute with big round eyeholes and a round mouth drawn on with sharpie. A quote bubble points to the mouth. "Boo!" it says.

                    MARY (CONT'D)
          Lovely!

                    MARK
          I don't want to be lovely. I want
          to be scary.

                    MARY
          It is scary. Very scary.

Mark looks down at himself and holds the sides of the costume
out.

                    MARK
          It's basically a dress. I wanted to
          be a spaceman.

                    MARY
          I thought you said you wanted to be
          scary?

Mark spins in a circle going "Boooooooo!". His sheet fans out
around him. He seems to be happy enough with his costume now.

                    MARK
          Can we bob for apples later?

                    MARY
          Maybe. Now go and play.

Mark starts running off.

                    MARY (CONT'D)
          Don't get dirty!

INT. BEDROOM - DAY

Mary is putting away neatly folded and ironed sheets.

She hears CHILDER GIGGLING outside.

She looks out the window and sees Mark running in circles in
the garden making spooky "WOOOOOOO!" sounds as his sheet
floats around him in the air.

The Childer can be seen in the trees, hanging from branches
and climbing. They are like an organic part of the forest.
They belong there. One of the boys WHISTLES and mark looks at
them. They beckon to him.

Mary RUNS downstairs.

INT. HALLWAY - DAY

She THROWS open the front door and Mark is nowhere to be
seen. She stands panting on the doorstep and then enters the
garden.

EXT. GARDEN - DAY

It is starting to get dark. Mary stands in the garden.

                              MARY
                    Mark?! Mark?!

Distant GIGGLING can be heard coming from the trees. Mary
gingerly approaches the trees.

A leaf lands on the neat grass.

She pauses on the edge of the neat garden and takes a
decisive STEP across to the wilder forest.

EXT. FOREST - DAY TO NIGHT

The first is WILD and ALIVE. Green living things surround
mary. It is unnaturally quiet. She follows the sound of
GIGGLING but never quite reaches it. The forest darkens
around her.

                              MARY
                      Mark? Mark?

No answer. She shivers and pulls her cardigan tighter.

Sounds begin to build up in the forest.

An owl HOOTS.

A breeze RUSTLES TREES.

A stream BABBLES.

More and more of the organic sounds of the forest build up
until the sound of nature there is deafening.

Mary covers her ears with her hands and SCREAMS.

INT. HALLWAY - NIGHT

Mary SLAMS the door behind herself and PANTS heavily.

She looks down at herself. Her clothes are dirty. Her tights
are torn.

She strips off as though her life depends on it.

INT. BATHROOM - NIGHT

Mary SCRUBS HERSELF RAW in the bath. She scrubs her arm so
hard it bleeds. Drops of blood swirl in the water.

INT. KITCHEN - NIGHT

Mary, wearing a dressing gown, stares at the washing machine
and the clothes roll around and around in suds.

From offscreen the front door CLOSES. Mary stops what she's
doing and looks up.

INT. HALLWAY - NIGHT

Mark stands there in the hallway. He is dirty from head to
toe. His nose is snotty. The ghost sheet is ripped and
filthy. He holds it in his hands. He and his mother stare at
one another.

                    MARY
          Come upstairs this instant and get
          washed. You are FILTHY!

INT. BATHROOM - NIGHT

Mark sits in the bath. Mary kneels beside him and scrubs at
his arm. He flinches in pain.

                    MARY
          Didn't I tell you not to play with
          those children? Didn't I tell you?
          Didn't I tell you not to play with
          those Children?!

She is furious. Terrifying to the child. Her eyes are wild.
She scrubs him till he bleeds.

                    MARK
          Mammy...mammy!

She stops and looks at him.

                    MARY
               (softer voice)
          I told you not to play with those
          Childer.

Then, suddenly. She GRABS HIM and PUSHES HIM under the water.
He KICKS and STRUGGLES.

                    MARY (CONT'D)
          Filthy! Filthy! Dirty BOY!

The camera slowly backs out of the room as Mary drowns Mark
and he continues to struggle.

The camera backs all the way down the stairs. We can hear the struggling continue. SPLASHING and Mary's exerted BREATHING.

The camera ends on a bowl filled with water and bobbing red apples. The struggling from upstairs stops. Silence.

EXT. CABBAGE PATCH - NIGHT

Mary PANTS with exertion. Her face is dirty.

She PATS a shovel on the earth on a finished shallow grave. It's a very neat grave. A little garden spike reads 'CABBAGES'. She pauses and wipes the sweat from her brow.

A GIGGLE echoes from behind her. She turns and walks, seeking the giggler.

EXT. GARDEN - NIGHT

The giggler is nowhere to be seen. She goes back to the house. Her clothes and skin are filthy.

INT. BATHROOM - NIGHT

Mary EMPTIES the bath and SCRUBS IT. She refills it and empties the bottle of bleach into the bath. She scrubs herself with the bleachy water.

INT. BEDROOM - NIGHT

Mary stands in front of the mirror. Scrubbed to within an inch of her life. She is now dressed and neat again. She puts a final hair back in place. And examines herself in the mirror. She sits on the bed and smoothes the neat white sheets.

There is a FLAT THUD and then a distant GIGGLE. Mary turns towards the door.

INT. HALLWAY - NIGHT

Another THUD. Mary opens the front door. Mark's green bouncy ball lies on the step. It is covered in mud.

GIGGLES.

Mary looks up at the forest straight ahead.

The Childer wind in between foliage and tree branches. One of them is Mark in his ghost costume, now covered in mud.

EXT. CABBAGE PATCH - NIGHT

The ground is disturbed. The grave is empty.

EXT. HOUSE - NIGHT

Mary stands motionless in the doorway as the Childer giggle in the forest beyond.

TEN

His Canon, Herself

Teaching Horror as Feminist Cinema

Dan Vena, Iris Robinson, and Patrick Woodstock

In constructing a course on Western horror cinema, one may be tempted to address a body of auteurs who commonly represent an intersection of privileged identities within filmmaking industries (e.g., white, male, straight, able-bodied, etc.) and who conversely remain markers of generic achievement and cultural capital within the genre. Names such as Mario Bava, Wes Craven, David Cronenberg, Brian De Palma, Alfred Hitchcock, Tobe Hooper, and Michael Powell are endlessly recycled in introductory studies on horror, which often frame the development of the genre chronologically and/or in relation to the technical and narrative achievements of these already privileged filmmakers (see Wells 2000; Worland 2007; Leeder 2018; Turnock 2019). This standard is reinforced in fan cultures, and academic conferences by extension, where devoted fan-scholars (and this is by no means pejorative) grapple with the legacies and, admittedly, often growing irrelevancies of these directors. As an example, at the annual conference for the Society of Cinema and Media Studies, I (Vena) attended a panel discussion on then-recently deceased horror maverick George A. Romero. Led by seasoned horror scholars and dear friends of Romero, the panel highlighted the filmmaker's ongoing influence, particularly with respect to zombie cinema and recent features like Jordan Peele's *Get Out* (2017). When I questioned why we ought to return to Romero's *Night of the Living Dead* (1968) as a milestone of black representation, especially when black filmmakers like Peele have achieved such mainstream success and cultural clout, I was met with disapproval. One scholar immediately responded that it was my *duty* to teach students the historical role Romero played in developing the political landscape of American horror cinema and that his work should serve as an origin point for the discussion that could *eventually* address Peele's accomplishments. As I noted at the time, I disagree with this suggestion.

Alongside two of my former students (Robinson and Woodstock), I suggest an alternative pedagogical approach to the horror canon that moves away from "cultural capital" teaching, which only serves to reproduce toxic fan cultures and overemphasize the legacies of privileged filmmakers. Instead, we argue for teaching horror *as* feminist cinema from the outset, thereby calling into question what precisely fan-scholars may mean when they discuss (often chronologically) the historical, political, or technical "achievements" of the genre. For us, this means repatriating women and other marginalized filmmakers and critics back to course syllabi and to resist framing their inclusion as a subversion of horror but rather as *the story of horror itself* (see Paszkiewicz 2018). While placing women directors and critics center stage in the learning process is an important intervention, we hold that this work must be done intersectionally to further unite anti-oppressive projects when it comes to canonization and recognition.

While ample work has been done on the topic of feminist pedagogy, much less has been done on the topic of feminist horror pedagogy, with Aalya Ahmad and Sean Moreland's edited anthology, *Fear and Learning: Essays on the Pedagogy of Horror* (2013), serving as a cornerstone text. The anthology as a whole works to redeem horror from (surely, now) outdated assumptions regarding the genre's progressiveness and thus usefulness to educators who may want to introduce students to more liberal ideas and modes of criticism (Ahmad and Moreland 2013, 12). These feelings of "guilt by association," which may serve as barriers for incorporating horror into the classroom, are interestingly mitigated by Ahmad and John Edgar Browning in their respective contributions, both harnessing the supposed disrepute of the genre to provoke politically nuanced insights from their students (Ahmad and Moreland 2013, 12). In each of their entries, Ahmad and Browning outline the tenets of their respective feminist horror classrooms, generally agreeing that a central focus of concern should be placed on the cultural work enacted by horror to address social inequities and on students' abilities to think reflexively about their participation in such systems, thereby constructing a "political awakening" (Stabile cited in Browning 2013, 43) via a process of "de/re-socialization" (Browning 2013, 46). Taken together, both pieces offer concrete pedagogical strategies (particularly Ahmad's) for negotiating popular assumptions students may have of horror and bringing them into more critical awareness of the genre's feminist possibilities.

Unlike the aforementioned works, this chapter does not provide the blueprints on *how* to create a feminist classroom. Rather, it explores the results of designing course material on horror as *already* feminist and what may emerge when students are introduced to horror filmmaking and criticism through an innately feminist lens (women-/BIPOC-/queer-/trans-/disabled-centered). What happens when the only story students are given of horror's histories, authors, audiences, images, pleasures, and affects are fundamentally organized around marginalized subjectivities, whether these bodies be on screen or off? To address these effects, I turn to former students, Iris Robinson and Patrick Woodstock, both of whom have gone on to study horror cinema at the graduate level. For her master's research, Robinson looked at the representation of "mad" women on screen, arguing that there is an intrinsic link between images of "madness" meant to scare and capitalist film production. In her contributions to this chapter, Robinson recounts the ways in which discovering horror through feminist film criticism allowed her to understand the genre as an intrinsic point of study for feminist scholarship. Like Robinson, Woodstock also recently completed his master's research, which focused on the depictions of aging women within classical Hollywood horror cinema and their capacity to undermine the system's patriarchal, heterosexist norms. In this piece, Woodstock recounts his initial understanding of horror as a problematic and often exclusionary "guilty pleasure," and how his encounter with a feminist-based approach prompted him to reconsider how the genre can speak to multiple, often marginalized, modes of subjectivity. Together, all three of us consider the design of as well as the insights and ongoing reflections provoked by a feminist horror classroom. Unlike other pedagogical essays, which may exclude students from speaking about their own experiences, this chapter extends feminist pedagogical practices outward, creating room for the often overlooked and undervalued voices of students/junior researchers.

COURSE DESIGN

I (Vena) have had the good luck of teaching horror in two very divergent settings: first, in a class broadly entitled "Women and Film," in which I met Robinson; and second, in a class of my own design called "A Cultural Study of the American Horror Film," in which I met Woodstock. As described in their respective syllabi, "Women and Film" introduces students to a number of foundational texts of feminist film criticism, while "American Horror" showcases the genre's ability to defend or destabilize the status quo. In both contexts, students have rarely been exposed to feminist film theory or psychoanalysis in any depth, which serve as the bedrock literatures for both courses (even though we may go on to challenge some of the latter's formulations). Names like Linda Williams and Carol Clover appear in both syllabi, alongside titles such as *American Psycho* (Mary Harron, 1991), *Ginger Snaps* (John Fawcett, 2000), *Jennifer's Body* (Karyn Kusama, 2009), and *American Mary* (Jennifer and Sylvia Soska, 2012) (see appendix).

Although both courses are self-selected by majors in the program, they tend to attract different types of students. "Women and Film," as one may guess, tends to enroll students who often already have an imagined set of ideals for feminist content and criticism. Courses such as "Women and Film" that explicitly deal with questions of identity and representation meanwhile tend to be "blacklisted" by students more attracted to the latter course on "American Horror," which they mistakenly assume to be an exercise in cinematic "appreciation" rather than analysis. Students in "American Horror" often expect a somewhat "easier" classroom experience where they will be allowed to watch some "fun" titles without having to tax their critical thinking skills. Surprisingly, in both contexts, my approach to the selected topics is equally disruptive: for those in "Women and Film," horror initially offers no redeeming qualities, let alone any worthwhile women directors to study, while students in "American Horror" seem outright annoyed that the syllabus does not include *enough* iconic directors such as Stanley Kubrick (this has been a repeated sentiment). In both cases, I consider my teaching a kind of "Trojan horse," one in which students are awakened to the political depth and impact of feminist horror cinema and criticism (the irony of the method's phallic name association notwithstanding). In the following passages, both Robinson and Woodstock speak to their initial experiences in their respective courses, reflecting on the ways in which the course set up and countered expectation.

I (Robinson) had only minimally encountered feminist film theory up until the third year of my undergraduate degree in film and media studies. Through Vena's "Women and Film" course, I discovered early writers such as Laura Mulvey, Mary Ann Doane, and Anneke Smelik as well as concepts such as the gaze, female spectatorship, and the extensive relationship between psychoanalysis and film studies. This proved to be a significant intervention into my learning. Prior to being introduced to this literature, my understanding of feminist criticism was limited to pop cultural analyses or my own personal issues regarding on-screen representation. I was attracted to the course because I wanted the opportunity to discuss the problematic images I was seeing using an academic vocabulary I so deeply needed. In this sense, "Women and Film" operated not just as a space for me to study inadequate representations of women *on screen* but also as a vehicle through which to confront the overall absence of female representation in the foundational undergraduate film studies syllabus.

Vena's syllabus explicitly argues for the course's function as an intervention into "traditional" film studies through its consideration of written and filmic texts produced by nonmale authors and artists. This framing allows students to recognize the subversive nature of writings by women and gender-variant folks from the outset. By the time our class had reached the horror unit, I had come to understand the genre not as a separate area of study but as *an intrinsic movement* in feminist film studies and, in particular, feminist psychoanalysis. Accordingly, prior to any discussion of horror theory, the syllabus incorporated films that contained major tenets of horror such as *Vertigo* (Alfred Hitchcock, 1958), *Thriller* (Sally Potter, 1979), and *Black Swan* (Darren Aronofsky, 2010) in order to reinforce the essential relationship between the genre and feminist writings. I came to recognize that feminist horror criticism was not an exclusive pushback against male horror filmmakers or male horror scholars, but on patriarchal film theory more generally and the inherent violence of representation itself. Exemplified by Tania Modleski's formulations of female spectatorship through Hitchcock's oeuvre, the feminist film studies classroom can likewise use the horror text as a means of tackling broader concerns in feminist film studies, such as representation, identification, and pleasure. In this sense, feminist horror writers should not be seen as secondary or subversive pedagogical tools but as essential inclusion in film/horror studies syllabi; their involvement in the discipline likewise mirrors that of female horror directors—fundamental rather than solely subversive. Framing horror criticism as an essential component to feminist film studies allows students to recognize women's knowledges as foundational rather than supplementary, and students can in turn bring that understanding to other areas of film studies.

I (Woodstock) took Vena's "American Horror" course. In his syllabus, Vena suggests that "personal improvement can range in meaning. For some, this may be learning to speak more *or less* in class." This quote acknowledges a familiar dynamic within postsecondary classrooms—the tendency for often privileged men to speak over, interrupt, or openly contradict the voices of those whose opinions or lived experiences differ from their own. While gendered inequality tends to shape a classroom's dynamics in any number of postsecondary settings (see Krupnick 1985; Maher 1985; Gabriel and Smithson 1990), it is made especially visible within a horror film classroom as this impulse to narrate over women's experiences has consistently shaped academic and nonacademic discussions around the genre as a whole.

Just as some students consciously or unconsciously exert their privilege to dictate the direction of their class's discussion, popular understandings of the horror genre tend to be dominated by its oft-celebrated male auteurs, many of whom are championed by these same students. Even as figures like Alfred Hitchcock, Roman Polanski, or Stanley Kubrick offer an inherently one-sided depiction of sexual violence in their films (and, in some cases, are also complicit in such violence offscreen), their prominence has a demonstrable effect on how students and consumers come to understand the horror genre in general. Not only does this narrow group of auteurs shape what is shown in classrooms and discussed in academic papers, they also inform what merchandise gets made, what celebrities get invited to conventions, and which films get restored and re-released in short. They and their canonization shape *what horror is* within popular culture and, in turn, what some students may *want it to be* in the classroom.

I begin with these auteurs and their films because they are also responsible for much of my interest (and skepticism) about the horror genre going into Vena's class. While I entered "American Horror" as a fan of horror films, my understanding of the genre was based almost entirely on these works, which had been marked as "important" by their omnipresence in popular culture and at the conventions I had attended. Instead of considering horror as any kind of feminist project, I thought the exact opposite was true. I believed that the appeal of the figures that tend to dominate discussions of horror fandom—John Carpenter, William Castle, Wes Craven—rested in the *appearance* of a rebellious subversion of "good taste," leaving, more often than not, the problematic hierarchies of mainstream culture untouched. But even if I viewed these films as apolitical at best and inescapably misogynistic at worst, it was my long-standing love for these filmmakers that led me into Vena's classroom in the first place. Based on my own experience, I would assume that other students (and especially the other men in the course) entered the classroom with a similar idea of what the horror genre is, regardless of their opinions of it. While this familiarity could be considered a roadblock, it is also central to what makes horror such a useful pedagogical tool—offering a common starting point in students' ideas of what the genre *should be* and the chance to build on these preexisting ideas by providing the fuller picture of what it *can be.*

From my (Vena) perspective as Robinson and Woodstock's instructor, both students flag the vital importance of taking women's knowledges and productions seriously, especially in the context of horror wherein male filmmakers and fans are given continued license to serve as tastemakers and gatekeepers of the genre. In *Learning How to Scream*, Linda Williams (1994) suggests women must be taught how to look at horror and mediate its supposedly masochistic offerings. While this point has already been scrutinized by authors like Rhona J. Berenstein (1996), Brigid Cherry (2001), and Isabel C. Pinedo (1997), Robinson's apprehension about studying horror in a feminist context is telling of the continued assumption women students may have about the genre (and, admittedly, the types of images they will be asked to encounter). As provoked by both responses, perhaps it is not just women who have to learn how to be in relationship to patriarchal horror, but rather students in general (and those most privileged, specifically) need to come into deeper awareness of marginalized artists' participation in horror in order to change the myopic assumptions they bring into the classroom. To extend Williams's conclusions, students—especially those who are used to occupying a privileged position in classes and fan circles—need to learn how to "look" at feminist horror *as* horror, in turn renarrativizing the genre's boundaries, its cultural status, and, perhaps most importantly, its ownership. In the next section, the students reflect on the experience of learning how to look at horror from a feminist perspective, referring to some of the personal insights inspired by their assignments.

INSIGHTS

I (Robinson) was assigned readings and screenings on the horror unit of Vena's "Women and Film" course, such as Linda Williams's (1991) *Film Bodies: Gender, Genre, and Excess* as well as Carol Clover's (1992) "Her Body, Himself" in combination with the Soska Sisters' film *American Mary*. Functioning as a means of actively working through questions of identification, fantasy, and pleasure, the unit forces students to uniquely engage with a female-driven work outside of the more traditional horror canon. True to Williams's formulations of "body genres," *American Mary* depicts graphic instances of underground body modification done by aspiring female surgeon Mary Mason. Mason's character arguably repurposes the knife that is normally used against women in the traditional slasher to be an object of female power. As per her surgical expertise, Mason uses her scalpel to perform consensual surgeries on other female clients and to enact nonconsensual procedures on her male rapist. The film's image of the surgical knife and of Mason's larger infliction of body horror importantly exemplifies the generic characteristics outlined by Williams and Clover without being complicit in the slasher film's oft terrorization of the female body. Rather than drawing from a more traditional horror "canon" as discussed in both of the readings— *Psycho* (Alfred Hitchcock, 1960), *The Texas Chain Saw Massacre* (Tobe Hooper, 1974), or *Halloween* (John Carpenter, 1978)—the course required students to comprehend as well as *apply* arguments made by Clover and Williams to the process of feminist horror filmmaking. This method contrasts perhaps more conventional approaches to content delivery, which may simply ask students to identify Clover's and Williams's arguments in relation to more canonical texts.

Assigning films outside of the canon likewise invited the opportunity for more inventive student responses. As per our class requirements, I submitted a reading response on Williams's article and *American Mary*, paying particular attention to identification and the mimetic response Williams describes between the viewer and the characters on screen. Noting in my paper that despite Mason's agency in the film, she continues to follow a similar trajectory as the female character in the slasher genre (powerless victim to active aggressor), I unpack the implications of having an agential female character of this nature and am resultingly critical of her representation. Since *American Mary* provokes a rich dissection of the effects of Mason's agency and power as a female character created within a feminist text, it allows for the application of Williams and Clover that is critical rather than diagnostic (i.e., "*Does* Mary Mason embody the 'Final Girl'?" rather than "Mary Mason *is* the 'Final Girl'"). Indeed, in looking back, I recall initial responses toward the film elicited a constructive and multilayered discourse rather than a simple debate surrounding "good" versus "bad" representation.

Since I entered Vena's classroom with the on-screen representation of women in mind, I was understandably critical of the horror genre. Horror, in its invitation toward identification, tailored a viewing experience for me that aligned myself as a female viewer with gender-based victimization. Admittedly, upon receiving our course syllabus, I was apprehensive to even approach the horror unit itself. Writing in my response paper that "*American Mary* is an unconventional horror film in that it seemingly features a woman in a position of power," I evidently was encountering this sort of female-driven horror narrative for the first time—an encounter that mirrored my initial exposure to feminist film scholars and the possibility for feminist study of the horror genre. In other words, studying *American Mary* in a feminist film studies context positioned my learning of horror as one driven by feminist discourse from the outset and framed my introduction to the study of the genre as a whole.

I (Vena) believe that what Robinson names here is worth emphasizing—by encountering horror cinema through Williams, Clover, and the Soska Sisters, her *primary* story of the genre became a markedly feminist one (admittedly, one still heavily grounded in whiteness). In turn this allowed her, as well as other students, to move beyond binary thinking of "good" and "bad" representation (a tendency that often plagues film instructors) and toward more dimensional conversations about women's contributions to the very textual fabrics of horror and film studies at large. Woodstock takes up similar threads in his response, thinking about the universalizing ways in which students already come to genre, alongside the harmful effects of siloing marginalized artists and thinkers in course syllabi.

I (Woodstock) only need to look as far as my own work for Vena's "American Horror" course to demonstrate the tendency for a male subjectivity to dominate discussion of horror films. As part of the course, students were required to complete two short reflection pieces (one at the beginning and one at the end of the semester) regarding their personal relationship to the horror genre. In my first response, I describe how I was "drawn to the genre because of its ability to provide profound emotional experiences to its audience," citing the comedy of *Evil Dead II* (Sam Raimi, 1987) and the tragedy of *The Fly* (David Cronenberg, 1986) as examples. Through the labels of comedy and tragedy (and the suggestion of a monolithic, singular "audience"), I am clearly trying to suggest a capacity for horror films to unite their audience by sparking a visceral, universal emotional experience. Of course, these films' spectacle of gendered and sexualized violence is anything but universal and apolitical—but as a white, male horror fan (a common demographic in this particular classroom), I had never really been asked to think much further than the specific subjectivity that the canon universalizes.

I discuss these shortcomings in my second response:

> [My first response was] limited by its focus on the emotional, rather than intellectual, aspects of the genre. [Through this course,] I was able to extend my interest in these films beyond the entertaining spectacle they provide, and towards the social issues they probe.

If the realization that I am coming to here—that, essentially, horror films are not experienced in the same way by all audiences—seems pretty obvious, I should emphasize that I had not come to it before "American Horror," which I took in the fourth and final year of my undergraduate degree. I would argue that this is less a failing of my specific institution and instead proof of film classes' tendency to think about the politics of representation as a specific topic of study (to be isolated in specific weeks—such as a "female filmmaker" week, a "race" week, and so on) instead of something inherent to all films.

Through my experience in film studies and production classes, I know that if so-called social justice issues are framed in this way, students understand them as things that they can "choose" to take up (or not). What is needed are more spaces that encourage students to understand such fundamental concepts as film reception, history, and theory as constructs, rather than universal givens upon which to build their analyses. Each of these concepts (including the syllabi made to cover them) are anything but objective, as they are constructed out of the same network of power relations that informs films themselves—and students ought to be trained to recognize this pattern. While the presence of films directed by women and other traditionally excluded filmmakers is absolutely essential, framing these contributions as a recent undoing of "how it has always been" does a disservice to the past and gives too much credit to the present.

All of which brings me to Vena's approach to the genre in "American Horror," which encouraged us to consider *how* we were watching films as an equally valid object of study as *what* we were watching. By constructing its syllabus around feminist scholars and films that specifically aim to invite marginalized forms of subjectivity, Vena's course encouraged students to problematize the perspective that many canonized films assume: a privileged male spectator. The class's explicit focus on subjectivity prompted me to reassess my initial assumption that horror cinema served only to further reinforce the centrality of this dominant perspective. By discussing how people in a variety of positions create and view horror cinema, I realized horror's potential to reveal and problematize the limitations of popular culture, rather than merely echo its exclusionary tendencies.

Instead of restricting questions of representation to one or two focused "weeks," "American Horror" framed its entire survey of the genre around these concerns. As such, it asked us to consider how these topics are always very much at play, even in films which are not explicitly "about" issues of marginalization. For instance, while *American Psycho* (Mary Harron, 1991) does not directly make race its focus, our study of the film focused on how it destabilizes whiteness by making it visible, prompting us to consider and problematize spectatorship itself. By making this element of the film one of multiple angles by which it was discussed—in addition to the more obvious work it does as a study of fragile masculinity by a female director—the course draws students' attention to how each of these discourses constantly work invisibly within any film, rather than localizing concerns over representation to a few specific texts.

ONGOING REFLECTIONS

My (Robinson) first encounter with horror film scholarship in Vena's "Women and Film" course was Williams and Clover; they offered pedagogic tools that established the horror genre for me as a point of feminist study. In continuing my studies of horror at the graduate level, it was then natural for me to explore foundational feminist writers such as Barbara Creed, Julia Kristeva, Tania Modleski, and Kaja Silverman principally before even beginning to encounter other so-named foundational thinkers such as Noël Carroll or Christian Metz, a progression that is once again deeply rooted in my discovery of horror studies within the context of a feminist film studies classroom. This approach expanded my understanding of not only film studies texts but research methodologies as a whole. In graduate school, I began to research based on feminist texts in dialogue with one another, compiling an understanding of psychoanalytic film studies through the interpretations of women writers. Having read Mulvey, Doane, and Smelik (among others) before other male scholars forced me into a consideration of identification with the horror film that was based in gender rather than, for example, determining aesthetic affect. In turn, when eventually moving to the area of aesthetic and narrative discourse in horror, films and writings constructed by women were unable to function solely as texts subverting what I already knew to be true about the horror genre because they were all that I knew to be true about horror in the first place.

Of course, rather soon into continuing my study of horror, I developed a broader understanding of scholarship within the genre's discipline. This expansion allowed me to comprehend the subversions as well as the broader cultural discourses in which early feminist horror scholars were engaged, while also preserving my initial understanding of feminist writings as innate to the development of horror studies. However, for a narrow window in my early academic pursuits, "horror" operated almost solely as a device that galvanized feminist critique against problematic films. I assumed that this counter-critique was all feminist thinkers and creators offered to the genre. By being exposed to horror through the context of two women directors in tandem with two female scholars, I was able to define the genre in relation to its feminist potential. This framing operated as the promised pedagogic intervention outlined in Vena's syllabus: namely, to increase the representation of nonmale voices throughout the undergraduate film studies curriculum, thereby offering a point of representation for women and gender-variant students both on- and offscreen.

Returning to my reading response on *American Mary*, I argued at the time that the film could not be seen as "fully feminist" since it contains aspects of male subjecthood as described by Williams and Clover; for example, feminine victimization and violence toward women, the possible trope of the Final Girl, and the murder (eventual punishment) of Mason at the end of the film. Though I was in the process of developing an understanding of the horror genre that would allow me to see *American Mary* for its revolutionary potential, it is evident in my initial response that I was perhaps uncomfortable with the level of graphic violence being displayed and the potential consequences to these sorts of radical risks of feminist empowerment that the Soska Sisters implied (ones that I had never encountered previously in a film studies classroom). What my response failed to see at the time was that regardless if Mason died at the film's conclusion, the greatest importance was that she was alive at all.

When I (Woodstock) reflect on Vena's "American Horror" course, I believe that it shifted my approach toward the horror genre—and toward film studies as a whole. This is best exemplified by the course's assignments. The single largest portion of the grade was devoted to four "Head-to-Head" response papers, which asked students to compare two films and to specifically focus on their differing models of representation (as per the assignment sheet, to ask yourself, "What is being filmed?" "How is it being filmed?" "Why is it being filmed that way?" and "What does that decision reveal about our cultural understanding of gender, race, sexuality, class, ability, age, ethnicity, and/or religion?"). As suggested above, encouraging students to link formal film analysis to discourses of representation is by no means a given in an undergraduate course. By foregrounding the differences in how films from different filmmakers and points in history approach similar subject matter, "American Horror" encouraged students to develop an understanding of film history more nuanced than representation simply being worse in the past and always improving.

Vena's gesture toward a more socially engaged form of criticism culminated in the course's final project: to produce a podcast episode as a group, in place of a standard research essay. This may seem like a subtle shift, but it suggests a fundamental shift in what constitutes valid academic discourse. The stylistic confines of a research essay are built to suggest objectivity (as, among other things, the use of "I" pronouns is often discouraged), while a podcast inherently makes students recognize and progress from their own specific subject positions. Thus, this project reminds students that the knowledge they create and produce is not objective but instead informed by the same network of underlying discourses as the films that they analyze.

While the literal focus that the podcast project places on students' individual voices may seem at odds with the syllabus's suggestion that students speak "more *or less*," I would argue that making students (especially those with the inherent privilege that is offered by a privileged postsecondary institution) confront their subjectivity is an essential exercise that horror films are uniquely suited to provide. Even as much of the horror canon invisibly reinforces a dominant subjectivity, they can be incredibly useful pedagogical tools to make the specificity and fragility of such a viewpoint apparent. Even though horror is often understood as an inherently misogynistic genre whose codes are only recently "undone" by female critics and filmmakers, it bears remembering that this is a genre whose current form can (within a Eurocentric historical narrative) be traced back to Mary Shelley. A privileged male subjectivity is not inherent to the genre but rather a learned element of film spectatorship that, if engaged with critically, can be unlearned.

From my (Vena) perspective as an instructor, and as Robinson and Woodstock make clear, introducing students to horror *as* feminist cinema from the outset denaturalizes the subjectivities and perspectives that continue to coopt popular and academic discourses of the genre. As an introductory exercise in both classes, I ask students to name words they have come to associate with "horror movies." Their answers are predictable: blood, gore, sex, nudity, teenagers, violence, jump scares, and so forth. Not once has someone gone beyond these basic traits to use terms like "feminist," "queer positive," or "black excellence" to define the genre. This needs to change. If we do not change the story of horror toward marginalized voices, we will continue to make invisible the very defining histories, stories, and political adeptness that make the genre so compelling (and teachable!) in the first place.

Of course, the road toward change can be fraught and by no means did I design, nor did the students conduct, a "perfect" course—if such a thing should exist, please contact me. In general, it was difficult at times to get students to "buy into" this approach, as they questioned why psychoanalytic theory explains the killer's knife to be a "phallus" and why the threat at the end of *Scream*, for instance, should be treated as homoerotic (interestingly, many of my queer students openly rejoiced when I finally exposed horror for its queer erotics). As Robinson reminded me, getting students to "buy into" the usefulness of theory at *all* is always a struggle, and patience rather than frustration should be given in these cases as students are on their own learning curves to understand and apply criticism. There were also flaws in the design of "American Horror." I did not *explicitly* broach intersectionality as a methodology and, in turn, potentially allowed students to leave thinking analyses of race, ability, and queerness can be "tacked on" to discussions of gender. I have since changed the introductory screening of the course to the documentary *Horror Noire* (Xavier Neal-Burgin, 2019), based on the research of Robin M. Means Coleman, so students have the benefit of understanding what intersectional, feminist horror criticism looks like from the outset. I also have them practice this approach early on by exploring the legacy of classical Hollywood's only female monster designer, Milicent Patrick, and her work on the deeply colonial film *Creature from the Black Lagoon* (Jack Arnold, 1954). This hopefully better spells out the project of feminist criticism to students and broaches what Woodstock raises as another pedagogical concern: since courses on representation are often elective, it may place an undue onus on students to open themselves up to these ways of thinking rather than putting the burden more on departmental curriculum design to train students for such content. Representation-driven courses cannot and ought not to stand alone in film studies curricula but complement dialogues already in progress across courses and levels.

Writing on the goals of a feminist classroom, Browning (2013) identifies bringing "awareness to perception itself" as a primary goal, suggesting students need to reconcile with "how [their perception] is influenced by cultural assumptions and 'common knowledge'" (48). When we frame horror as already belonging to marginalized artists and scholars, we allow students to rethink their relationship not only to genre, film history, and academic study but to reality itself. As feminist theorists have already guided, the story of genre is the story of world-making and the subject's position within these processes. It is time students learn as such.

BIBLIOGRAPHY

Ahmad, Aalya. "When the Women Think: Teaching Horror in Women's and Gender Studies." In *Fear and Learning: Essays on the Pedagogy of Horror*, ed. Aalya Ahmad and Sean Moreland, 56–74. Jefferson, NC: McFarland, 2013.

Ahmad, Aalya, and Sean Moreland, eds. *Fear and Learning: Essays on the Pedagogy of Horror*. Jefferson, NC: McFarland, 2013.

Berenstein, Rhona J. *Attack of the Leading Ladies: Gender, Sexuality, and Spectatorship in Classic Horror Cinema*. New York: Columbia University Press, 1996.

Browning, John Edgar. "Towards a Monster Pedagogy: Reclaiming the Classroom for the Other." In *Fear and Learning: Essays on the Pedagogy of Horror*, ed. Aalya Ahmad and Sean Moreland, 40–53. Jefferson, NC: McFarland, 2013.

Cherry, Brigid. "Refusing to Refuse to Look: Female Viewers of the Horror Film." In *Horror, the Film Reader*, ed. Mark Jancovich, 169–182. New York: Routledge, 2001.

Clover, Carol. "Her Body, Himself." In *Men, Women, and Chain Saws: Gender in the Modern Horror Film*, 2nd ed., 21–64. Princeton, NJ: Princeton University Press, 2015.

Gabriel, Susan L., and Isaiah Smithson, eds. *Gender in the Classroom: Power and Pedagogy*. Urbana: University of Illinois Press, 1990.

Krupnick, Catherine G. "Women and Men in the Classroom: Inequality and Its Remedies." *On Teaching and Learning: The Journal of the Harvard-Danforth Centre* 1, no. 1 (1985): 18–25.

Leeder, Murray. *Horror Film: A Critical Introduction*. New York: Bloomsbury Publishing, 2018.

Maher, Frances. "Pedagogies for the Gender-Balanced Classroom." *Journal of Thought* 20, no. 3 (1985): 48–64.

McCollum, Victoria. *Make America Hate Again: Trump-Era Horror and the Politics of Fear*. London: Routledge, 2019.

Paszkiewicz, Katarzyna. "When the Woman Directs (a Horror Film)." In *Women Do Genre in Film and Television*, ed. Mary Harrod and Katarzyna Paszkiewicz, 41–56. New York: Routledge, 2018.

Pinedo, Isabel Cristina. *Recreational Terror: Women and the Pleasures of Horror Film Viewing.* Albany: State University of New York Press, 1997.

Turnock, Bryan. *Studying Horror Cinema.* Leighton Buzzard, UK: Auteur Publishing, 2019.

Wells, Paul. *The Horror Genre: From Beelzebub to Blair Witch.* New York: Wallflower Press, 2000.

Williams, Linda. "Film Bodies: Gender, Genre, and Excess." *Film Quarterly* 44, no. 4 (1991): 2–13.

———. "Learning to Scream." *Sight and Sound* 4, no. 12 (1994): 14–17.

Worland, Rick. *The Horror Film: An Introduction.* Malden, MA: Blackwell Publishing, 2007.

Appendix

A Cultural Study of the (Western) Horror Film (Abridged Viewing List)

Note: This is an updated version of the syllabus used for "American Horror," which has been expanded to a broader survey on the socio-political dimensions of (mostly) Western horror. Although my original course design stressed an engagement with feminist politics through key women thinkers and creators (sometimes not directors but producers, screenwriters, and even fans), the syllabus still retained an unbalanced number of male filmmakers. While I have not reached full gender parity in this new list, I retain that it is important to treat "women in horror" as a category that includes scholars, filmmakers, and audiences. A feminist horror classroom is arguably one that can profile all types of women contributors to the genre and one that can champion an intersectional approach to topics and texts profiled.

Horror, Inviting Otherness
Screening: *Horror Noire* (2019, Xavier Neal-Burgin)
Key Scholars: Robin M. Means Coleman; Linda Williams

Storying Horror History
Screening: *Creature from the Black Lagoon* (1954, Jack Arnold) and *Twilight* (2008, Catherine Hardwicke)
Key Scholars: Linda Williams; Rhona J. Berenstein

Psychoanalysis and Repression
Screening: *Texas Chainsaw Massacre* (1974, Tobe Hooper)
Key Scholar: Robin Wood

Slashers and Final Girls
Screening: *Scream* (1996, Wes Craven)
Key Scholar: Carol Clover

Revenge Films
Screening: *A Girl Walks Home Alone at Night* (2014, Ana Lily Amirpour)
Key Scholar: Carol Clover

The Abject
Screening: *Raw* (2016, Julia Ducournau)
Key Scholars: Julia Kristeva; Barbara Creed

Fearing the Body
Screening: *Freaks* (1932, Tod Browning) and *Chained for Life* (2018, Aaron Schimberg)
Key Scholar: Travis Sutton

Queers Who Kill
Screening: *Jennifer's Body* (2009, Karyn Kusama)
Key Scholar: Harry M. Benshoff

Reclaiming Zombie Lore
Screening: *Get Out* (2017, Jordan Peele)
Key Scholar: Robin M. Means Coleman

Return of the 1980s and Trump-Era Horror
Screening: *American Psycho* (1991, Mary Harron)
Key Scholars: Robin Wood; Victoria McCollum

Index

abject, 5, 16, 25, 28, 32, 44, 46
absurdity, 14, 65
abuse, 6, 8, 55, 81
academia, 7, 10, 11, 14, 16, 17, 97, 99, 105, 110, 116, 150, 174, 188, 213, 216, 217, 218, 223, 224, 225
Academy (Oscars), 3, 7, 8, 10, 51, 63, 99, 101
acting, 4, 7, 13, 28, 44, 46, 48, 49, 53, 56, 58, 59, 61, 62, 64, 65, 71, 84, 85, 107, 118, 146, 170, 174, 181, 184, 189, 191
activism, 13, 16, 103
adaptation, 1, 7, 13, 24, 28, 29, 30, 170
adolescence, 6, 70, 77, 118, 119, 170, 175, 225
aesthetics, 10, 13, 15, 17, 23, 26, 28, 32, 69, 70, 72, 73, 74, 75, 77, 78, 80, 81, 82, 83, 85, 86, 115, 175, 181, 182, 183, 186, 194, 195, 223
affect, 4, 16, 75, 76, 116, 125, 126, 184, 215, 223
African American, 17, 115, 117, 125, 127, 147
agency, 6, 23, 24, 25, 31, 79, 107, 122, 185, 220
agents, 16, 172, 183, 220
aggression, 4, 7, 39, 45, 119, 220
aging, 31, 75, 99, 104, 117, 122, 149, 155, 215, 224

Ahmad, Aalya, 214
allegory, 75, 103, 104
Amirpour, Ana Lily, 3, 63, 145, 168
animation, 12, 31, 33, 34, 177
anthologies, 10, 39, 56, 65, 154, 175, 214
antifeminism, 167, 173
appeal, 17, 31, 99, 102, 109, 151, 190, 218
archetypes, 6, 99, 119, 193
Arden, Jane, 101
Argento, Dario, 5, 7, 86
Aronofsky, Darren, 217
art, 4, 23, 24, 25, 27, 44, 65, 75, 77, 84, 123, 182, 187, 190, 194
Artaud, Antonin, 43, 44, 51
Asia, 17, 71, 77, 150, 156
assault, 5, 25, 55, 80, 81, 104, 111
atmosphere, 27, 33, 45, 85, 102, 190
attitudes, 24, 75, 77, 83, 84, 85, 102, 193
Atwood, Margaret, 70
audiences, 2, 3, 5, 8, 14, 16, 22, 24, 26, 30, 42, 55, 58, 63, 71, 99, 103, 110, 116, 123, 153, 169, 173, 190, 221
Australian horror, 2, 42, 145, 147, 149, 150, 158, 172
auteurs, 16, 108, 111, 195, 213, 218
authorship, 2, 3, 7, 10, 35, 43, 49, 99, 107, 108, 110, 111, 215
avant-garde, 7, 21, 25, 26, 34, 34, 35, 51

awards, 3, 8, 63, 101, 151, 167, 172
Ax Wound Film Festival, 145, 148, 151,
   154, 162

Babadook (Jennifer Kent), 2, 3, 42, 60,
   63, 151, 168
barriers, 125, 178, 190, 214
Baskova, Svetlana, 10, 39, 46, 47
Bava, Mario, 213
BBC, 107, 233
beasts, 33, 71, 83
beauty, 57, 65, 69, 71, 72, 73, 75, 76, 77,
   78, 79, 80, 81, 82, 83, 84, 85, 86, 120
belonging, 73, 75, 86, 171
Berlin (Final Girls), 31, 34, 107, 145,
   151, 152, 164, 173
Bettis, Angela, 13, 48, 49, 53, 54, 55, 56,
   57, 58, 59, 60, 61, 62, 63, 64, 65
Bewailing (Jennifer Trudrung), 191, 195
BFI, 101, 102, 111
Bias, 9, 15, 106, 109, 117, 127, 148, 156,
   188, 193
Bier, Susanne, 42
Bigelow, Kathryn, 8, 63, 146
Biller, Anna, 70, 73, 84, 86, 168, 175
Bird, Antonia, 102, 146
birth, 5, 6, 33, 186
Blaché, Alice Guy, 12, 22, 23, 27, 28, 29,
   30, 31, 34, 35, 36, 146, 178
black filmmakers, 14, 17, 115, 116, 117,
   118, 119, 120, 121, 122, 123, 124, 125,
   126, 127, 213, 225
blood, 6, 28, 40, 47, 77, 81, 82, 84, 148,
   149, 174, 175, 184, 225
Blum, Jason, 3, 154, 155
bodies, 5, 25, 28, 36, 44, 46, 47, 83, 84,
   214
body-horror, 46, 47, 72, 79, 219
Bogutskaya, Anna, 2, 7, 15, 167
borders, 17, 61, 69, 71, 72, 195
boundaries, 23, 24, 31, 84, 152, 156
Bowen, Lori, 149, 150
Boyle, Danny, 104, 106
British horror, 13, 14, 39, 52, 85, 97, 98,
   99, 100, 101, 102, 103, 104, 105, 106,
   107, 108, 109, 110, 110,112, 113, 145,
   148, 173, 175, 182, 183

Browning, John Edgar, 214, 226
brutal, 4, 108
brutality, 4, 29, 72, 108
budgets, 59, 98, 101, 102, 104, 105, 106,
   110, 153, 191, 192, 193, 195, 196
Buffy The Vampire Slayer, 177

Canadian horror, 3, 7, 10, 13, 17, 69, 70,
   71, 72, 73, 74, 75, 76, 77, 78, 79, 80,
   82, 83, 84, 85, 85, 151
Cannes, 107, 155
canonization, 16, 21, 29, 35, 117, 121,
   121, 213, 214, 219, 220, 221, 221, 222
career, 11, 27, 31, 53, 64, 108, 146, 150,
   154, 168, 172, 178, 179, 182, 183, 188,
   189, 191, 196
careers, 15, 31, 64, 146, 154, 168, 172,
   178, 182
carnivalesque, 24, 47, 75
Carpenter, John, 2, 6, 218, 219
Carrie (Brian De Palma), 6, 9, 54, 55,
   174, 178
Carrillo, Sofía, 168, 175, 177
Carroll, Noël, 27, 32, 34, 222
challenges, 2, 14, 15, 17, 85, 99, 103,
   105, 167, 188
Cherry, Brigid, 9, 71, 99, 218
Chevalier (Athina Rachel Tsangari),
   12, 39
Childer (Aislinn Clarke), 15, 16, 17, 181,
   189, 195
children, 16, 31, 33, 56, 122, 126, 182, 184
cinematography, 8, 10, 14, 46, 59, 60,
   147, 152
Clarke, Aislinn, 1, 4, 6, 8, 15, 16, 17, 58,
   169, 181, 182, 183, 185, 186, 187, 188,
   189, 190, 192, 194, 195
classics, 4, 24, 44, 45, 46, 170, 184, 215
class, 107, 123, 116, 224
clichés, 9, 61, 156
Clover, Carol, 4, 5, 6, 7, 9, 46, 72, 99,
   170, 215, 219, 220, 222, 223
Cobb, Shelley, 97, 98, 105, 106, 107, 110
Cocteau, Jean, 83, 84
Cody, Diablo, 8, 78, 79, 84
collaboration, 14, 54, 57, 74, 84, 145,
   149, 150, 158, 196

collectives, 2, 7, 11, 15, 23, 127, 146, 154, 169, 170, 172, 174, 175, 176, 177
comedy, 21, 65, 108, 109, 221
commercialization, 17, 23, 192
community, 14, 15, 50, 64, 75, 80, 124, 125, 145, 146, 147, 148, 150, 153, 154, 157, 158, 167, 170, 171, 176, 183, 189, 189, 189, 189, 189, 190, 194, 195
competitions, 152, 155, 173, 190
consumption, 2, 11, 26, 81, 117, 189
controversy, 7, 8, 43, 51, 170
conventions, 2, 3, 15, 26, 44, 70, 80, 84, 167, 220
Cooper, Jennifer, 149, 153, 155, 156, 157
costumes, 77, 82, 83, 155
COVID, 17, 177
Craven, Wes, 2, 4, 7, 104, 213
Creature of the Black Lagoon (Jack Arnold), 225
Creed, Barbara, 5, 7, 9, 99, 222
crews, 86, 155, 184, 188
criticism, 5, 7, 8, 16, 42, 75, 80, 98, 125, 169, 171, 178, 193, 214, 215, 216, 217, 224, 225, 225, 225
critics, 2, 8, 8, 8, 22, 26, 29, 32, 33, 40, 41, 41, 43, 44, 51, 70, 73, 85, 98, 99, 119, 150, 167, 168, 173, 177, 178, 178, 214, 224, 225
Cronenberg, David, 71, 73, 75, 81, 82, 213, 221
cult film, 13, 45, 46, 48, 50, 64, 72, 175, 234, 234
curation, 15, 41, 170, 179
Curtis, Jamie Lee, 174

dada, 25, 34
Dale, Holly, 73
Daughters of Darkness (Harry Kümel), 70, 72, 83, 84, 85, 86, 88
debut, directorial, 13, 31, 58, 61, 62, 84, 108, 115, 121, 168
Delano, Leslie, 149
Denis, Claire, 7, 174
desire, 5, 6, 27, 43, 55, 56, 56, 59, 74, 79, 80, 82, 115, 119, 125, 169
Destroyer (Karyn Kusama), 8, 53

Devil's Doorway (Aislinn Clarke), 17, 169, 181
difference, 5, 6, 63, 70, 194
directing, 8, 49, 54, 54, 59, 61, 62, 63, 64, 64, 64, 64, 80, 182, 193, 193
distribution, 15, 26, 69, 88, 106, 107, 110, 120, 148, 150, 157, 169, 175
diversity, 14, 28, 35, 39, 42, 50, 105, 106, 107, 110, 111, 157, 158
Do, Mattie, 3, 168, 169
Doane, Mary Ann, 5, 216, 223
documentary, 73, 107, 178, 225, 235
Dracula, 75, 170
Ducornau, Julia, 3, 168
Dulac, Germaine, 34, 39, 43, 44, 44
Duvernay, Ava, 120
Dzialoszynski, Krista, 151, 153, 154, 157

Ebert, Roger, 102, 121
economics, 47, 98, 103, 105, 106, 107, 181, 182, 183, 184, 191, 196
editing (film), 23, 27, 97, 103, 152, 187
education, 17, 24, 24, 145, 145, 149, 158, 233
Edwards-Behi, Nia, 148, 149
Egomaniac (Kate Shenton), 14, 99, 108, 109, 110, 112
emotional, 15, 65, 108, 117, 122, 123, 184, 194, 221
empathy, 59, 60, 126, 156, 186
employment, 97, 104, 107, 195
empowerment, 6, 9, 58, 79, 81, 116, 123, 124, 153, 223
equality, 6, 49, 65, 107, 108, 194, 195, 217
erasure, 111, 120, 126
Etheria (Film Night), 145, 147, 151, 154, 158, 160, 163, 173
ethnicity, 74, 127, 127, 224
European film, 17, 29, 37, 70, 182, 192, 195
Eve's Bayou (Kasi Lemmons), 121, 124, 128
exclusion, 41, 50, 105, 117, 215, 222
executive producers, 97, 117, 168, 172, 187
exploitation, 73, 80, 84, 84, 146
exposure, 11, 127, 220

extremity, 7, 29, 47, 82
exuberance, 69, 75, 77, 79, 80, 81, 83, 83, 85

family, 17, 24, 55, 76, 100, 101, 106, 115, 121, 122, 123, 124, 182, 184
fandom, 15, 64, 151, 153, 157, 167, 169, 170, 171, 172, 173, 176, 177, 178, 184
fantastic, 27, 33, 59, 146, 154, 154, 183
Fargeat, Coralie, 145, 168
fashion, 21, 24, 73, 75, 77, 78, 81, 82
fathers, 55, 74, 117, 122
Fawcett, John, 70, 86, 216
fear, 6, 24, 26, 28, 29, 32, 44, 45, 70, 80, 81, 156, 182, 184, 188, 214, 233
feature (filmmaking), 5, 8, 32, 33, 39, 75, 150, 154, 169, 183, 213, 220
femininity, 40, 49, 77
feminism, 6, 8, 9, 13, 17, 51, 62, 69, 167, 169, 175, 234, 234
feminization, 44, 46, 47, 50
festivals, 2, 3, 10, 11, 14, 15, 16, 42, 72, 99, 103, 145, 146, 147, 148, 149, 150, 151, 152, 153, 154, 155, 157, 158, 167, 168, 170, 171, 172, 173, 176, 178, 183, 185, 188, 189, 190, 191, 194, 233
foreignness, 70, 74, 76, 77, 82
Forman, Hannah (Neurotica), 148, 149, 153, 154, 156, 157
Fox, Megan, 8, 79
fragility, 119, 124, 224
French horror, 3, 7, 10, 31, 83, 41, 84, 152
franchises, 73, 184, 193
Frankenstein (Mary Shelley), 170
Freitag, Gina, 71, 72, 75
frustration, 110, 151, 169, 225
Fujiwara, Kei, 7, 10, 39, 46, 47
funding, 14, 15, 17, 103, 103, 104, 105, 106, 107, 108, 109, 110, 145, 147, 182, 185, 187, 192, 192, 195
future, 12, 17, 26, 31, 40, 115, 121, 127, 156, 173

games, 24, 233
gatekeepers, 10, 14, 110, 145, 167, 172, 172, 173, 218
Gaumont, Leon, 27, 35, 36

gaze, 5, 6, 7, 9, 12, 57, 69, 79, 156, 184, 192, 216
Geena Davis Institute, 170
gendered, 14, 15, 16, 35, 44, 46, 47, 49, 51, 63, 65, 72, 86, 97, 100, 101, 109, 185, 186, 194, 217, 221
generations, 84, 119, 121, 123, 127
genre, 7, 8, 10, 31, 34, 21, 22, 23, 24, 25, 26, 28, 31, 40, 41, 42, 45, 48, 49, 51, 55, 58, 59, 62, 64, 65, 66, 70, 71, 72, 73, 75, 77, 80, 85, 97, 103, 105, 120, 169, 184, 219
German horror, 10, 25, 31, 34, 82, 145, 152, 155, 168, 173
Gerwig, Greta, 98
Gevargizian, Jill Six, 149, 154, 158
ghettoization, 42, 187, 193
ghosts, 23, 24, 33, 33
Giallo, 71
Gibson-Hudson, Gloria, 123, 124
Ginger Snaps (John Fawcett), 13, 69, 70, 71, 74, 74, 75, 76, 77, 78, 79, 80, 81, 82, 86, 86, 146, 216, 234
Girolamo, Laura Di, 151, 157
global trends:, 7, 10, 14, 17, 42, 88, 104, 111, 145, 1590, 167, 196
gothic, 2, 4, 19, 23, 24, 35, 87, 100, 103
Green Elephant (Svetlana Baskova), 39, 46, 47, 48, 51
Guerrero, Gigi Saul, 3, 17, 74, 86, 149, 154, 155, 158

Halberstam, Judith, 9
Hammer horror, 4, 14, 100, 100, 101, 102, 103
Harron, Mary, 7, 146, 216, 222
haunted, 16, 64, 118, 124
health, 14, 34, 49, 79, 81, 124, 125, 182
Hellbound Train (James and Eloyce Gist), 121
Heller-Nicholas, Alexandra, 12, 39, 40, 42, 44, 46, 48, 50, 72,168
heritage, 13, 75, 85, 115, 127
Hill, Debra, 6, 146
historical, 2, 4, 10, 10, 12, 14, 22, 23, 40, 42, 106, 110, 116, 118, 123, 186, 213, 214, 224

Hitch-Hiker (Ida Lupino), 39, 40, 44, 45, 46, 47, 146
Hitchcock, Alfred, 187, 213, 217, 218, 219
Hollywood, 1, 14, 42, 44, 70, 71, 97, 98, 111, 117, 120, 121, 147, 178, 191, 194, 195, 215, 225
Home, 3, 24, 35, 50, 55, 57, 60, 76, 80, 119, 126, 150, 154, 168, 189
Honeycutt, Heidi, 17, 147, 148, 149, 150, 152, 153, 154, 157
Hooper, Tobe, 213, 219
Hulu, 154, 158

identity, 3, 11, 12, 15, 55, 71, 72, 78, 79, 83, 84, 69, 71, 105, 106, 107, 108, 115, 118, 123, 176, 181, 194, 216
ideology, 5, 35, 41, 74, 171
imagination, 27, 31, 33, 71, 75, 76, 118, 121, 182, 184
impact, 7, 8, 21, 31, 43, 46, 47, 116, 157, 172, 183, 187, 216
inclusion, 65, 105, 112, 120, 123, 129, 177, 186, 190, 214, 217
indie (filmmaking), 10, 15, 70, 121, 147, 189, 191, 194
industry, 2, 3, 8, 9, 10, 11, 14, 15, 17, 18, 21, 22, 27, 41, 42, 63, 70, 83, 97, 98, 99, 102, 103, 104, 105, 106, 108, 109, 110, 112, 116, 152, 156, 157, 169, 172, 173, 182, 183, 184, 185, 187, 188, 189, 190, 192, 193
influences, 23, 28, 45, 48, 51, 52, 61, 70, 78, 124, 168, 213, 226
innovation, 13, 24, 27, 28, 30, 36, 51, 64, 66, 75
insecurity, 54, 75, 79, 80, 81, 85
internationalism, 17, 69, 70, 71, 72, 74, 75, 76, 76, 77, 78, 82, 83
intersectionality, 16, 120, 156, 177, 225
interviews, 14, 15, 17, 44, 59, 67, 71, 82, 108, 109, 119, 145, 181, 194, 195
intimacy, 15, 29, 47, 53, 57, 61, 71, 84, 121, 125, 194
Invitation (Karyn Kusama), 3, 39, 48, 49, 50, 168, 220
Iranian horror, 2, 63

Irish horror, 17, 15, 16, 17, 169, 181, 189, 195

Jackson, Shirley, 2
Janisse, Kier-La, 146, 150
Japanese horror, 7, 10, 17, 46, 52, 87, 145, 173
Jelly Dolly (Susannah Gent), 105, 106, 107
Jennifer's Body (Karyn Kusama), 3, 8, 8, 9, 17, 70, 78, 79, 80, 81, 82, 86
Jeter, Stephanie, 126, 127
journalism, 100, 119, 129, 147, 168, 174, 175
Juno (Jason Reitman), 78, 86
Jusu, Nikyatu, 115, 127

Kahlo, Frida, 25
Kajutaijuq (Nyla Innuksuk), 74
Kent, Jennifer, 3, 60, 63, 145, 168
Kidd, Briony, 64, 149, 150, 153, 154, 155, 156, 157, 158, 172
Kidman, Nicole, 8
killing, 45, 58, 79
Kolesnik, Samantha, 152, 195
Kristeva, Julia, 5, 222
Kümel, Harry, 70, 84, 86
Kusama, Karyn, 3, 8, 18, 19, 39, 48, 49, 52, 168, 172, 175, 216

La Belle et la Bête (Jean Cocteau), 83, 84
Labour party, 104, 106, 107
La Coquille et le Clergyman (Germaine Dulac), 34, 39, 43, 44, 51
Lambert, Mary, 1, 7, 17, 146
landscape, 2, 7, 13, 22, 26, 31, 35, 39, 42, 78, 102, 103, 104, 111, 120, 213
Lark, Shannon, 146, 147, 149, 150, 153, 154, 156
Lauzen, Martha, 1, 97, 98, 98, 120, 155, 195
leadership, 2, 64, 105
legacies, 34, 40, 43, 51, 67, 86, 174, 225
Lemmons, Kasi, 121, 122
Lewis, Herschell Gordon, 146
Lewy, Elinor, 151, 152, 156, 156, 157
LGBTQIA, 56, 72, 75, 77, 104, 187, 192, 215, 225

literature, 10, 23, 23, 24, 34, 35, 170, 216, 234
López, Issa, 3, 145, 168
low-budget, 53, 54, 101, 106, 146, 191
Lowenstein, Adam, 25
Love Witch (Anna Biller), 70, 83, 84, 85, 158, 168, 175
Lugosi, Bela, 6, 170
Lupino, Ida, 44, 45, 46, 47, 51, 146
Lynch, David, 43, 51

Magdalene Laundries, 17
magic, 31, 32, 33, 36, 118, 122, 127, 177, 151, 190
mainstream, 4, 15, 26, 42, 57, 62, 101, 117, 120, 122, 151, 158, 167, 167, 167, 171, 172, 173, 190, 213, 218
makeup, 79, 83, 155, 178, 184, 184
male-dominated, 8, 50, 50, 64, 81, 171, 184, 191
marginalization, 10, 17, 35, 64, 105, 105, 108, 214, 215, 219, 221, 222, 225
margins, 57, 60, 117
marketing, 11, 16, 27, 27, 28, 31, 101, 120, 147, 148, 150, 157, 171, 174, 175, 176, 188, 190
masculinity, 6, 12, 13, 39, 39, 40, 42, 46, 60, 107, 222
masks, 25, 57, 79
masochism, 9, 218
Mathijs, Ernest, 13, 69, 70, 71, 72, 73, 74, 76, 77, 78, 80, 82, 83, 84, 86
May (Lucky McKee), 54, 55, 56, 57, 58, 59
McKee, Lucky, 13, 48, 449, 53, 54, 55, 57, 58, 59, 61, 62, 65, 67
McMurdo, Shellie, 17
media, 22, 23, 24, 26, 31, 34, 35, 35, 88, 98, 108, 111, 115, 117, 120, 124, 126, 148, 153, 170, 171, 175, 178, 190, 190, 190, 191, 194, 213, 216,
melodrama, 28, 46
memory, 79, 107, 110, 122, 123, 124
men, 1, 5, 6, 7, 9, 12, 13, 14, 39, 40, 43, 45, 46, 47, 48, 60, 62, 65, 81, 106, 107, 107, 108, 110, 111, 149, 155, 156, 158,

170, 171, 187, 188, 192, 193, 195, 217, 218
mentorship, 150, 151
merchandise, 175, 218
#MeToo, 3, 110
Metz, Christian, 5, 222
Mexican horror, 3, 45, 74
militarization, 47, 48, 107
minorities, 102, 125, 157, 189, 192
mirrors, 36, 64, 81, 217
misogyny, 6, 14, 108, 108, 109, 109, 111, 172
monstrosity, 5, 6, 33, 43, 55, 57, 74, 83, 99, 125, 168, 176, 184
morality, 47, 57, 81, 121
motherhood, 1, 5, 16, 17, 47, 54, 63, 69, 70, 76, 122, 156, 185, 190, 193
Mulvey, Laura, 4, 5, 9, 72, 216, 223
murder, 5, 39, 49, 50, 53, 57, 59, 60, 223
music, 7, 116, 171, 233
myth, 5, 27, 28, 74, 76, 99, 115, 122

Nakanashi, Mai, 149, 150, 151, 152, 153, 154, 156
narratives, 6, 23, 25, 31, 34, 39, 54, 57, 58, 99, 115, 123, 127, 234
networking, 14, 145, 147, 150, 158, 173, 178, 183, 190
Nicolodi, Daria, 7, 146
non-binary, 151, 173, 178, 188
normativity, 22, 24, 54, 55, 59, 72, 80, 84, 156
nudity, 156, 225

O'Brien, Edmond, 45, 84
objectification, 9, 43, 44, 77, 82
obsession, 13, 53, 57, 58, 59, 62, 65, 71, 75, 79, 193
opportunities, 11, 14, 15, 103, 106, 108, 110, 116, 118, 145, 146, 150, 151, 153, 155, 157, 158, 173, 178, 183, 192, 195
opposition, 12, 116, 117
oppression, 41, 45, 104, 115, 116, 186, 122, 123
Organ (Kei Fujiwara), 7, 39, 46, 47, 48
originality, 42, 152, 153, 157, 186

Orphan Black, 71, 74, 88
Otherness, 5, 41, 71, 75
Oughton, Charlie, 21, 108, 110
outrage, 45, 46, 51, 125
Outrage (Ida Lupino), 51
outsider, 53, 55, 56, 57, 59, 61, 62, 65, 171

pain, 50, 59, 60, 69, 119
Palma, Brian De, 6, 213
Paralysis (R. Shanea Williams), 14, 16, 17, 124, 125
parenthood, 54, 109, 118, 182, 184
Paszkiewicz, Katarzyna, 7, 8, 9, 42, 63, 100, 167, 169, 171, 214
patriarchy, 5, 15, 41, 74, 83, 99, 101, 167, 215, 217, 219
Patrick, Milicent, 178, 179, 225
pedagogy, 16, 214, 215, 217, 218, 222, 223, 224, 225
Peele, Jordan, 213, 214
Peirce, Kimberly, 9, 172
Peirse, Alison, 9, 10, 62, 63, 100
performance, 8, 23, 25, 26, 35, 53, 54, 55, 56, 57, 58, 59, 60, 61, 71, 73, 84, 108
Phillips, Kendall, 26
physicality, 56, 59, 61
pioneers, 2, 12, 14, 21, 27, 31, 37, 44, 45, 98, 111, 178
Pit and the Pendulum (Alice Guy Blaché), 28, 29, 30, 36, 37
pitching, 1, 81, 117, 150, 174
pleasure, 5, 9, 28, 215, 217, 219
podcasting, 153, 177, 178, 224
Poe, Edgar Allan, 28, 29, 30, 37
policy, 13, 71, 178
political, 3, 6, 8, 10, 11, 13, 17, 25, 39, 40, 41, 42, 44, 46, 48, 50, 51,69, 71, 72, 74, 116, 103, 104, 123, 151, 185, 193, 213, 214, 216, 225
porn, 31, 101, 168
possession, 5, 44, 79, 101
precarity, 60, 99, 109
prestige, 71, 122, 167
privilege, 14, 111, 213, 214, 217, 219, 222, 224,

producing, 1, 3, 6, 10, 27, 28, 79, 86, 97, 101, 104, 109, 147, 152, 168, 172, 175, 181, 191, 192, 193
production, 2, 7, 10, 11, 17, 21, 22, 24, 28, 36, 48, 63, 64, 69, 70, 71, 74, 78, 84, 86, 88, 97, 100, 101, 102, 103, 106, 107, 108, 111, 152, 155, 176, 183, 184, 191, 192, 193, 195, 215, 221
protagonists, 1, 4, 9, 14, 47, 79, 81, 107, 115, 120, 127
psychoanalysis, 5, 43, 99, 215, 216, 217, 223, 225
publicity, 15, 169, 172, 175, 176

Rabid (Jen and Sylvia Soska), 13, 70, 78, 79, 80, 81, 82, 86
race, 63, 70, 111, 116, 118, 119, 123, 126, 127, 149, 151, 170, 221, 222, 224, 225
Radcliffe, Anne, 2, 23, 24
Ramsay, Lynne, 12, 39, 145
rape, 4, 46, 47, 51, 81, 104, 111, 219
Raw (Julia Ducornau), 3, 168
reception, 3, 13, 40, 42, 43, 50, 59, 70, 71, 72, 98, 190, 221
recognition, 2, 7, 16, 45, 65, 71, 107, 148, 157, 214
regional, 13, 15, 69, 152, 167
Reilly, Phoebe, 9, 63
Reiniger, Lotte, 12, 22, 23, 31, 32, 33, 34, 35, 36
rejection, 25, 41, 57, 83
relatability, 6, 54, 56, 57, 60, 81
remakes, 9, 53, 82, 100, 157
representation, 11, 25, 26, 51, 56, 72, 82, 106, 107, 145, 150, 177, 192, 194, 213, 215, 216, 217, 220, 221, 222, 223, 224, 225
repression, 43, 152, 185
resistance, 50, 123, 125, 189
revenge, 6, 58, 79, 81, 104, 108, 118, 193
Rhodes, Gary, 28, 29, 36
risks, 28, 63, 63, 97, 98, 106, 111, 157, 182, 192
Roman, Angela Bettis, 13, 39, 48, 49, 53, 54, 54, 58, 59, 59, 60, 61, 62, 64, 65
Romero, George A., 2, 74, 213

Rothman, Stephanie, 146, 173
Russian horror, 46, 48, 51

Satan, 36, 79, 121, 154
satire, 14, 32, 109
screenings, 43, 48, 121, 147, 149, 150,
 151, 169, 174, 175, 177, 190, 225
screenwriting, 2, 6, 7, 10, 16, 17, 43, 59,
 76, 79, 86, 97, 124, 146, 152, 173, 187,
 190, 191, 195
self-reflexivity, 73, 79, 80, 82, 84, 108,
 109
sequels, 1, 7, 77, 146
settings, 75, 76, 77, 80, 82, 120, 158,
 173, 215, 217
sex, 43, 77, 79, 84, 109, 118, 123, 185,
 194, 225
sexism, 44, 65, 104, 116, 152, 185, 185
Shelley, Mary, 2, 150, 170, 224
Shenton, Kate, 14, 99, 108, 109, 110
shorts, 86, 149, 150, 152, 154, 175, 176,
 177, 181, 182, 183, 186, 187, 189, 194
Simpson, Mike, 100, 101, 103, 104, 111
slashers, 45, 104, 125, 151, 168, 185,
 219, 220
society, 22, 25, 47, 56, 57, 59, 61, 69, 71,
 77, 81, 104, 115, 117, 119, 123, 125,
 126, 127, 192, 213, 229
Soska Sisters, 10, 13, 70, 78, 80, 81, 82,
 84, 86, 149, 216, 219, 220, 223
space, 10, 40, 41, 53, 56, 58, 62, 64, 86,
 101, 115, 125, 147, 148, 151, 153, 155,
 157, 169, 172, 173, 188, 216
Spanish horror, 30, 174
spectatorship, 6, 8, 9, 29, 29, 216, 217,
 222, 225
Spencer, Octavia, 118, 119
spirituality, 35, 118, 121, 123, 127
splatter, 46, 31
statistics, 97, 98, 116, 127, 155
stereotypes, 6, 41, 41, 54, 60, 76, 80, 98,
 100, 101, 106, 108, 115, 117, 120, 122,
 123, 127, 150, 153, 156, 171
stigma, 14, 118, 156
storytelling, 10, 64, 115, 116, 125, 145,
 149, 158, 183, 186, 187

students, 16, 173, 182, 213, 214, 215,
 216, 217, 218, 219, 220, 221, 222, 223,
 224, 225
studios, 1, 3, 10, 26, 28, 57, 70, 100, 101,
 105, 106, 106, 157, 192, 192, 194, 195
style, 21, 23, 33, 41, 43, 45, 51, 71, 73,
 77, 78, 79, 82, 83, 84, 85, 117, 153,
 168, 181, 224
subgenre, 14, 42, 45, 48, 72, 117, 167,
 168, 174
subjectivity, 4, 43, 44, 49, 64, 72, 184,
 215, 221, 222, 224
subversion, 5, 12, 16, 21, 22, 26, 41, 42,
 43, 49, 84, 86, 184, 214, 217, 218, 223
success, 2, 3, 11, 15, 21, 31, 42, 64, 80, 98,
 99, 100, 101, 102, 104, 105, 145, 153,
 154, 158, 167, 172, 185, 192, 195, 213
suicide, 70, 77, 101, 115
supernatural, 2, 14, 23, 24, 32, 33, 53,
 58, 74, 79, 104, 115, 116, 118, 121,
 122, 123, 124, 125, 126, 127
surrealism, 7, 25, 34, 37, 43, 44, 50, 51,
 106, 108
survival, 6, 21, 27, 46, 50, 70, 74, 81,
 102, 116, 117, 124
suspense, 28, 29, 45, 183
Suspiria (Dario Argento), 7, 146
symbolism, 43, 56, 60, 61, 116

Takal, Sophia, 155, 168, 172
taste, 47, 51, 77, 99, 170, 218
teaching, 16, 213, 214, 215, 216
techniques, 25, 27, 28, 30, 33, 35, 36,
 60, 176
technology, 23, 25, 27, 34, 153
Teeth (Mitchell Lichtenstein), 6
television, 9, 31, 53, 60, 88, 97, 120, 126,
 147, 173, 177, 178, 196
terror, 4, 4, 28, 29, 44, 46, 46, 51, 85,
 125, 126, 175, 219
theaters, 31, 46, 81, 117, 147, 151, 187,
 190
themes, 3, 11, 12, 13, 21, 22, 23, 26, 34,
 40, 42, 50, 56, 57, 58, 69, 71, 74, 77,
 78, 79, 107, 116, 121, 174, 177, 183,
 185, 186

thrillers, 27, 41, 150, 173, 176, 183, 217
torture, 29, 30, 31, 36, 55, 58, 168
toxicity, 44, 46, 54, 214
transgression, 19, 41, 42, 71
transnationalism, 84, 98, 102
trauma, 12, 38, 49, 51, 554, 119, 120
Trim (Mayumi Yoshida), 13, 16, 17,
    85, 86
tropes, 21, 22, 23, 26, 36, 70, 73, 75, 76,
    77, 99, 104, 118, 153, 168, 174, 183,
    223
Trudrung, Jennifer, 15, 181, 182, 183,
    184, 185, 186, 188, 189, 190, 191, 194,
    195
Tsangari, Athina Rachel, 12, 39
Twilight (Catherine Hardwicke), 86,
    184

ugliness, 5, 33, 58, 72, 73, 81, 83
uncanniness, 16, 23, 24, 34, 37
underrepresentation, 4, 10, 11, 14, 80,
    105, 151, 155, 156, 157,

vampires, 5, 72, 73, 82, 83, 84, 88, 104,
    115, 177
victims, 3, 4, 5, 29, 30, 48, 55, 58, 69, 99,
    103, 156, 185, 220, 223
villain, 53, 55, 57, 58
violence, 6, 7, 9, 25, 39, 43, 44, 45, 46,
    47, 48, 49, 49, 50, 55, 57, 82, 101, 119,
    171, 185, 186, 193, 217, 218, 221, 223,
    225
virginity, 1, 4, 6, 77, 79, 82, 149
Viscera Film Festival, 145, 146, 147,
    148, 149, 150, 150, 156, 159
visibility, 3, 7, 10, 11, 14, 73, 120, 124,
    126, 145, 150, 155, 157, 171, 185, 187,
    190, 217, 222

Voodoo, 118, 120, 122, 124
Vuckovic, Jovanka, 73, 74, 86, 88, 154,
    168, 175

Walker, Johnny, 103, 104, 105, 106
Walton, Karen, 74, 76, 84, 86, 146
war film, 7, 8
Weinstein, Harvey, 110, 111
weirdness, 59, 169, 169, 171, 175, 176,
    177
werewolves, 70, 76, 78
western genre, 7, 213
Women in Horror Film Festival, 189,
    190, 191
Women in Horror Month, 11, 148, 149,
    153
Williams, Linda, 5, 9, 72, 99, 215, 218,
    219, 220, 222, 223
Williams, R. Shanea, 16, 17, 124, 125,
    127, 131
witches, 5, 33, 36, 40, 177
women-authored, 97, 99, 103, 105, 109,
    110
women-led, 13, 14, 83, 85, 99, 105, 167,
    184, 185, 186, 187, 189, 189, 190, 194
wounds, 46, 56, 72, 145, 148, 151, 154,
    162
Wright, Edgar, 104, 106
Wright, Vanessa Ionta, 15, 152, 153,
    181, 183, 184, 185, 186, 187, 189, 190,
    191, 193, 194, 195

XX (Roxanne Benjamin, Jovanka
    Vuckovic, Karyn Kusama, St.
    Vincent), 155, 168, 175

zines, 148, 153, 174
zombies, 73, 88, 108, 118, 213

About the Editors and Contributors

Victoria McCollum is a researcher and educator in cinematic arts at Ulster University, Northern Ireland. Victoria has published several cutting-edge books on film, media, and TV, including the recent *Make America Hate Again: Trump-Era Horror and the Politics of Fear* (2019). She is co-investigator on a Higher Education Research Capital project that will deliver £536,000 investment in a new Virtual Production Facility at Ulster University, addressing genuine industry need in four key strands of film, animation, immersive, and games. Victoria has previously held positions at BBC, ITV, MTV, and HBO (Time Warner Inc.) and has collaborated on projects with Apple, Cartoon Network, Cinemax, Facebook, New Line Cinema, *Sesame Street*, Telltale Games, Time Warner, Twitter, and Universal Music Group.

Aislínn Clarke is an award-winning writer and director. Her debut feature film, *The Devil's Doorway* (2018), was released internationally by IFC Midnight following a run at international genre film festivals (Sitges, Fright Fest, etc.). Along with a number of awards on the festival circuit, Aislínn was awarded the Academy of Motion Pictures Gold Fellowship in 2020. Aislínn currently has original TV work in development with major broadcasters in the UK, Ireland, and the United States. She also has feature film work in development with Disney and Hulu in Los Angeles and with the BFI, Northern Ireland Screen, and Screen Ireland closer to home. Aislínn lectures in creative writing and film at Queen's University and is repped by CAA in LA and Dench Arnold in London.

* * *

Erica Tortolani is an award-winning doctoral researcher in film studies at the University of Massachusetts, Amherst. Her research interests include silent cinema, horror films, German Expressionist film, and avant-garde and experimental film.

Alexandra Heller-Nicholas is an Australian film critic and academic who has written eight books on cult and horror film with a focus on gender politics, including *Rape-Revenge Films* (2011) and the forthcoming *1000 Women in Horror*. Alexandra is an adjunct professor in film and television at Deakin University and a programmer at Fantastic Fest in Austin, Texas, the largest genre film festival in the US.

James Francis Jr. conducts doctoral research focused on horror narratives and children's literature. His book *Remaking Horror: Hollywood's New Reliance on Scares of Old* (2013) examines the American horror film remake. James is currently a professor in English at Middle Tennessee State University.

Shelby Shukaliak is a Vancouver-based film producer and graduate of the University of British Columbia's Media Studies program. Shelby is a key collaborator on UBC's recent research project *Queen Bee: Women, Feminism and Genre Film* (2019).

Eve O'Dea is a graduate of the Film Studies program of the University of British Columbia. Eva is a key collaborator on UBC's recent research project *Queen Bee: Women, Feminism and Genre Film* (2019).

Ernest Mathijs is professor of film studies at the University of British Columbia. He has published on horror and cult cinema, including *Ginger Snaps* (2013) and *The Cinema of David Cronenberg* (2008).

Amy Harris is a doctoral researcher in the Cinema and Television History Institute at De Montfort University. She supports teaching on an "Introduction to Global Film History" module and works as an archiving and digitization intern in the Institute of Cinema and Television History Hammer horror archives.

Ashlee Blackwell is a Philadelphia native and Temple University graduate with an MA in liberal arts. She is the creator of *Graveyard Shift Sisters*, a digital resource that archives Black women in the horror/sci-fi genres.

She's also the cowriter/producer of the Shudder documentary *Horror Noire: A History of Black Horror.*

Kate R. Robertson is an Australian-born, New York–based writer and academic affiliate of the University of Sydney, where she taught for several years. She has written about art, film, and culture for a range of publications. Her current project, *Man-Eater: Cannibal Women in Contemporary Visual Culture*, presented at the Art Association of Australia and New Zealand (2013) and the Miskatonic Institute of Horror Studies (2020), explores ever-present social anxieties about the tense and endlessly complicated relationship between gender, hunger, desire, sex, autonomy, and power.

Anna Bogutskaya is a film programmer, podcaster, creative producer, and writer. Previously, she worked at Pedro Almodóvar's El Deseo, ran Shooting People, and programmed for BFI. She is currently the head of arts and culture at DICE, cohost of The Bigger Picture podcast, festival director of BAFTA-recognized Underwire Film Festival, and cofounder of horror film collective The Final Girls.

Brian Hauser is a horror films scholar, screenwriter, filmmaker, and novelist. He was coeditor of *The Journal of Short Film* from 2009 to 2016. His debut novel, *Memento Mori: The Fathomless Shadows* (2019), is about a fictional woman director of underground short horror films in the late 1970s.

Dan Vena is a SSHRC Postdoctoral Fellow at Carleton University and an adjunct instructor at Queen's University specializing in trans, queer, and feminist approaches to horror cinema and superhero comics. Dan has published in *Transformative Works and Culture*, *Studies in the Fantastic*, and several anthologies on gender, sexuality, and genre.

Iris Robinson recently completed her MA in cinema studies at the University of Toronto. Her research navigates the domestic, medical, and urban spaces in visual culture using feminist theory, photography, and urban studies with a particular interest in horror, documentary, and the evolution of "madness" on screen.

Patrick Woodstock is currently completing his MA in film studies at Concordia University in Montréal. His research focuses on the application of queer and feminist perspectives toward contemporary and historical popular visual cultures, with a specific interest in classical Hollywood, horror media, and the aesthetics of camp and decadence.